GRIND
HOUSE
DOORS OPEN
AT MIDNIGHT
DOUBLE FEATURE

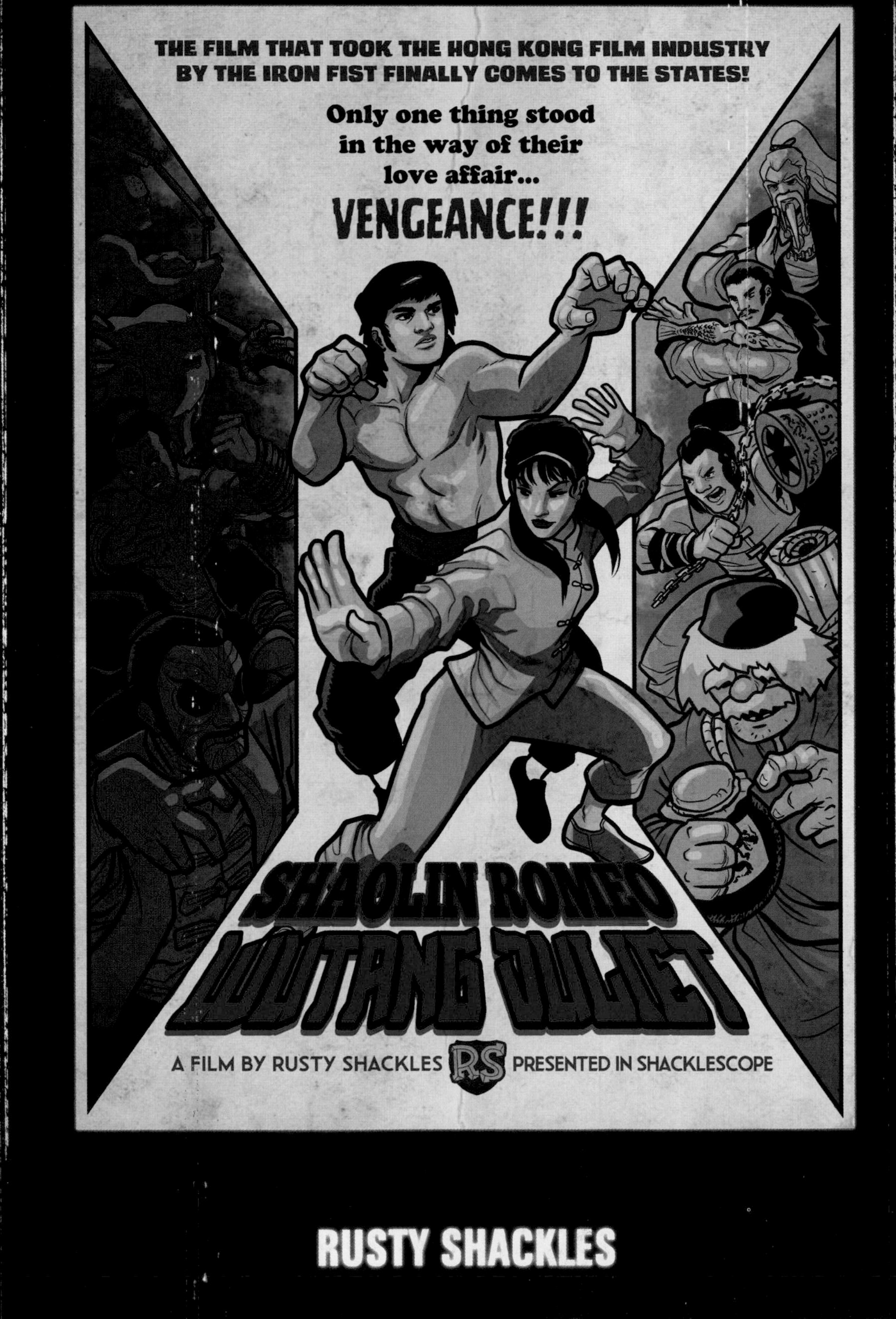
THE FILM THAT TOOK THE HONG KONG FILM INDUSTRY BY THE IRON FIST FINALLY COMES TO THE STATES!
Only one thing stood in the way of their love affair...
VENGEANCE!!!
SHAOLIN ROMEO
WUTANG JULIET
A FILM BY RUSTY SHACKLES
RS
PRESENTED IN SHACKLESCOPE

RUSTY SHACKLES

COMING SOON

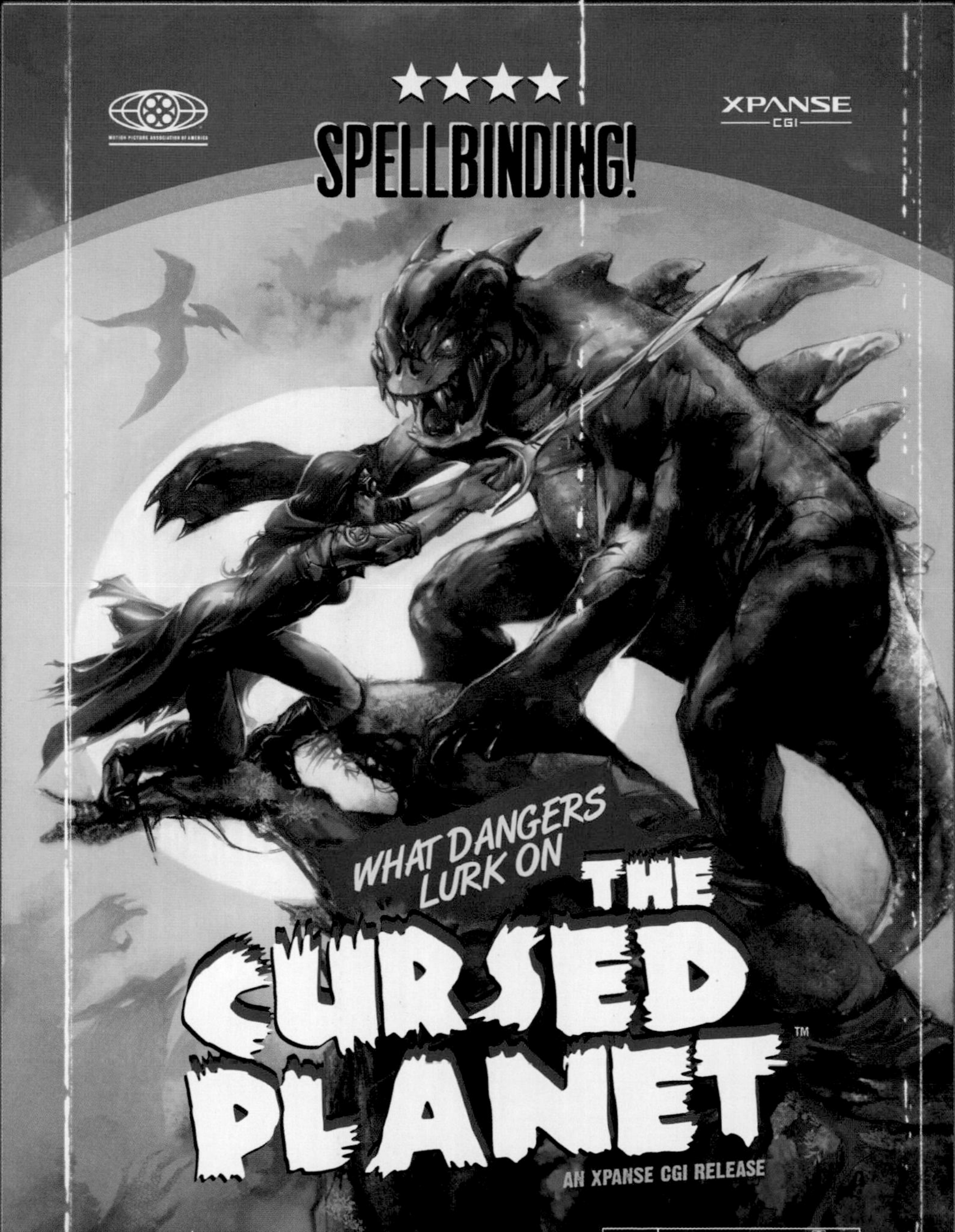
★★★★
SPELLBINDING!
XPANSE
CGI
WHAT DANGERS
LURK ON
THE
CURSED
PLANET™
AN XPANSE CGI RELEASE
ASHRAF GHORI
R
RESTRICTED
UNDER 17 REQUIRES ACCOMPANYING
PARENT OR ADULT GUARDIAN

ASHRAF GHORI

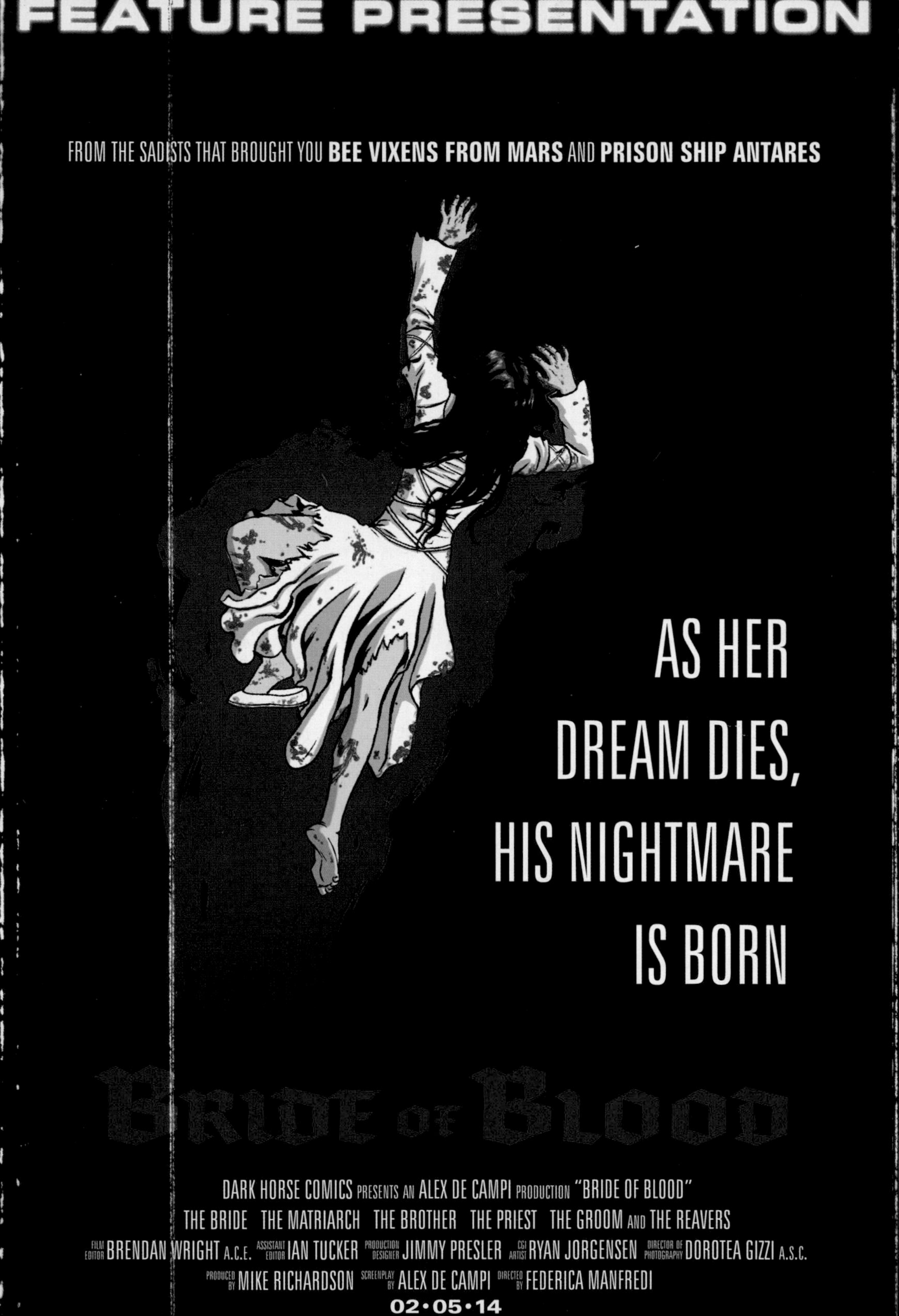
FEATURE PRESENTATION
FROM THE SADISTS THAT BROUGHT YOU BEE VIXENS FROM MARS AND PRISON SHIP ANTARES
AS HER DREAM DIES, HIS NIGHTMARE IS BORN
BRIDE OF BLOOD
DARK HORSE COMICS PRESENTS AN ALEX DE CAMPI PRODUCTION "BRIDE OF BLOOD"
THE BRIDE THE MATRIARCH THE BROTHER THE PRIEST THE GROOM AND THE REAVERS
FILM EDITOR BRENDAN WRIGHT A.C.E. ASSISTANT EDITOR IAN TUCKER PRODUCTION DESIGNER JIMMY PRESLER CGI ARTIST RYAN JORGENSEN DIRECTOR OF PHOTOGRAPHY DOROTEA GIZZI A.S.C.
PRODUCED BY MIKE RICHARDSON SCREENPLAY BY ALEX DE CAMPI DIRECTED BY FEDERICA MANFREDI
02•05•14

Bride of Blood

SCRIPT AND LETTERS
ALEX DE CAMPI

ART AND TITLE PAGE
FEDERICA MANFREDI

COLOR ASSISTANCE
DOROTEA GIZZI
ANDREA PRIORINI
DIEGO FARINA

COVER
FRANCESCO FRANCAVILLA

DARK HORSE BOOKS

EDITOR
BRENDAN WRIGHT

ASSISTANT EDITOR
IAN TUCKER

DESIGN
JIMMY PRESLER

DIGITAL PRODUCTION
RYAN JORGENSEN

PUBLISHER
MIKE RICHARDSON

PUBLISHED BY DARK HORSE BOOKS, A DIVISION OF DARK HORSE COMICS, INC.
10956 SE MAIN STREET MILWAUKIE, OR 97222 DARKHORSE.COM

TO FIND A COMICS SHOP IN YOUR AREA, CALL THE COMIC SHOP LOCATOR SERVICE TOLL-FREE AT (888) 266-4226.

INTERNATIONAL LICENSING: (503) 905-2377

FIRST EDITION: NOVEMBER 2014

LIBRARY OF CONGRESS CATALOGING-IN-PUBLICATION DATA

De Campi, Alex, author.
Grindhouse, Doors Open at Midnight Double Feature Volume 2 : Bride of Blood/Flesh Feast of the Devil Doll / script and letters , Alex De Campi ; Bride of Blood art, Federica Manfredi ; Flesh Feast of the Devil Doll art, Gary Erskine ; covers, Francesco Francavilla, Dan Panosian. -- First edition.
pages cm. -- (Grindhouse, Doors Open at Midnight ; Volume 2)
Summary: "A comic-book double feature mining the exploitation genres of the 1970s for stories of Medieval-era revenge and Puritan-era curses, filled with sex and violence"-- Provided by publisher.
"This volume collects issues #5-#8 of the Dark Horse comic-book series Grindhouse: Doors Open at Midnight."
ISBN 978-1-61655-378-4 (paperback)
1. Graphic novels. 2. Horror comic books, strips, etc. I. Manfredi, Federica, illustrator. II. Erskine, Gary, illustrator. III. Francavilla, Francesco, illustrator. IV. Panosian, Dan, illustrator. V. Title. VI. Title: Bride of Blood. VII. Title: Flesh Feast of the Devil Doll.
PN6737.D4G76 2014
741.5'973--dc23

2014022135
1 3 5 7 9 10 8 6 4 2
PRINTED IN CHINA

THIS VOLUME COLLECTS ISSUES #5—#8 OF THE DARK HORSE COMIC-BOOK SERIES *GRINDHOUSE: DOORS OPEN AT MIDNIGHT.*

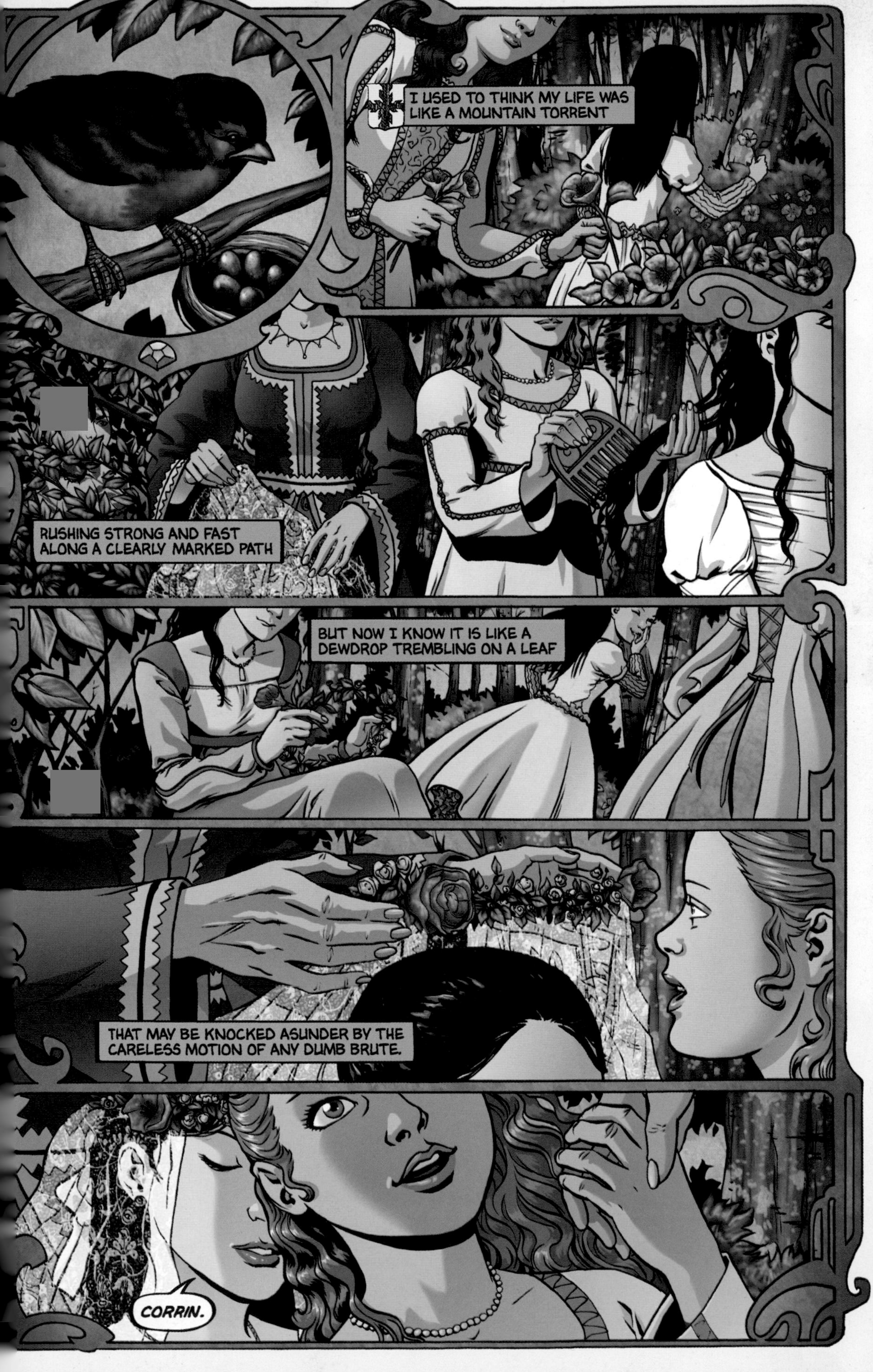
I USED TO THINK MY LIFE WAS LIKE A MOUNTAIN TORRENT
RUSHING STRONG AND FAST ALONG A CLEARLY MARKED PATH
BUT NOW I KNOW IT IS LIKE A DEWDROP TREMBLING ON A LEAF
THAT MAY BE KNOCKED ASUNDER BY THE CARELESS MOTION OF ANY DUMB BRUTE.
CORRIN.

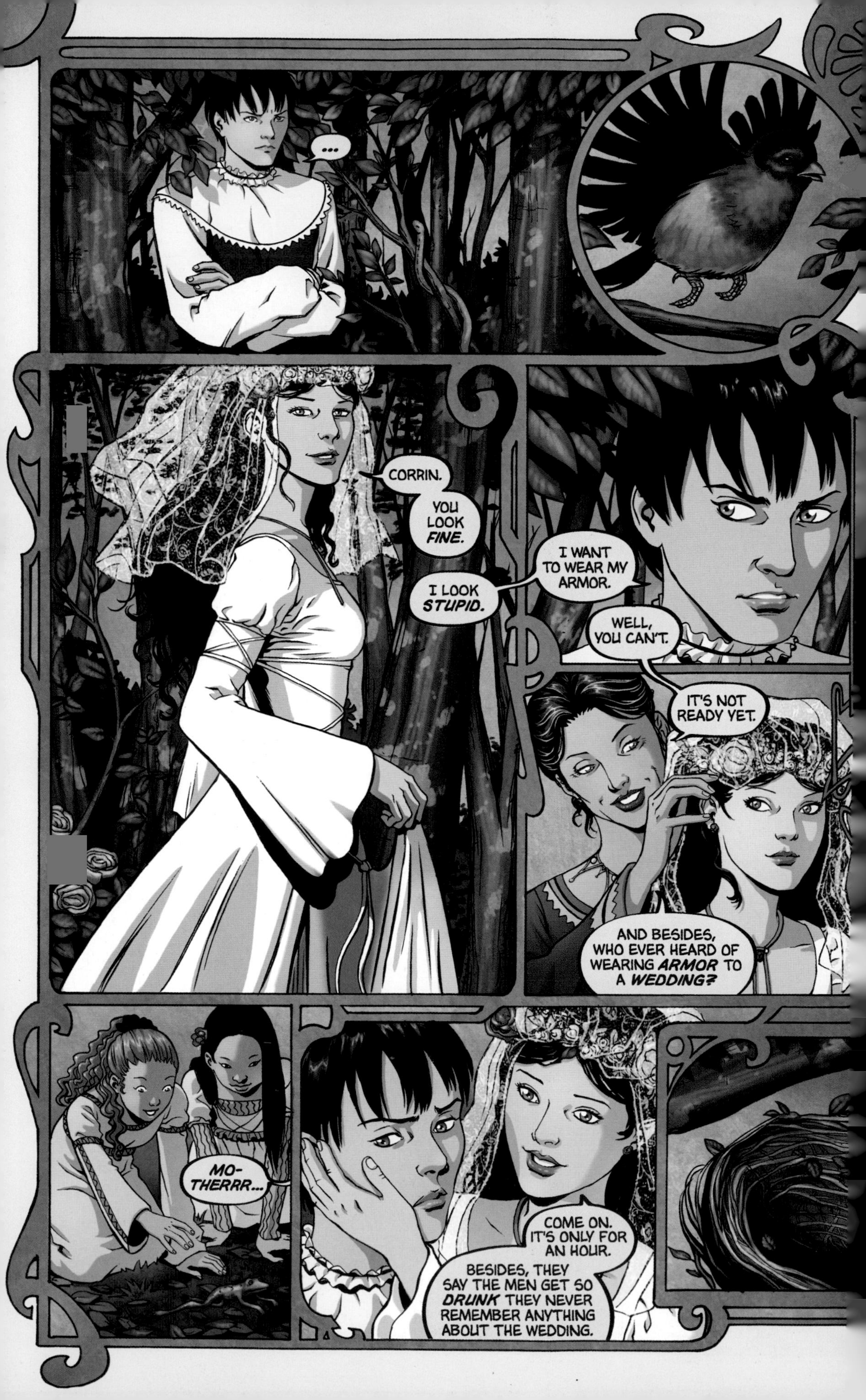
...
CORRIN.
YOU LOOK FINE.
I LOOK STUPID.
I WANT TO WEAR MY ARMOR.
WELL, YOU CAN'T.
IT'S NOT READY YET.
AND BESIDES, WHO EVER HEARD OF WEARING ARMOR TO A WEDDING?
MO-THERRR...
COME ON. IT'S ONLY FOR AN HOUR.
BESIDES, THEY SAY THE MEN GET SO DRUNK THEY NEVER REMEMBER ANYTHING ABOUT THE WEDDING.

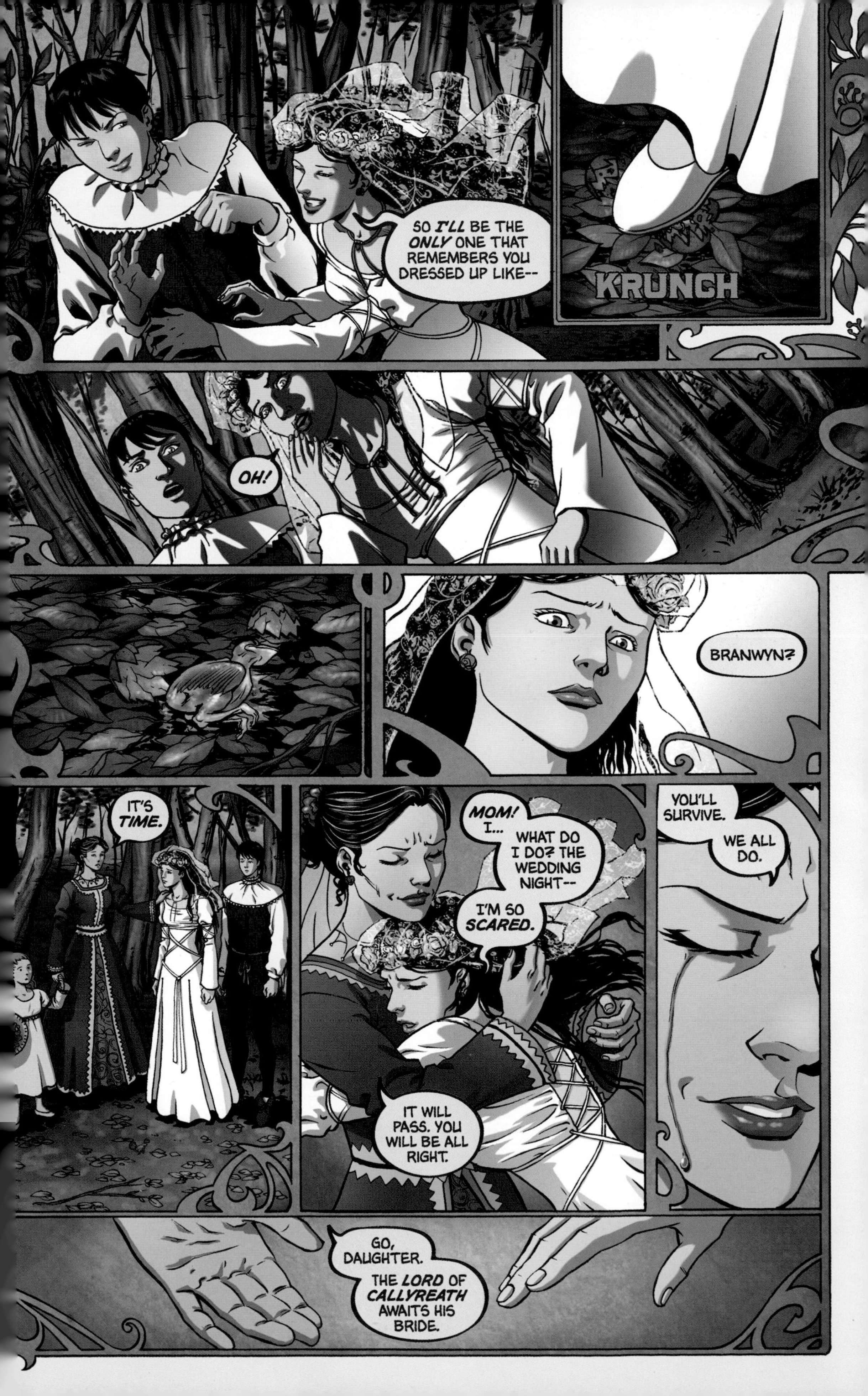
SO I'LL BE THE ONLY ONE THAT REMEMBERS YOU DRESSED UP LIKE--
KRUNCH
OH!
BRANWYN?
IT'S TIME.
MOM! I...
WHAT DO I DO? THE WEDDING NIGHT--
I'M SO SCARED.
IT WILL PASS. YOU WILL BE ALL RIGHT.
YOU'LL SURVIVE.
WE ALL DO.
GO, DAUGHTER.
THE LORD OF CALLYREATH AWAITS HIS BRIDE.

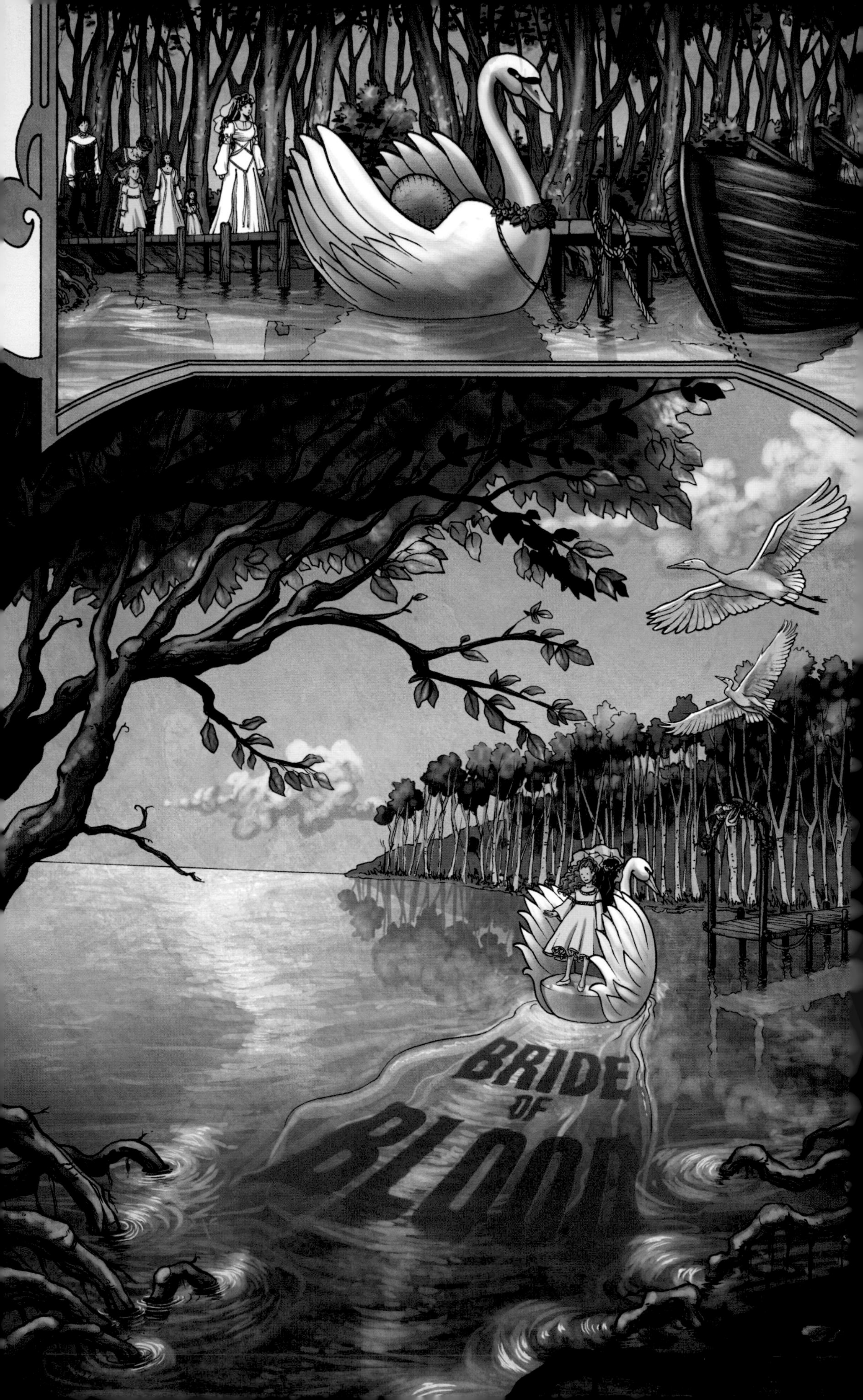
BRIDE
OF
BLOOD

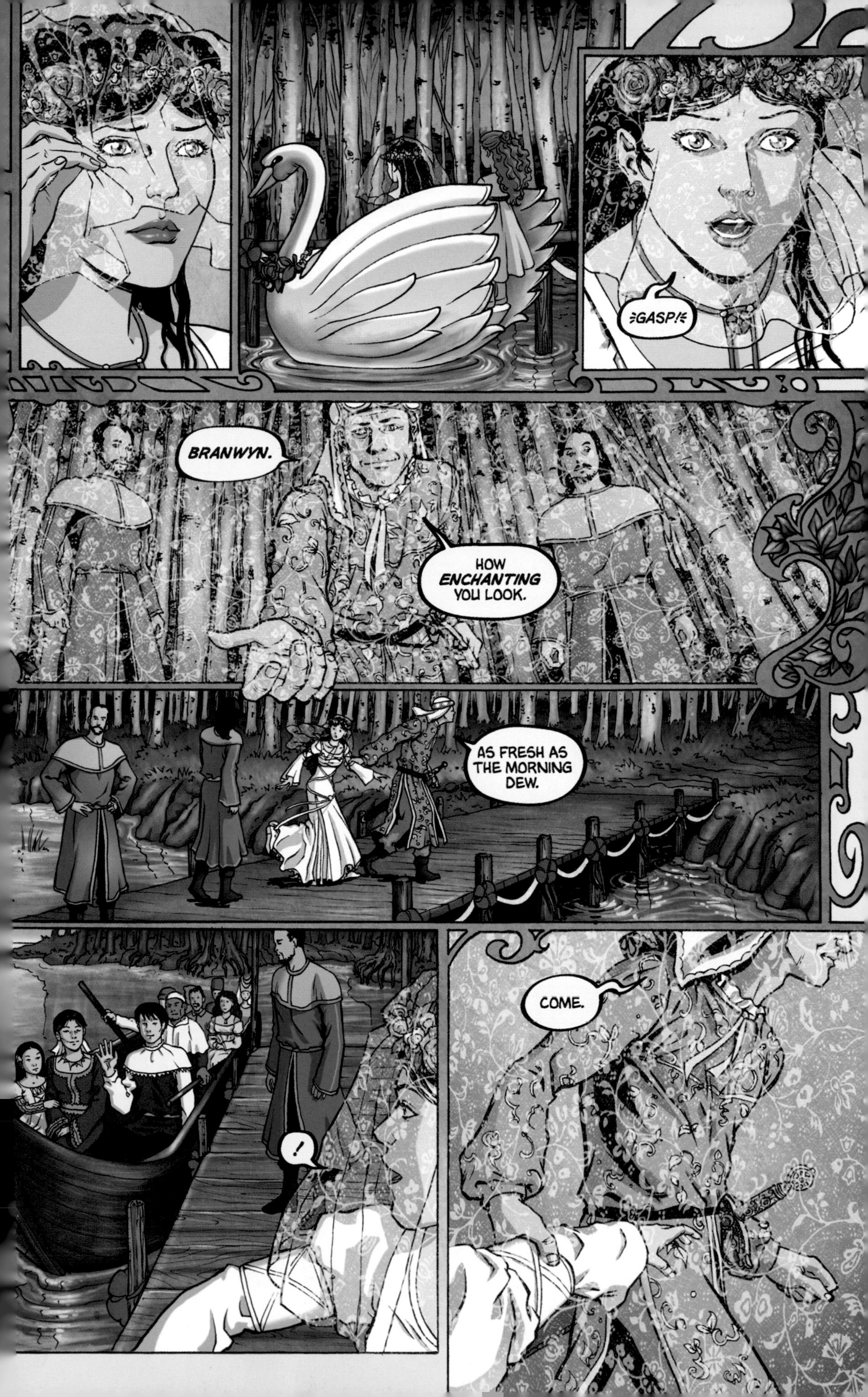

GASP!
BRANWYN.
HOW ENCHANTING YOU LOOK.
AS FRESH AS THE MORNING DEW.
!
COME.

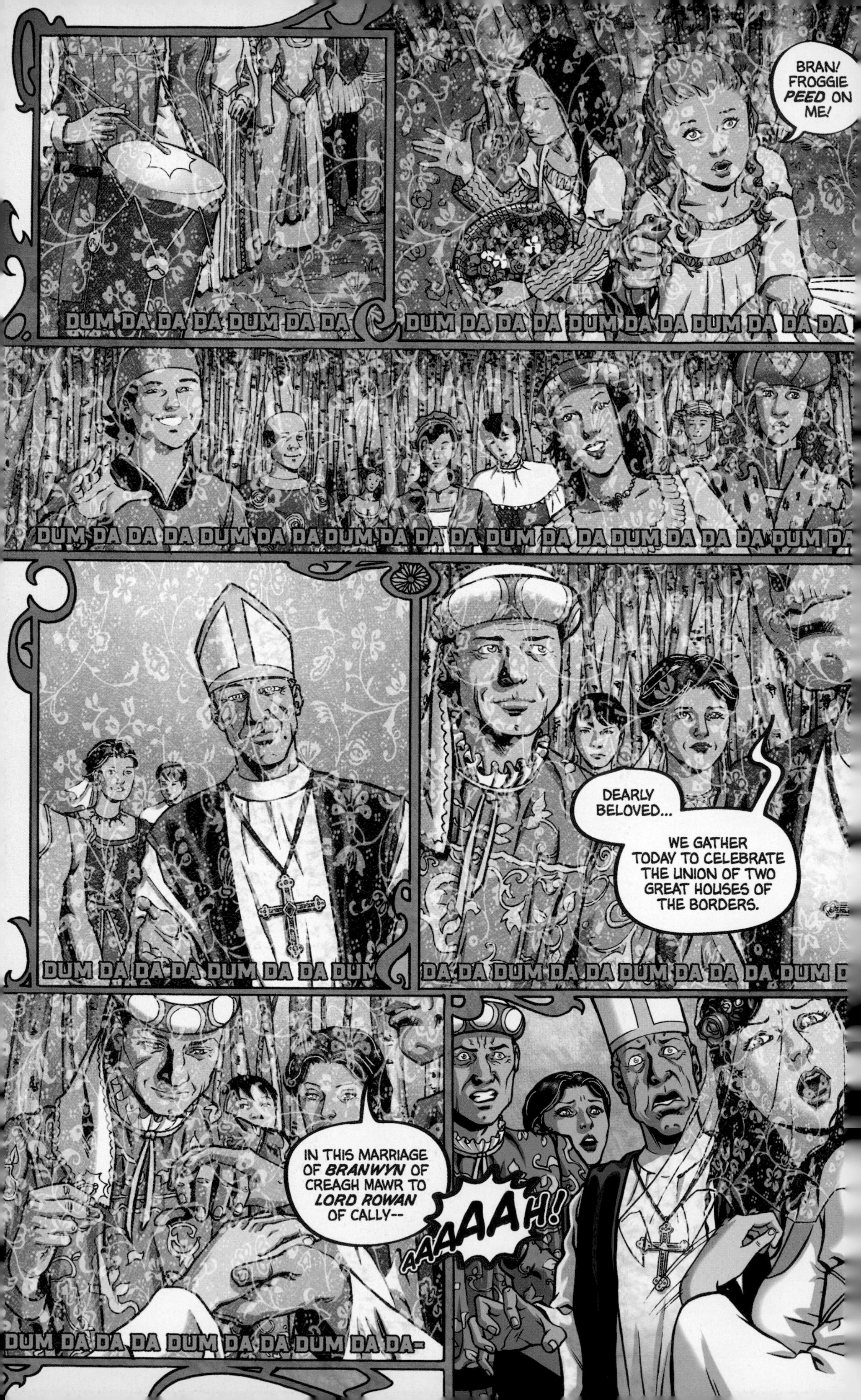
DUM DA DA DA DUM DA DA
BRAN! FROGGIE PEED ON ME!
DUM DA DA DA DUM DA DA DUM DA DA DA
DUM DA DA DA DUM DA DA DUM DA DA DA DUM DA DA DUM DA DA DA DA
DUM DA DA DA DUM DA DA DUM
DEARLY BELOVED...
WE GATHER TODAY TO CELEBRATE THE UNION OF TWO GREAT HOUSES OF THE BORDERS.
DA DA DUM DA DA DA DUM DA DA DA DUM D
IN THIS MARRIAGE OF BRANWYN OF CREAGH MAWR TO LORD ROWAN OF CALLY--
DUM DA DA DA DUM DA DA DUM DA DA-
AAAAAH!

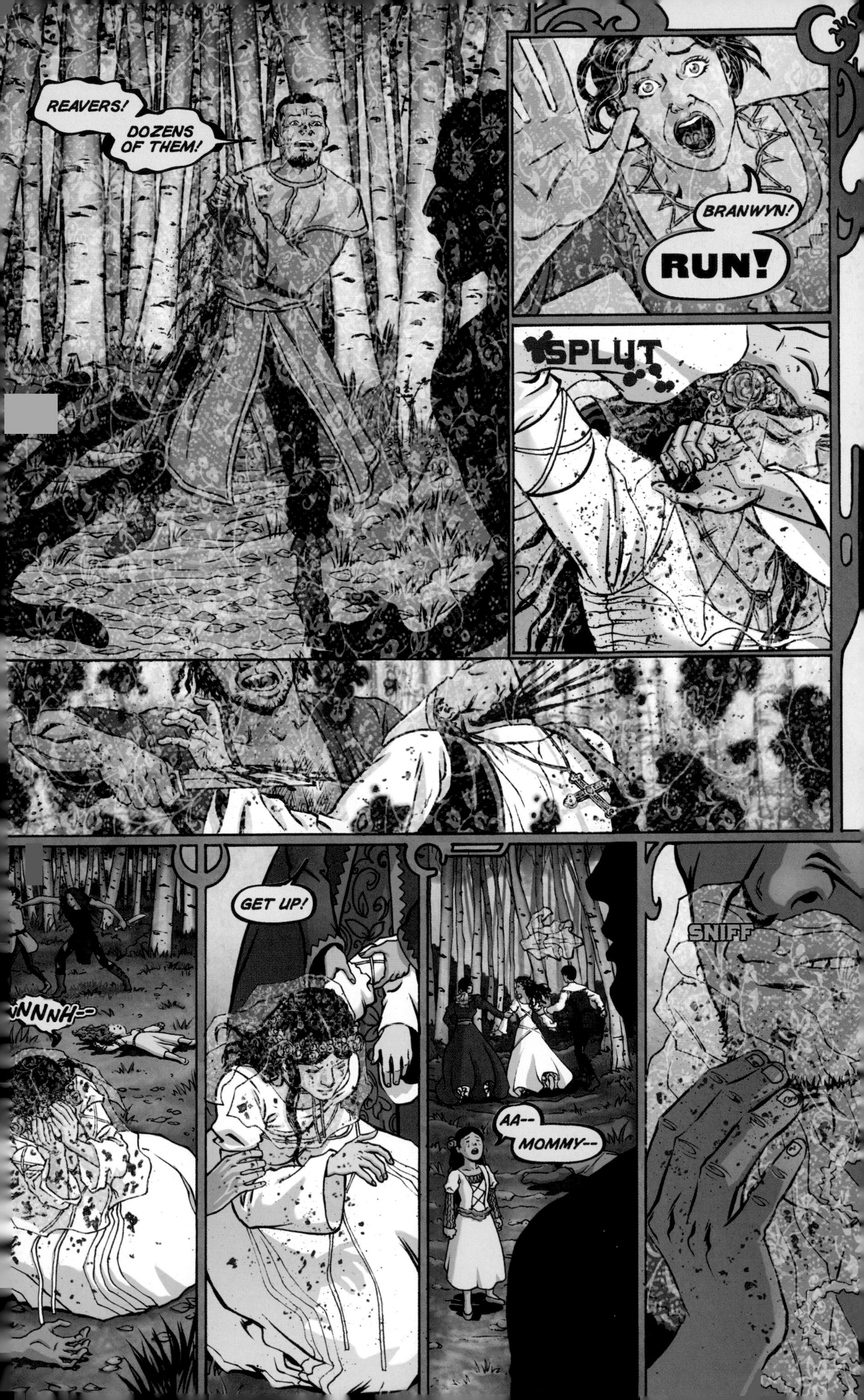
REAVERS!
DOZENS OF THEM!
BRANWYN!
RUN!
SPLUT
NNNH--
GET UP!
AA-- MOMMY--
SNIFF

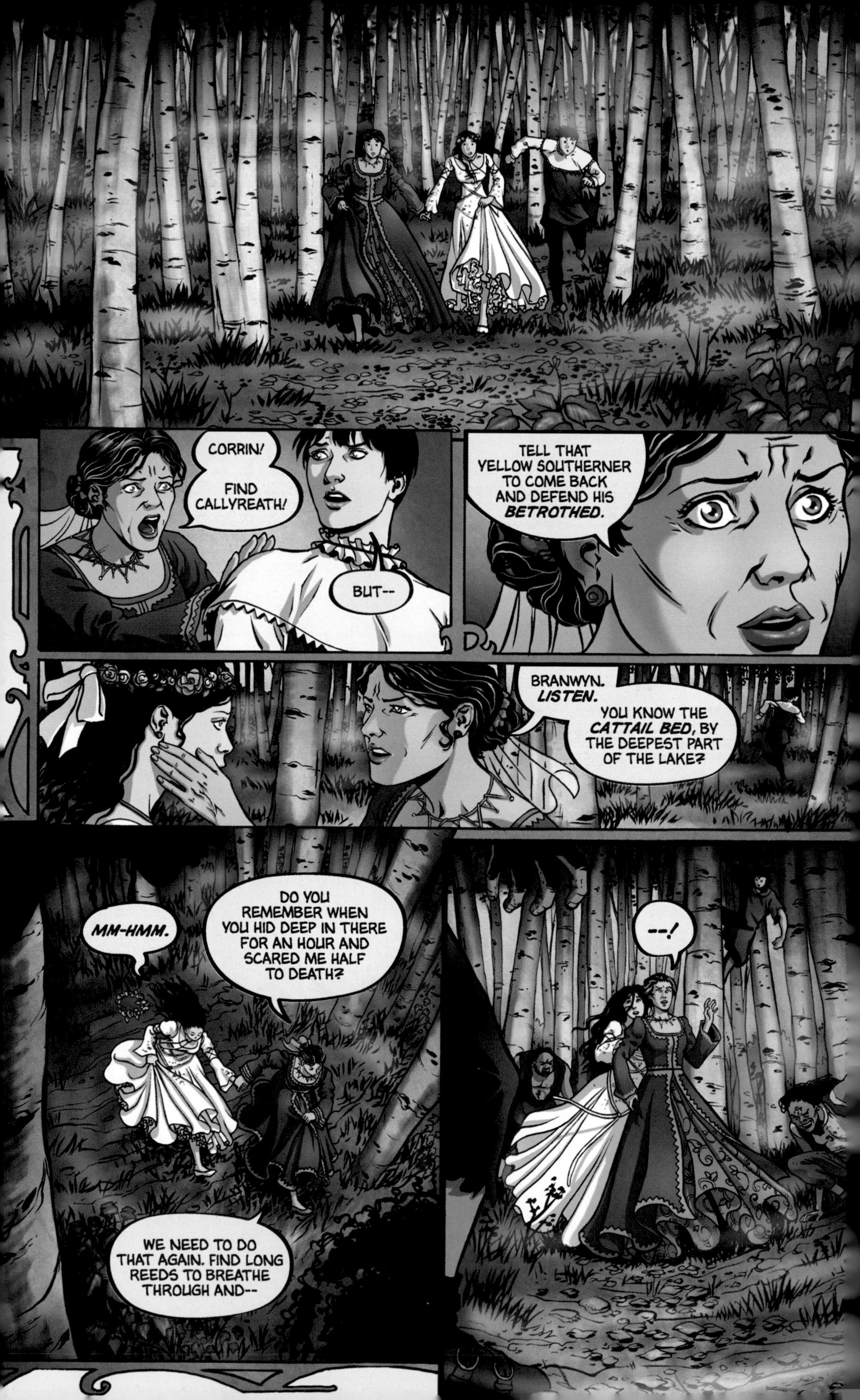
CORRIN!
FIND CALLYREATH!
BUT--
TELL THAT YELLOW SOUTHERNER TO COME BACK AND DEFEND HIS BETROTHED.
BRANWYN. LISTEN.
YOU KNOW THE CATTAIL BED, BY THE DEEPEST PART OF THE LAKE?
DO YOU REMEMBER WHEN YOU HID DEEP IN THERE FOR AN HOUR AND SCARED ME HALF TO DEATH?
MM-HMM.
WE NEED TO DO THAT AGAIN. FIND LONG REEDS TO BREATHE THROUGH AND--
--!

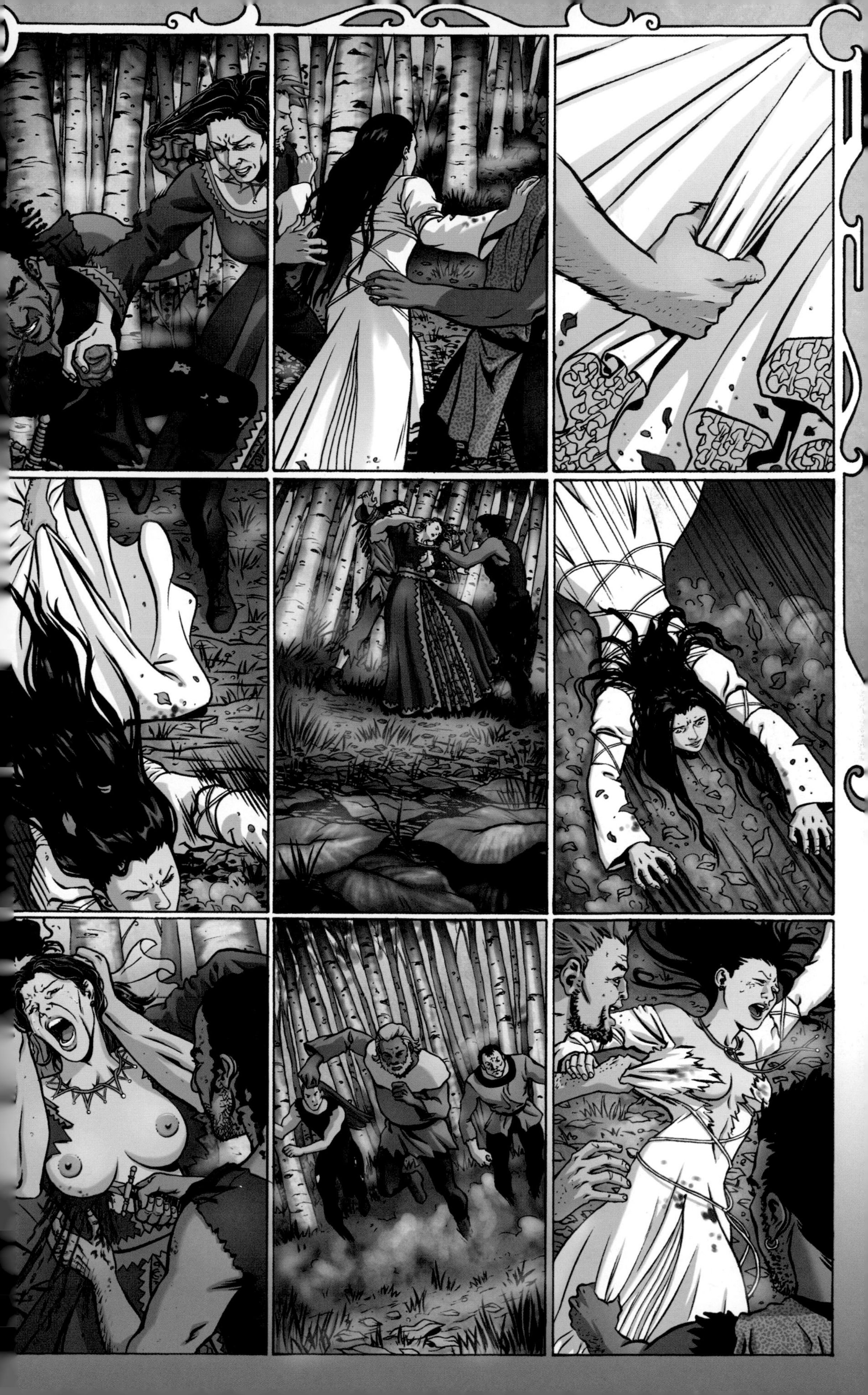

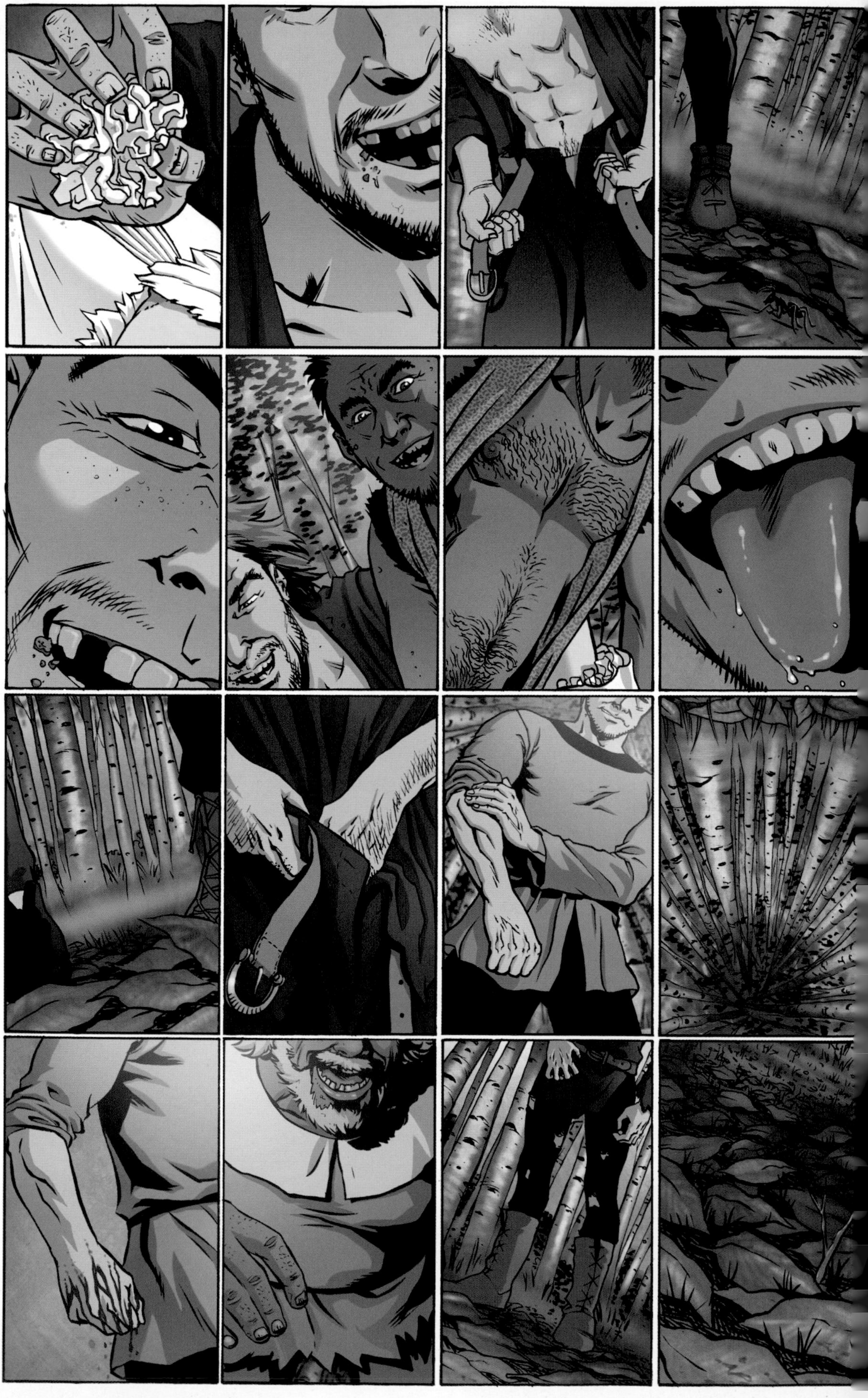

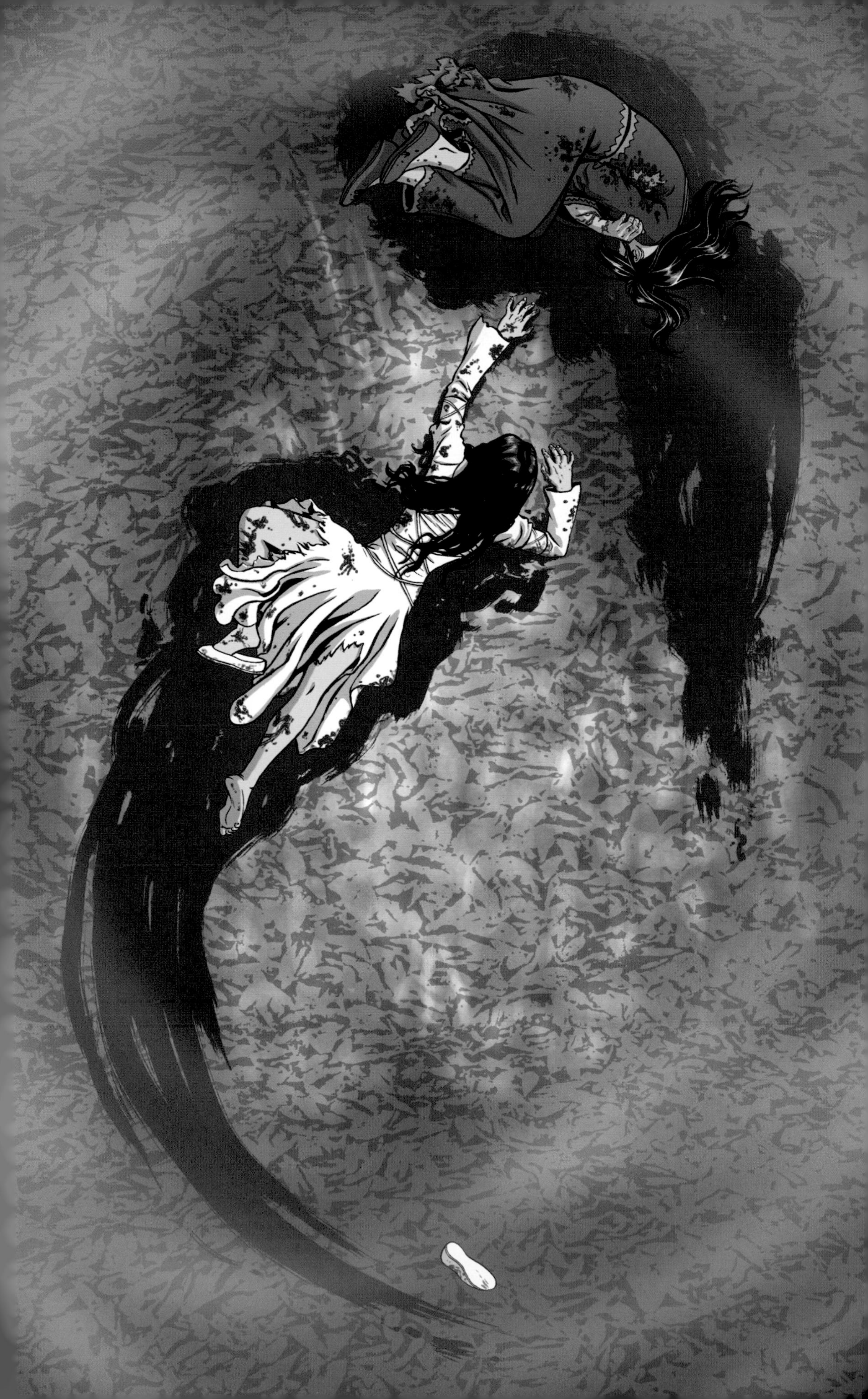

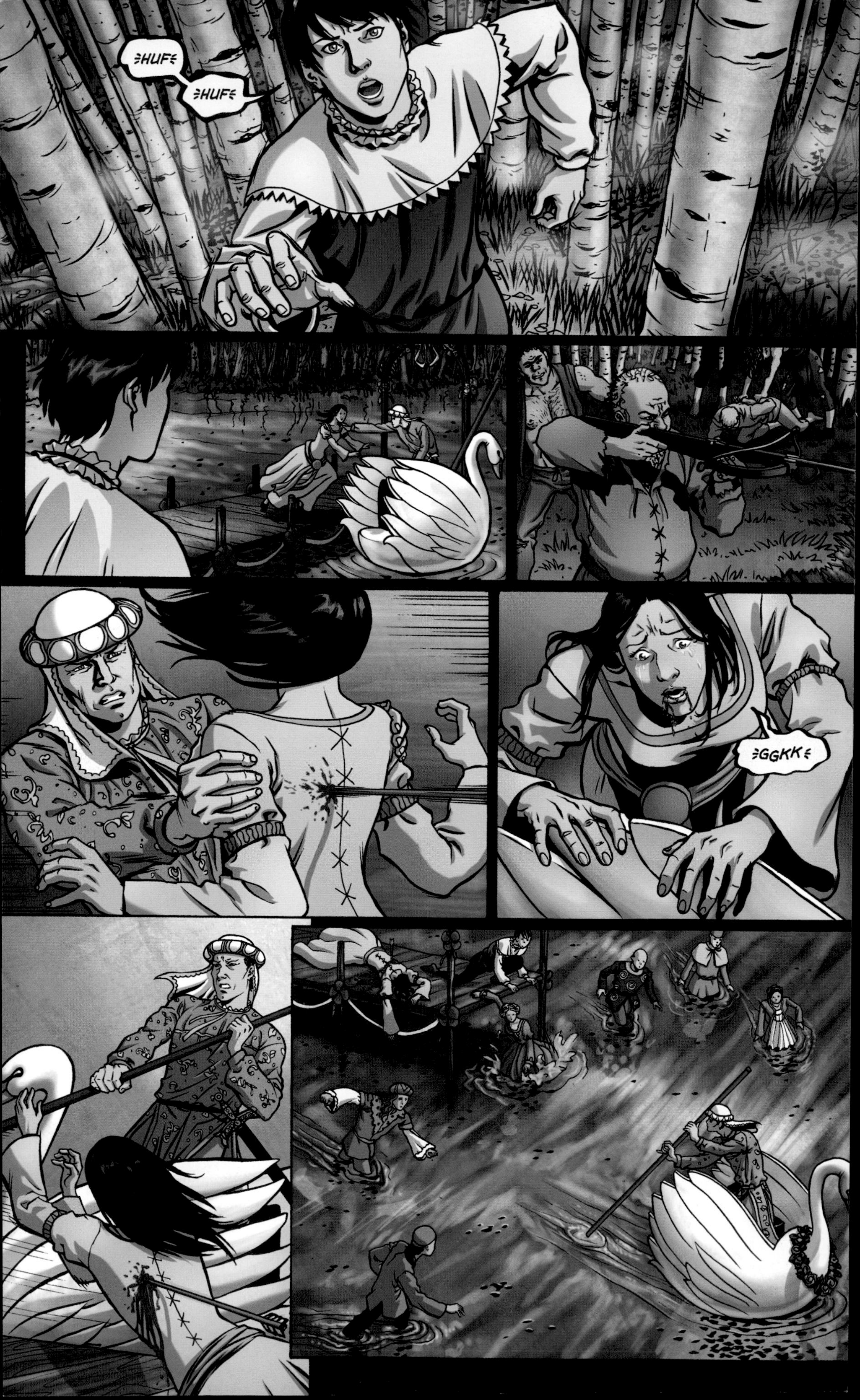
HUF
HUF
GGKK

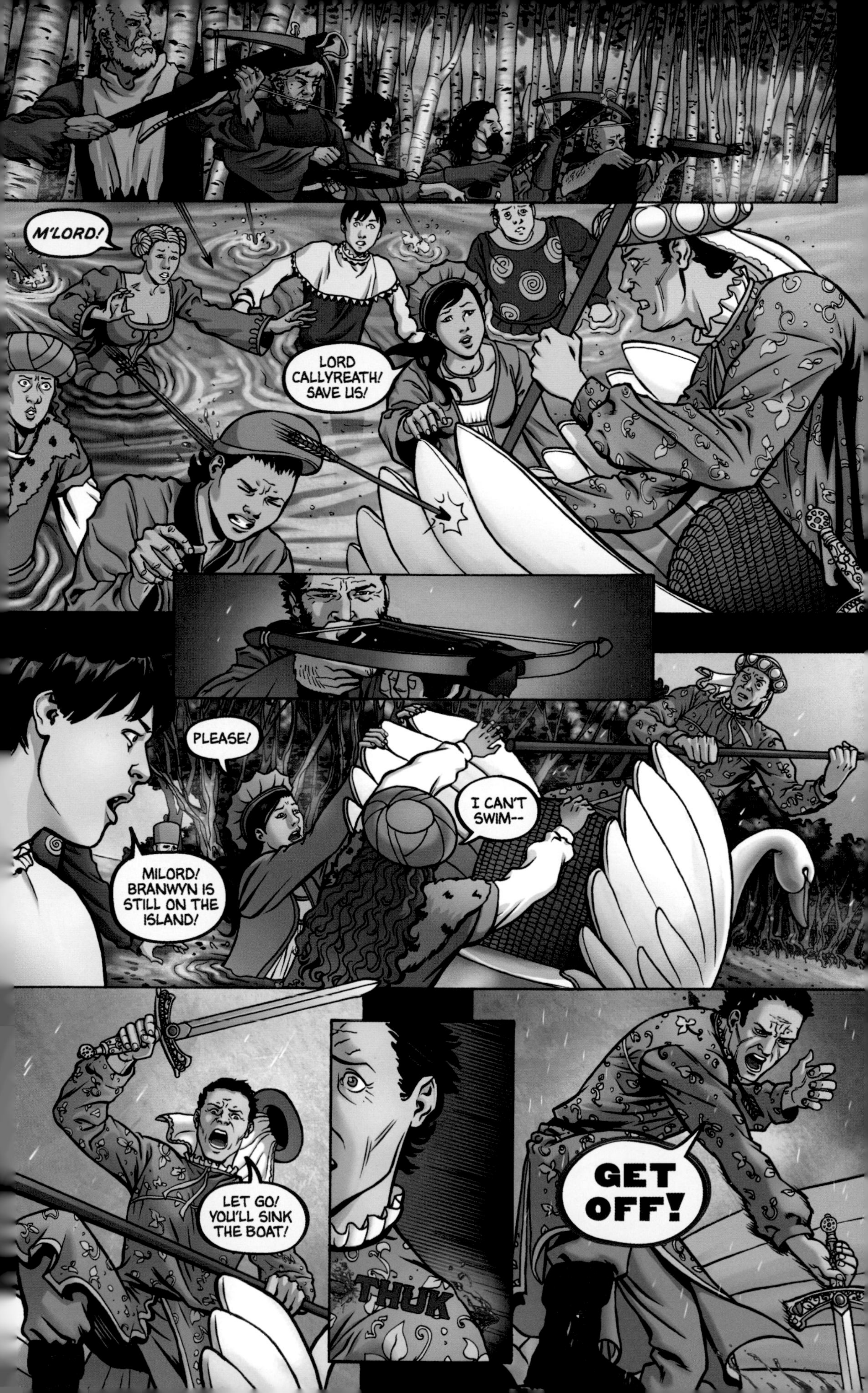

M'LORD!
LORD CALLYREATH! SAVE US!
PLEASE!
MILORD! BRANWYN IS STILL ON THE ISLAND!
I CAN'T SWIM--
LET GO! YOU'LL SINK THE BOAT!
THUK
GET OFF!

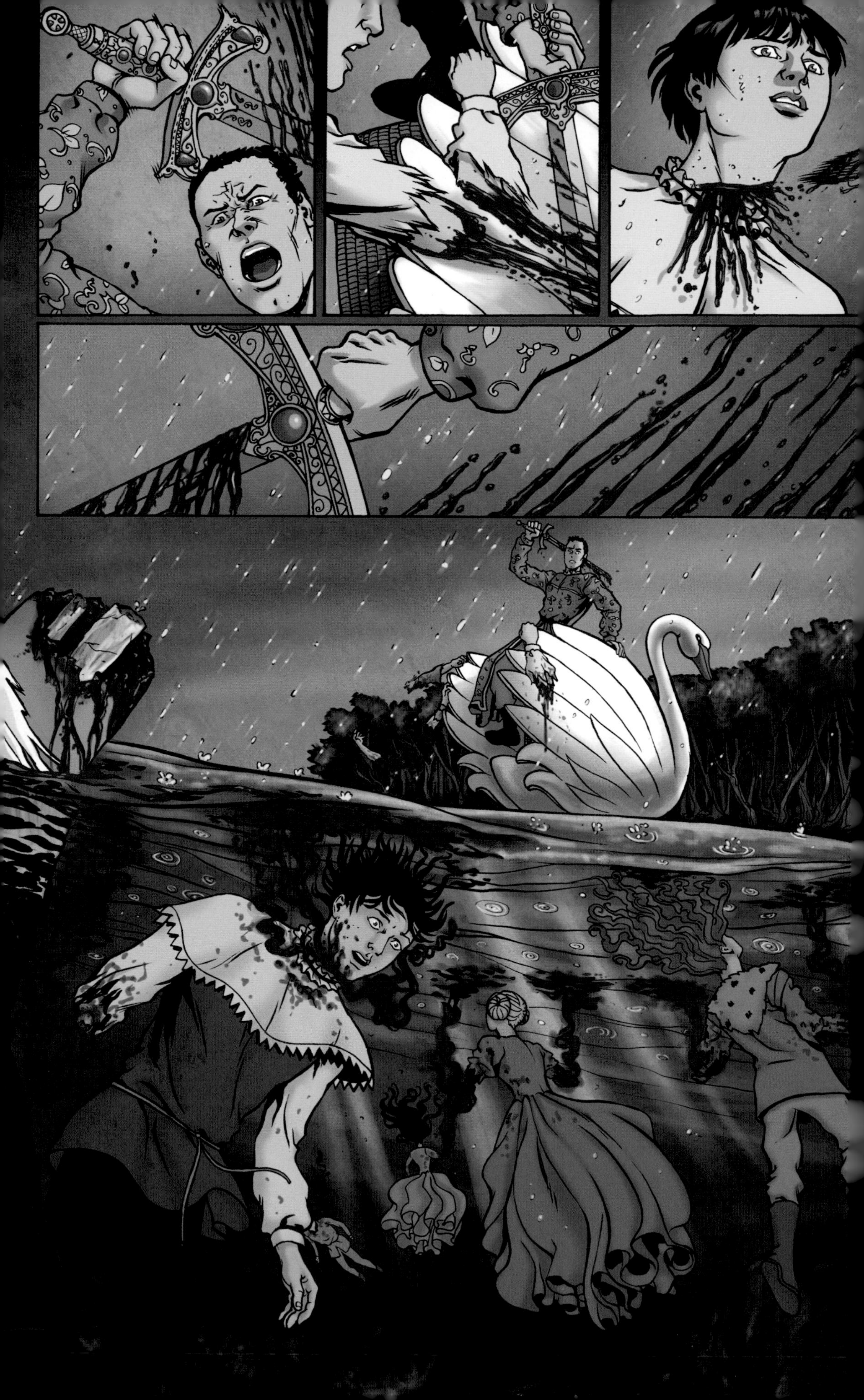

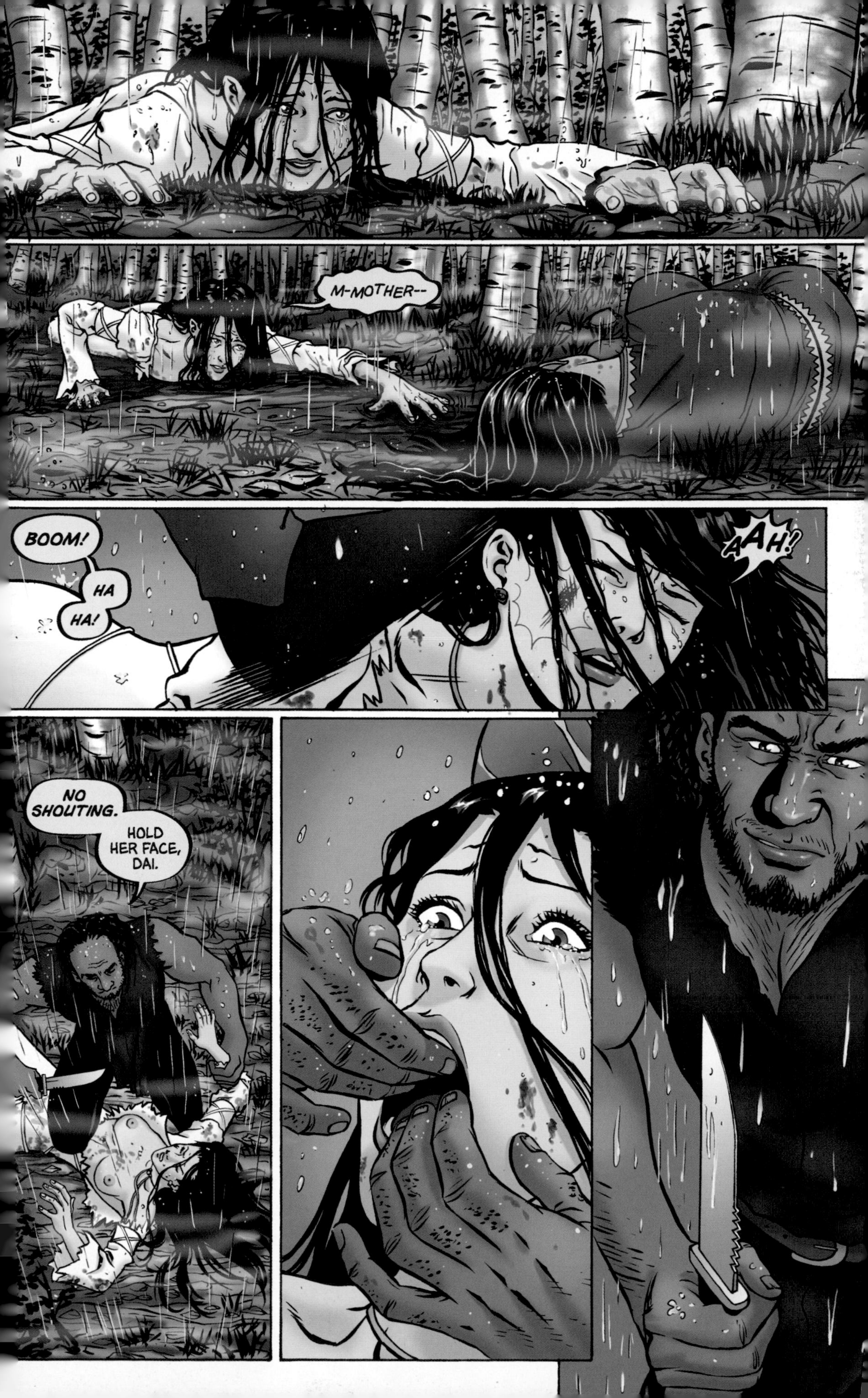
M-MOTHER--
BOOM!
HA
HA!
AAH!
NO SHOUTING.
HOLD HER FACE, DAI.

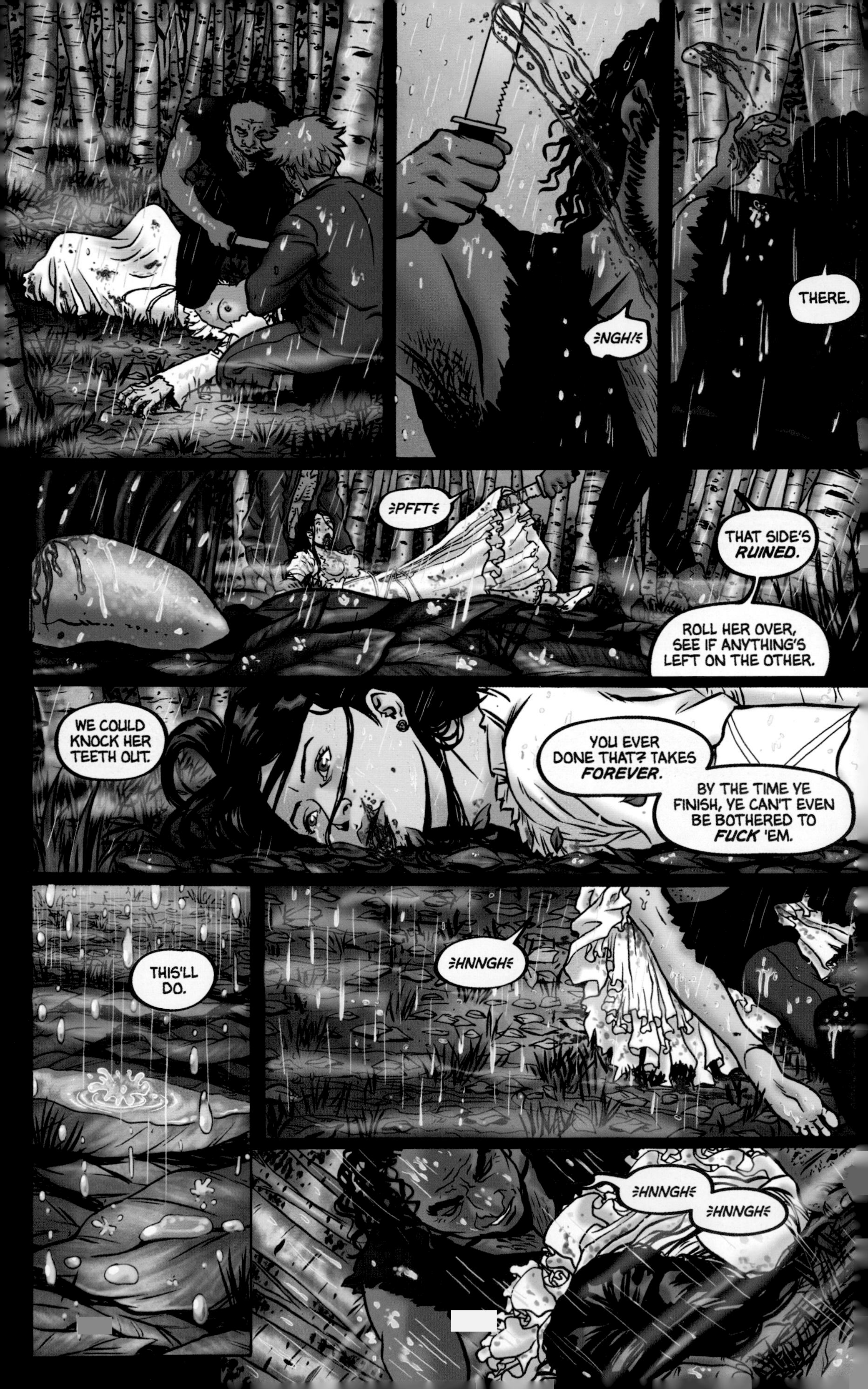
NGH!
THERE.
PFFT
THAT SIDE'S *RUINED.*
ROLL HER OVER, SEE IF ANYTHING'S LEFT ON THE OTHER.
WE COULD KNOCK HER TEETH OUT.
YOU EVER DONE THAT? TAKES *FOREVER.*
BY THE TIME YE FINISH, YE CAN'T EVEN BE BOTHERED TO *FUCK* 'EM.
THIS'LL DO.
HNNGH
HNNGH
HNNGH

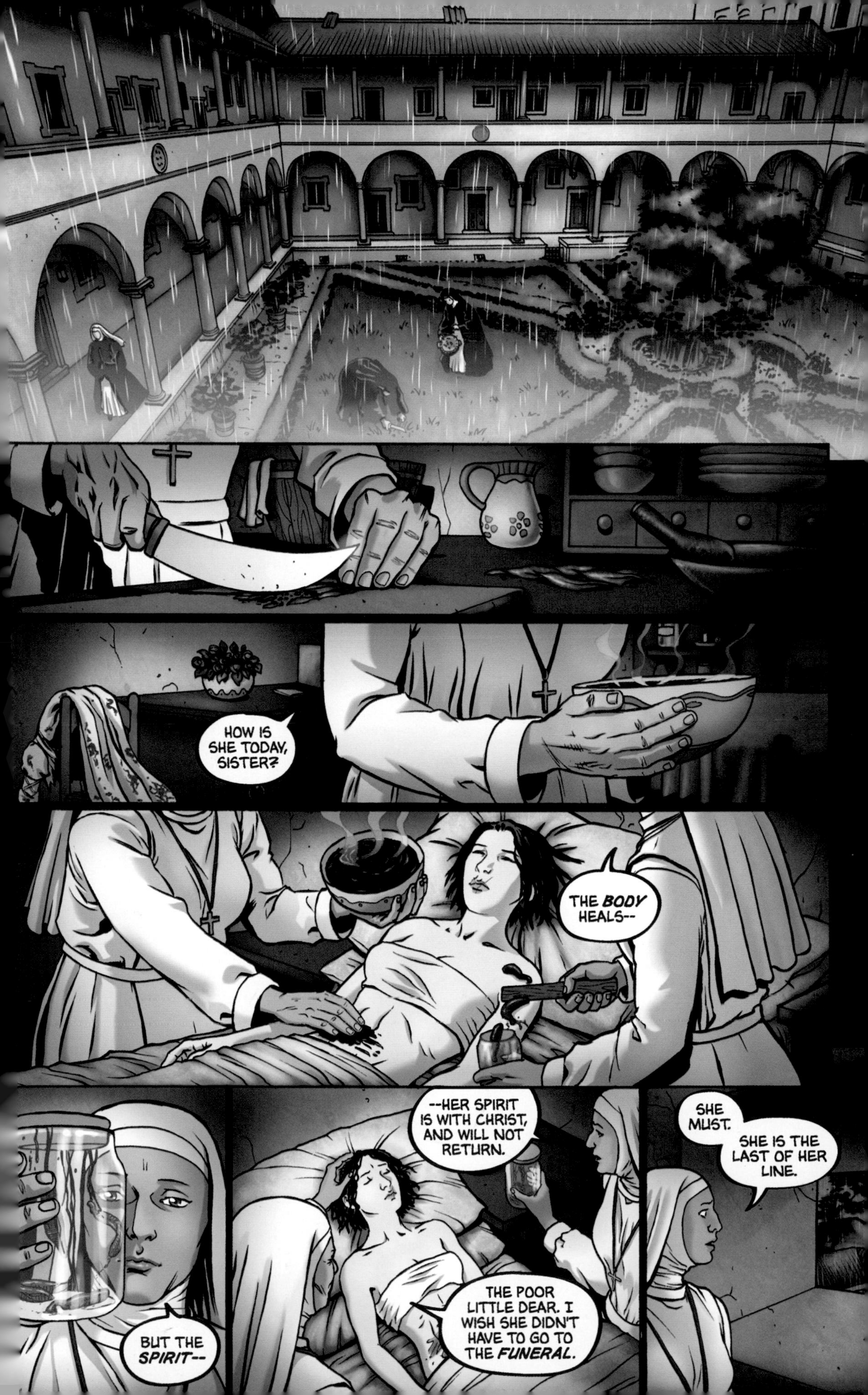
HOW IS SHE TODAY, SISTER?
THE *BODY* HEALS--
BUT THE *SPIRIT*--
--HER SPIRIT IS WITH CHRIST, AND WILL NOT RETURN.
THE POOR LITTLE DEAR. I WISH SHE DIDN'T HAVE TO GO TO THE *FUNERAL*.
SHE MUST.
SHE IS THE LAST OF HER LINE.

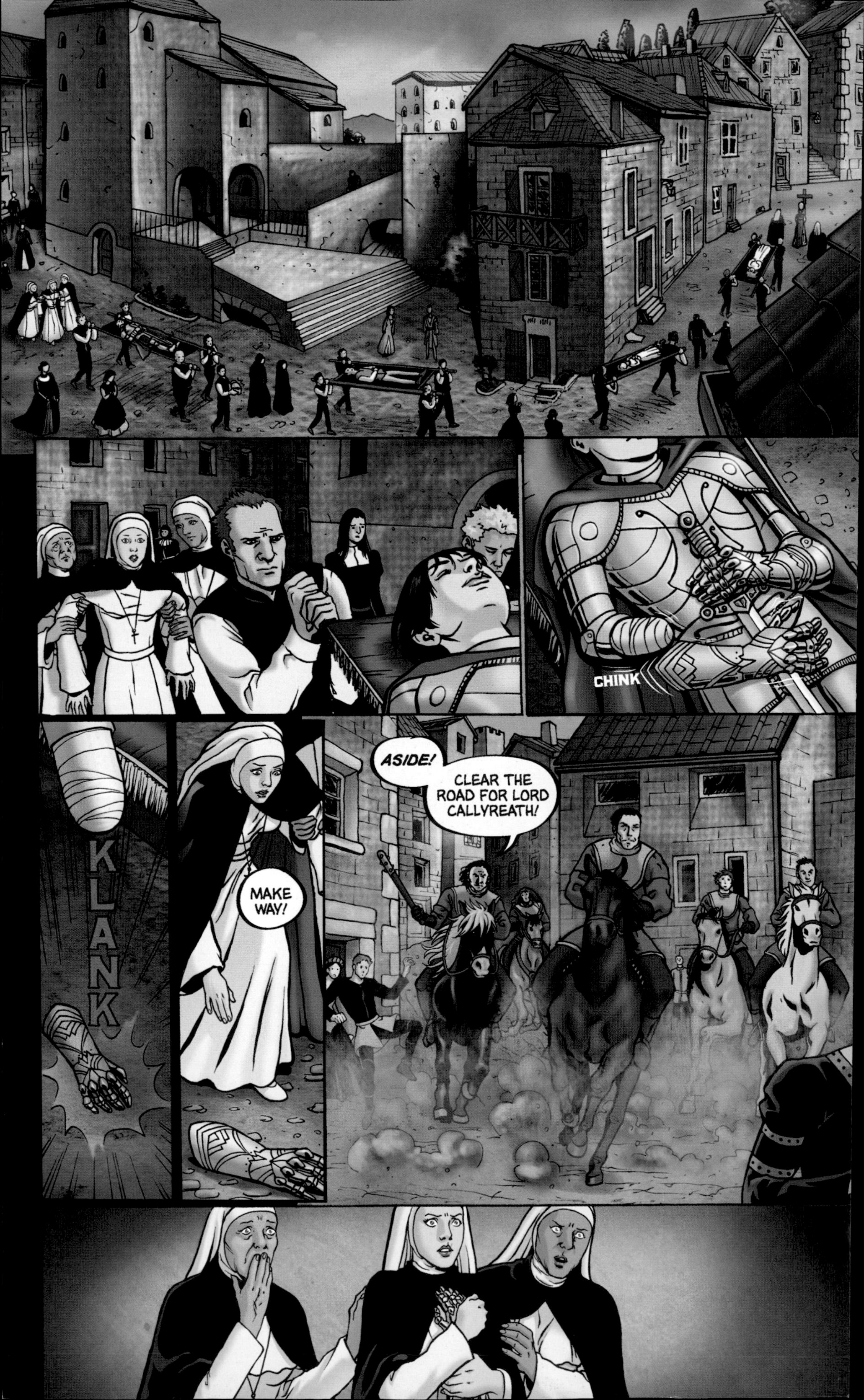
CHINK
KLANK
MAKE WAY!
ASIDE!
CLEAR THE ROAD FOR LORD CALLYREATH!

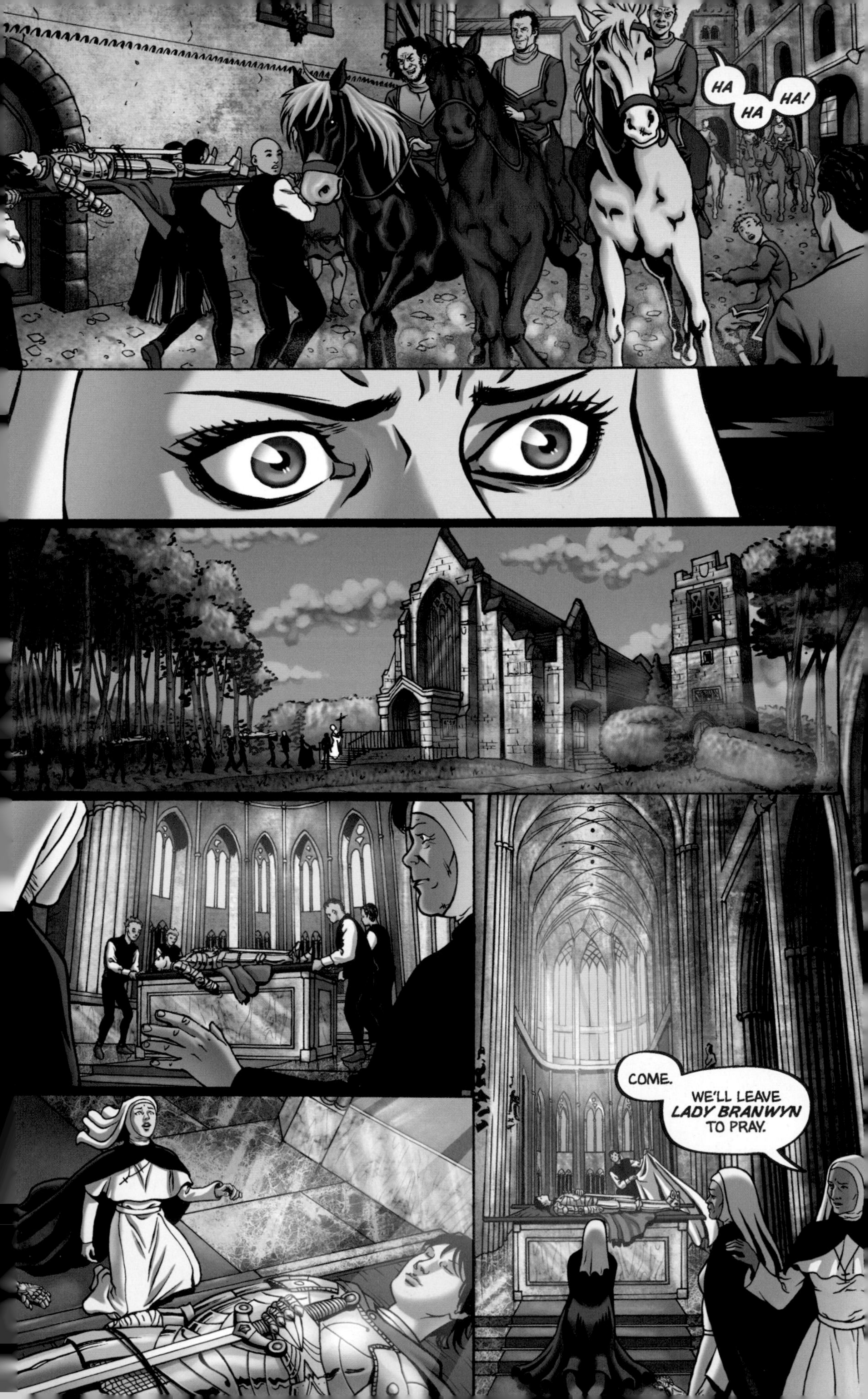
HA HA HA!
COME.
WE'LL LEAVE *LADY BRANWYN* TO PRAY.

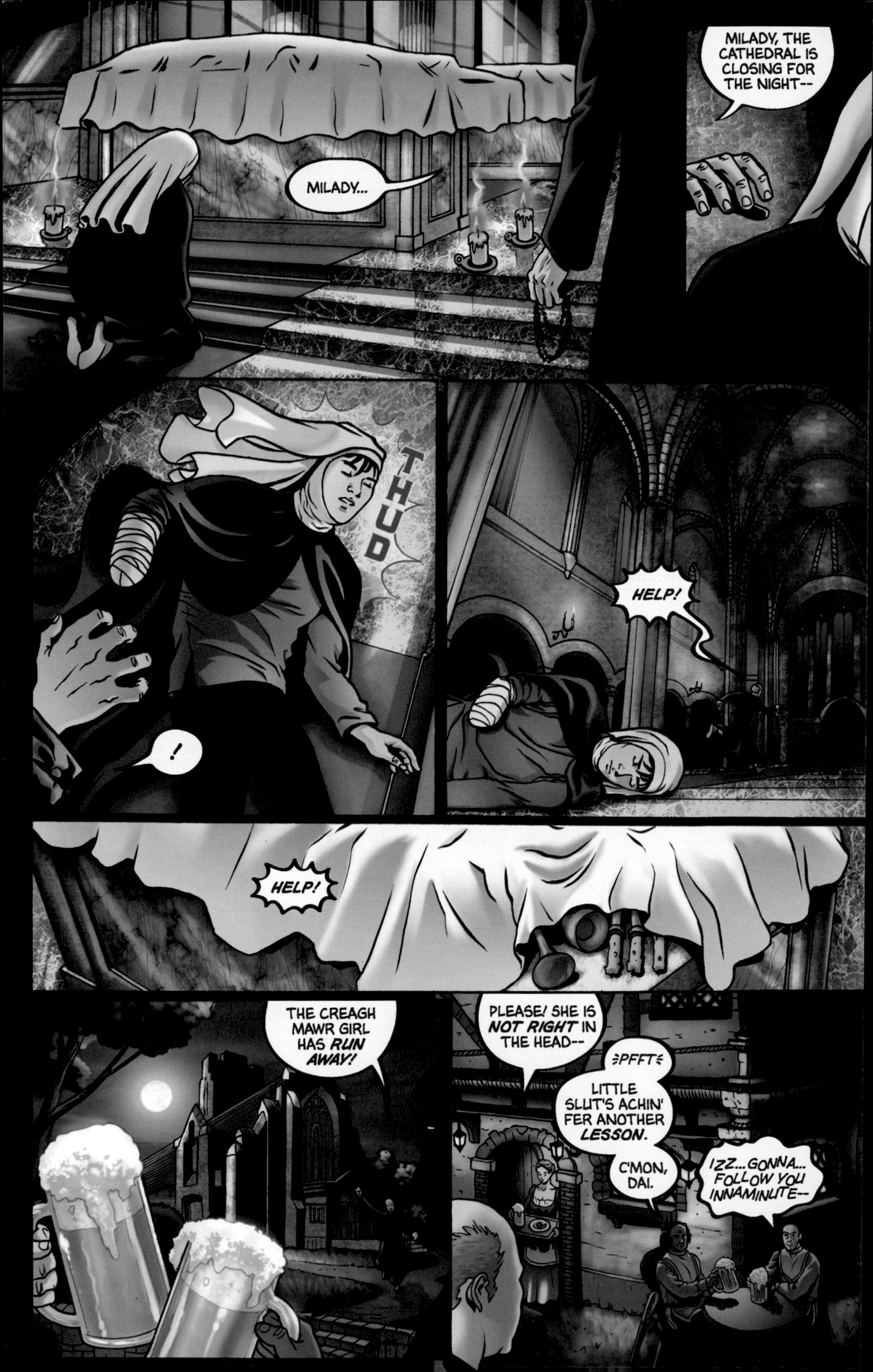
MILADY...
MILADY, THE CATHEDRAL IS CLOSING FOR THE NIGHT--
THUD
!
HELP!
HELP!
THE CREAGH MAWR GIRL HAS *RUN AWAY!*
PLEASE! SHE IS *NOT RIGHT* IN THE HEAD--
PFFT
LITTLE SLUT'S ACHIN' FER ANOTHER *LESSON.*
C'MON, DAI.
IZZ...GONNA... FOLLOW YOU INNAMINUTE--

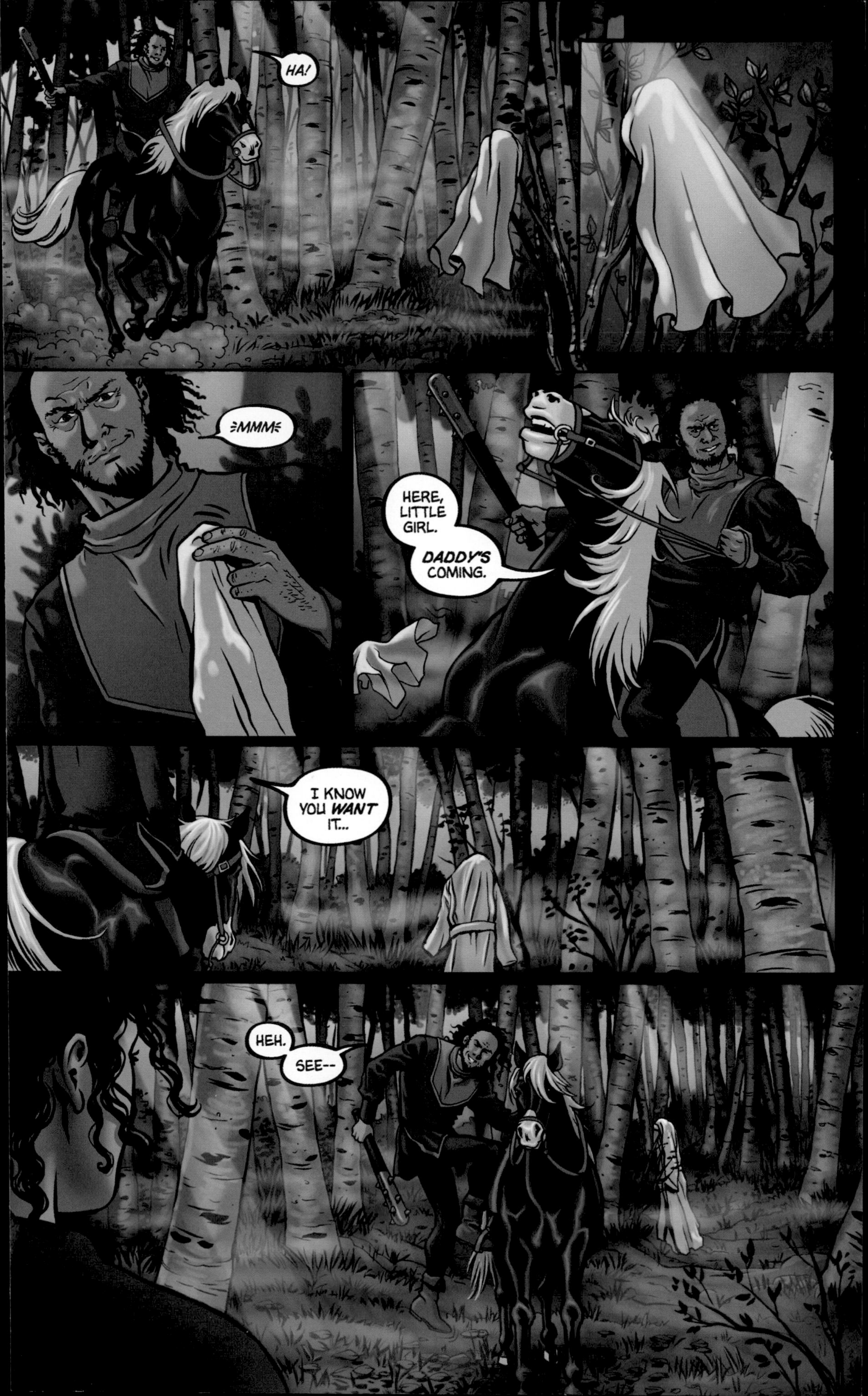
HA!
MMM
HERE, LITTLE GIRL.
DADDY'S COMING.
I KNOW YOU WANT IT...
HEH.
SEE--

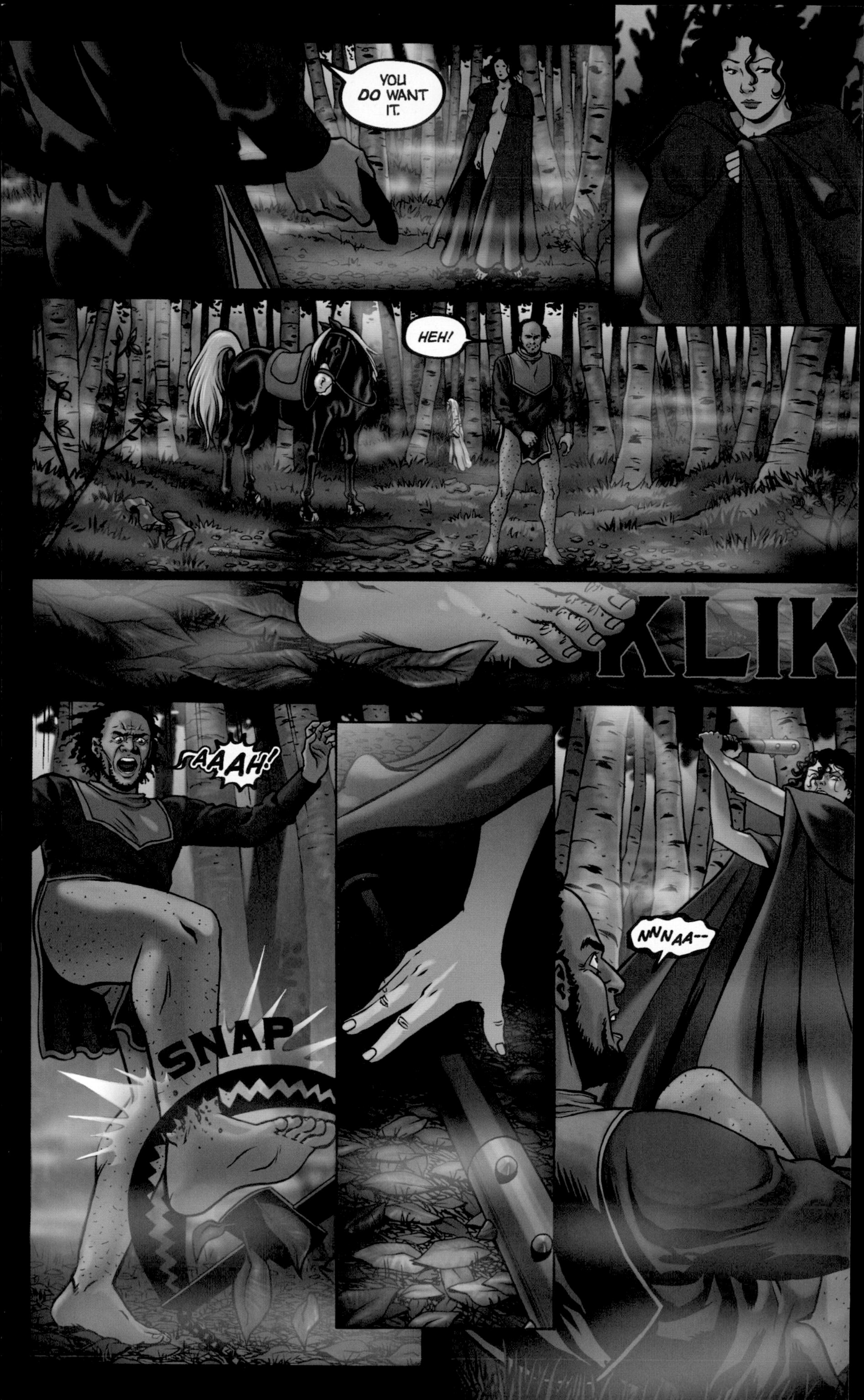
YOU DO WANT IT.
HEH!
KLIK
AAAH!
SNAP
NNNAA--

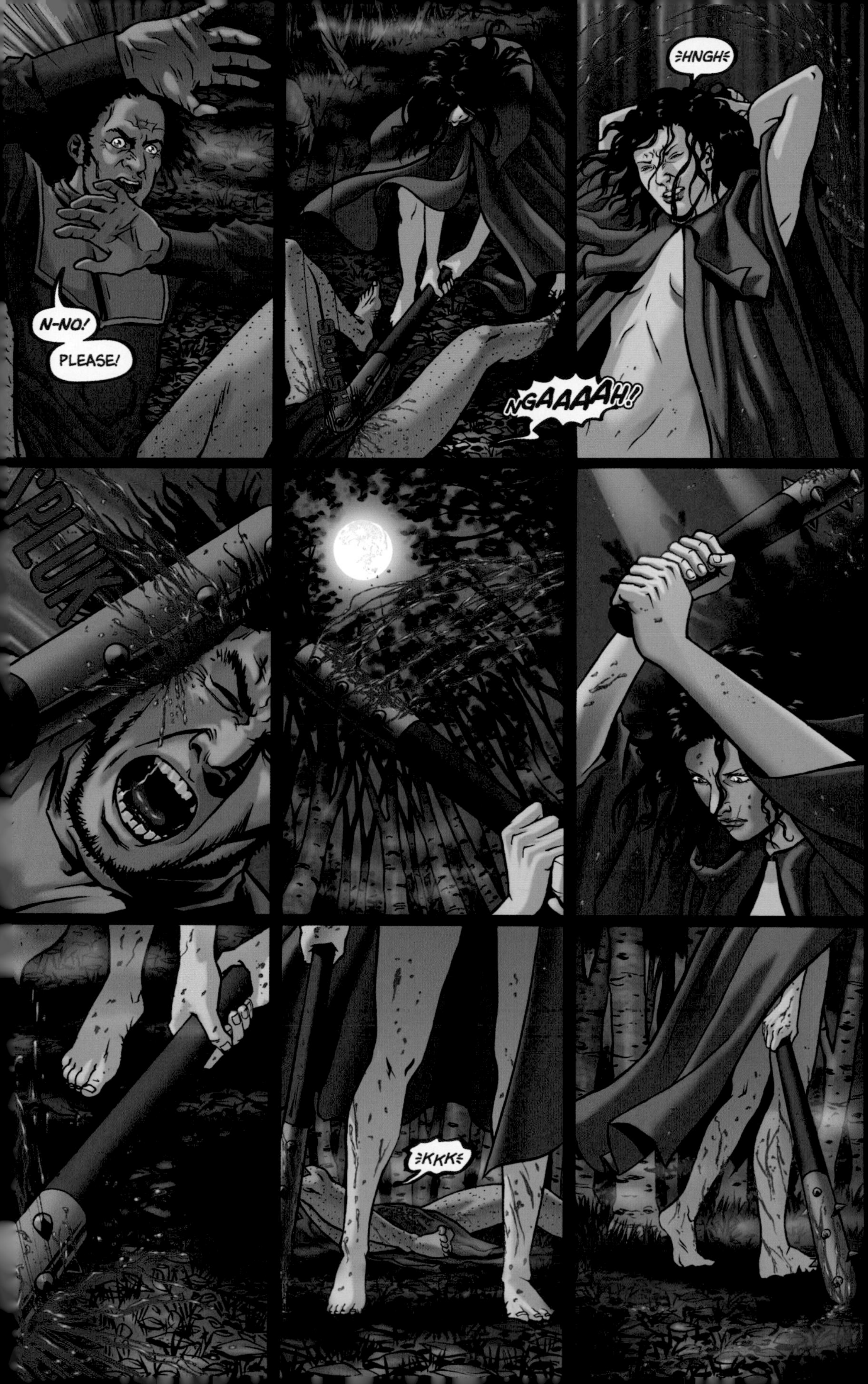
N-NO!
PLEASE!
SQUISH
HNGH
NGAAAAH!
SPLUK
KKK

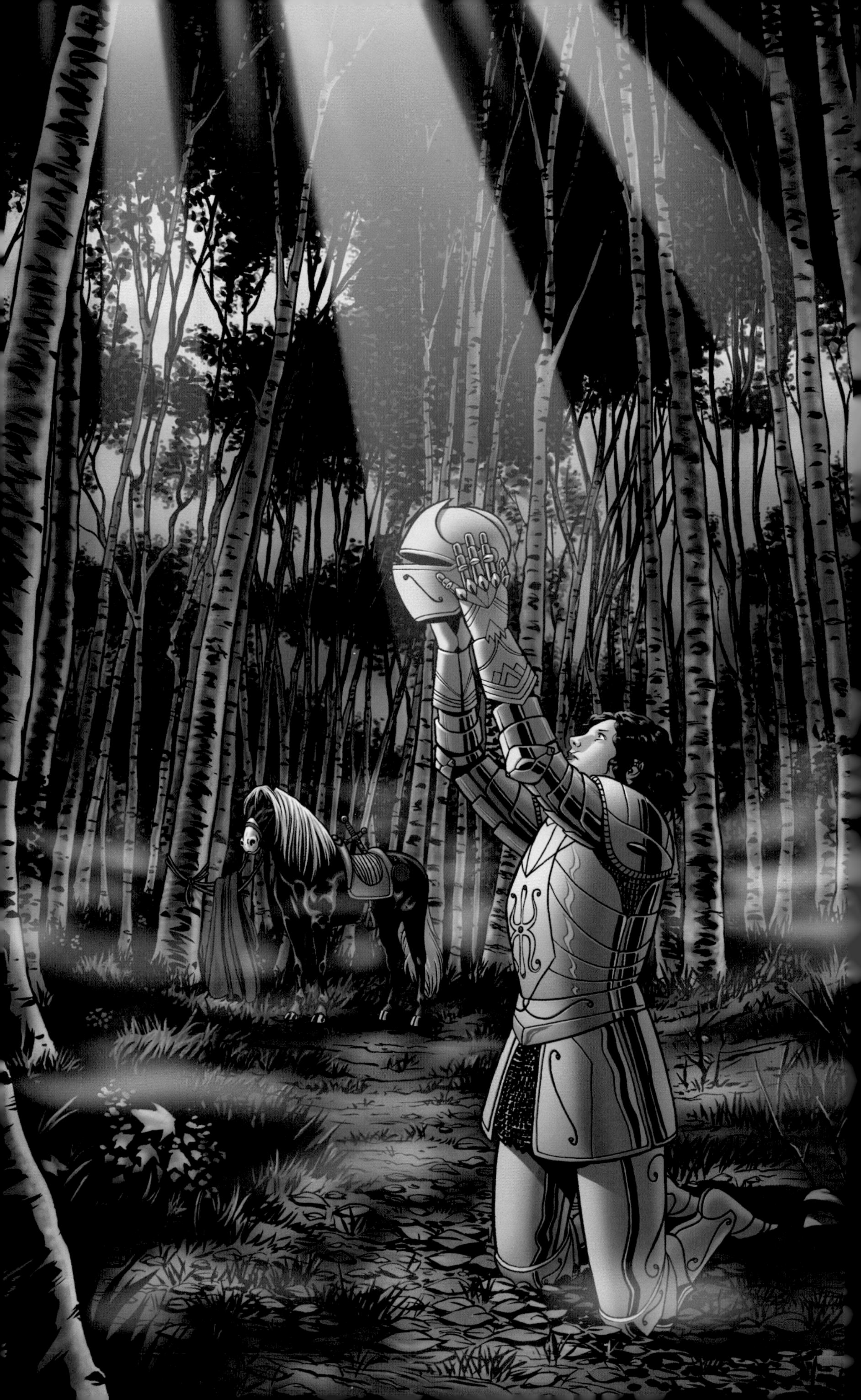

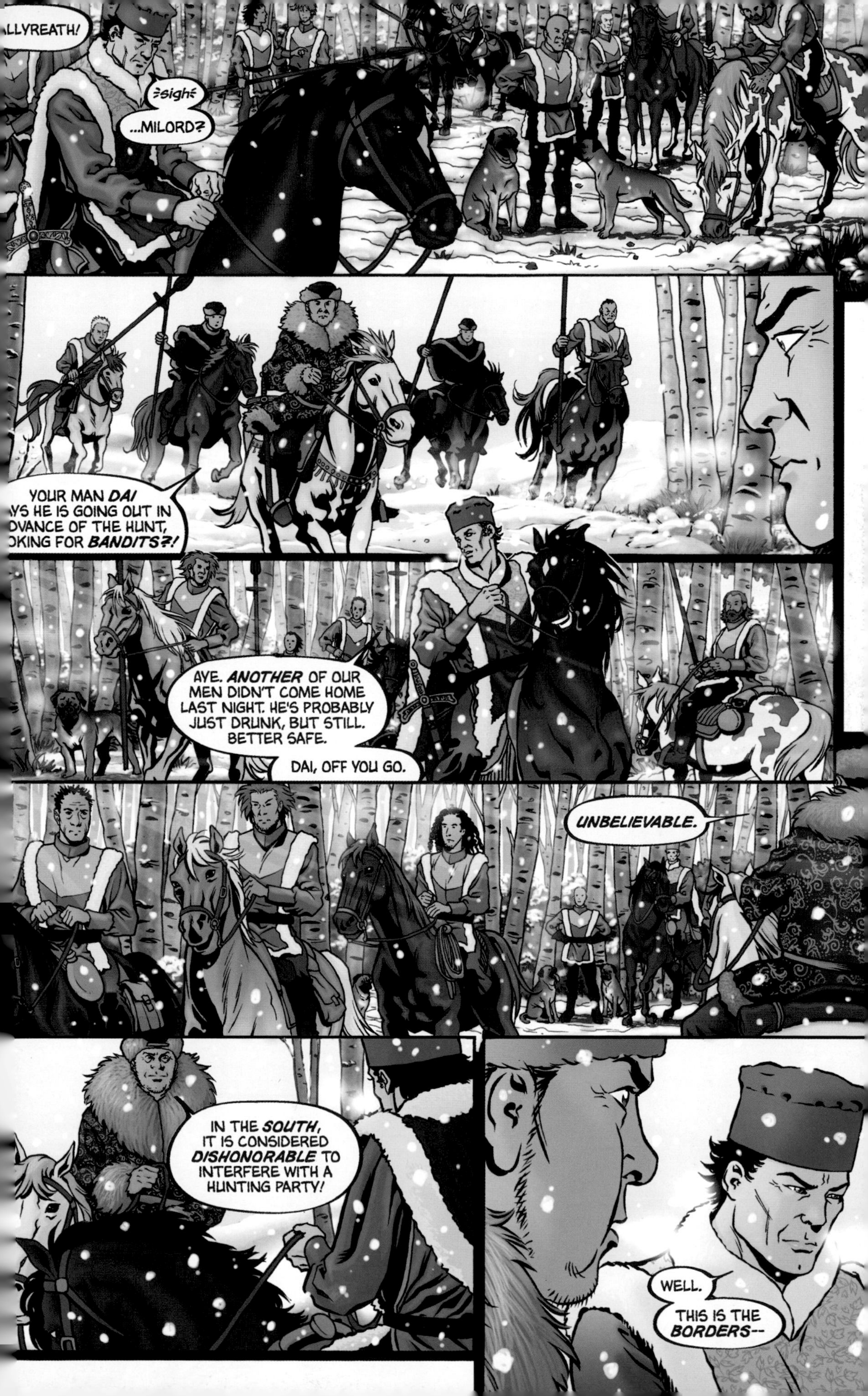
...ALLYREATH!
>sigh<
...MILORD?
YOUR MAN DAI ...AYS HE IS GOING OUT IN ...DVANCE OF THE HUNT, ...OKING FOR BANDITS?!
AYE. ANOTHER OF OUR MEN DIDN'T COME HOME LAST NIGHT. HE'S PROBABLY JUST DRUNK, BUT STILL. BETTER SAFE.
DAI, OFF YOU GO.
UNBELIEVABLE.
IN THE SOUTH, IT IS CONSIDERED DISHONORABLE TO INTERFERE WITH A HUNTING PARTY!
WELL.
THIS IS THE BORDERS--

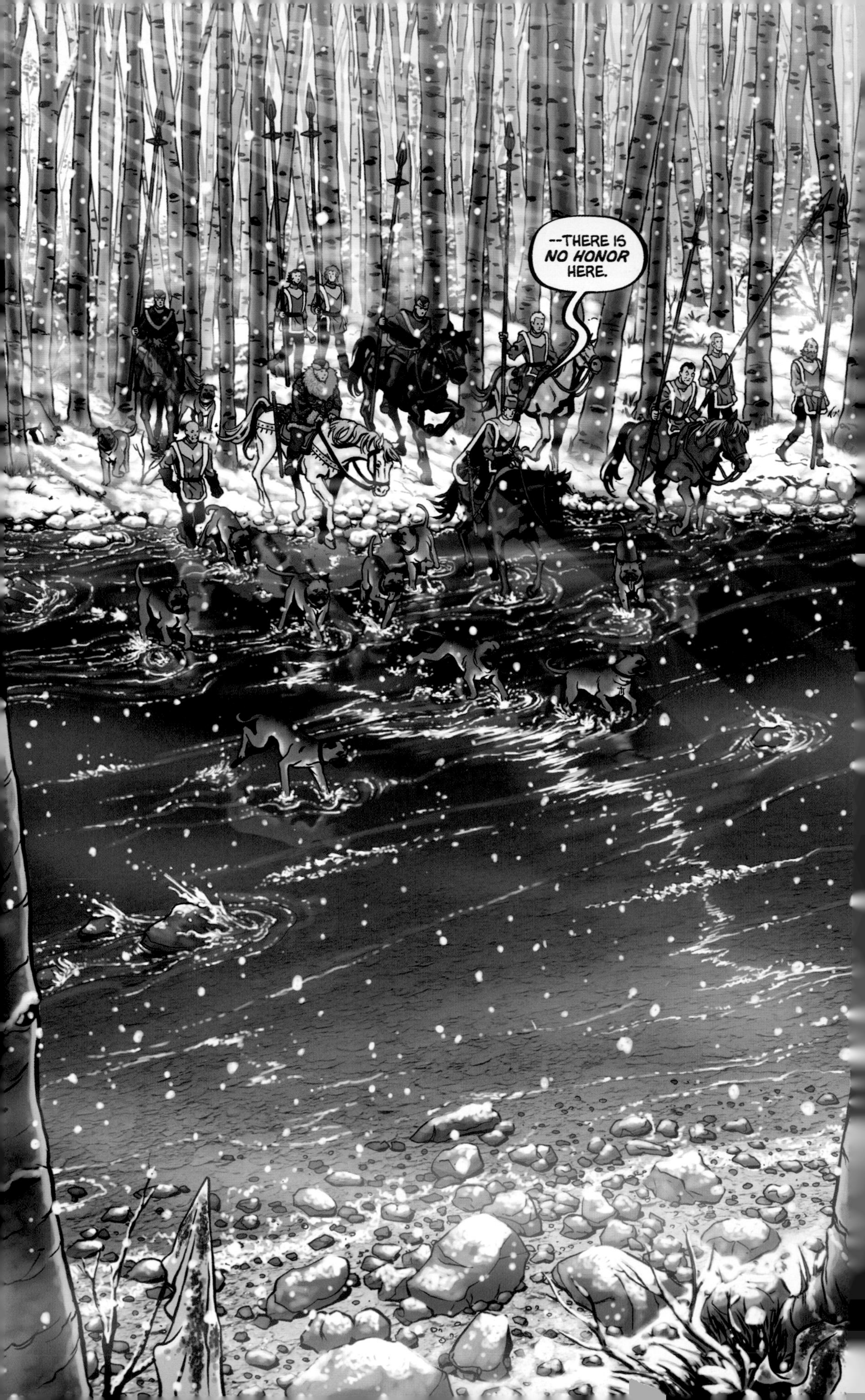
--THERE IS *NO HONOR* HERE.

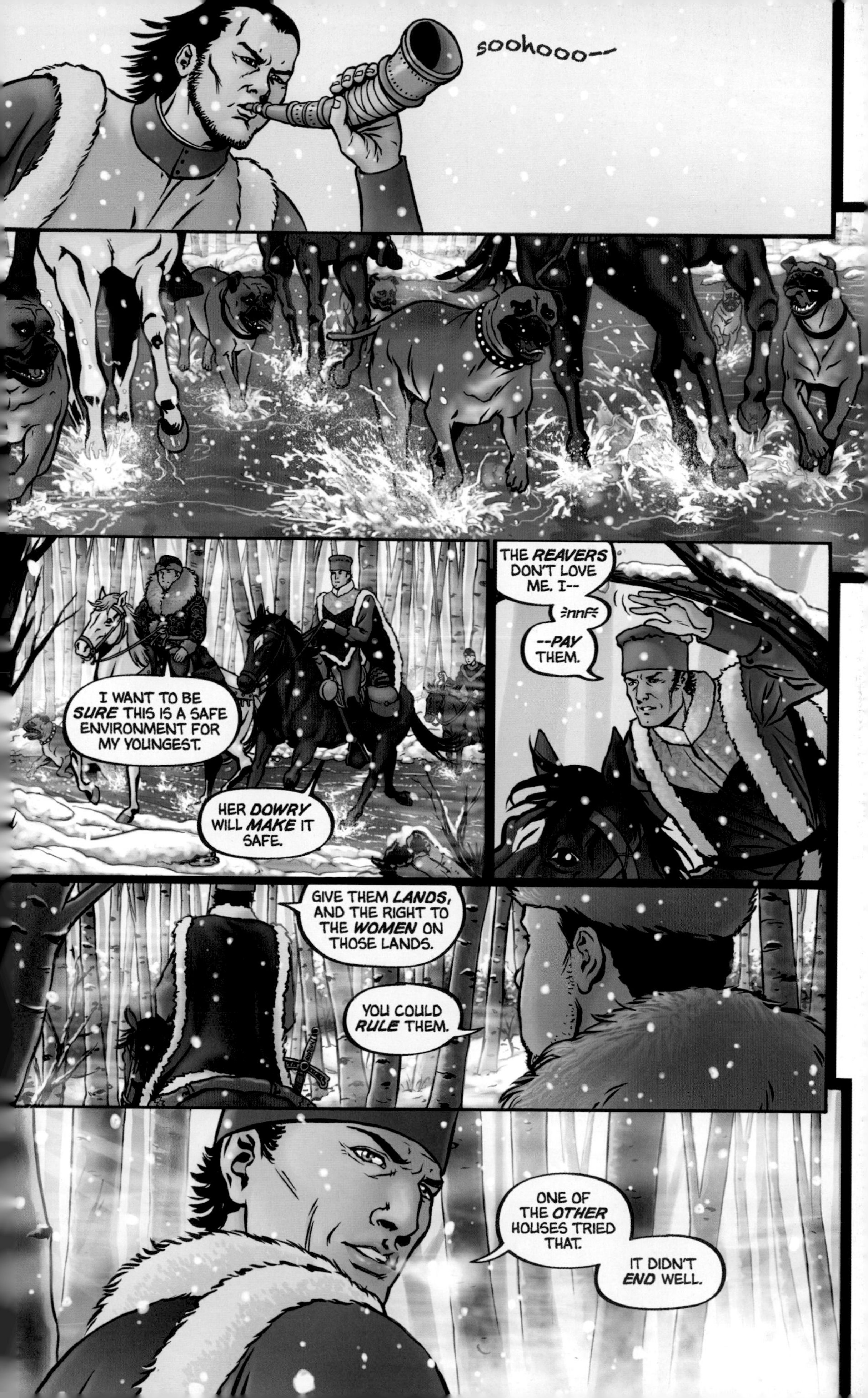
soohooo--
I WANT TO BE SURE THIS IS A SAFE ENVIRONMENT FOR MY YOUNGEST.
HER DOWRY WILL MAKE IT SAFE.
THE REAVERS DON'T LOVE ME. I--
nnf
--PAY THEM.
GIVE THEM LANDS, AND THE RIGHT TO THE WOMEN ON THOSE LANDS.
YOU COULD RULE THEM.
ONE OF THE OTHER HOUSES TRIED THAT.
IT DIDN'T END WELL.

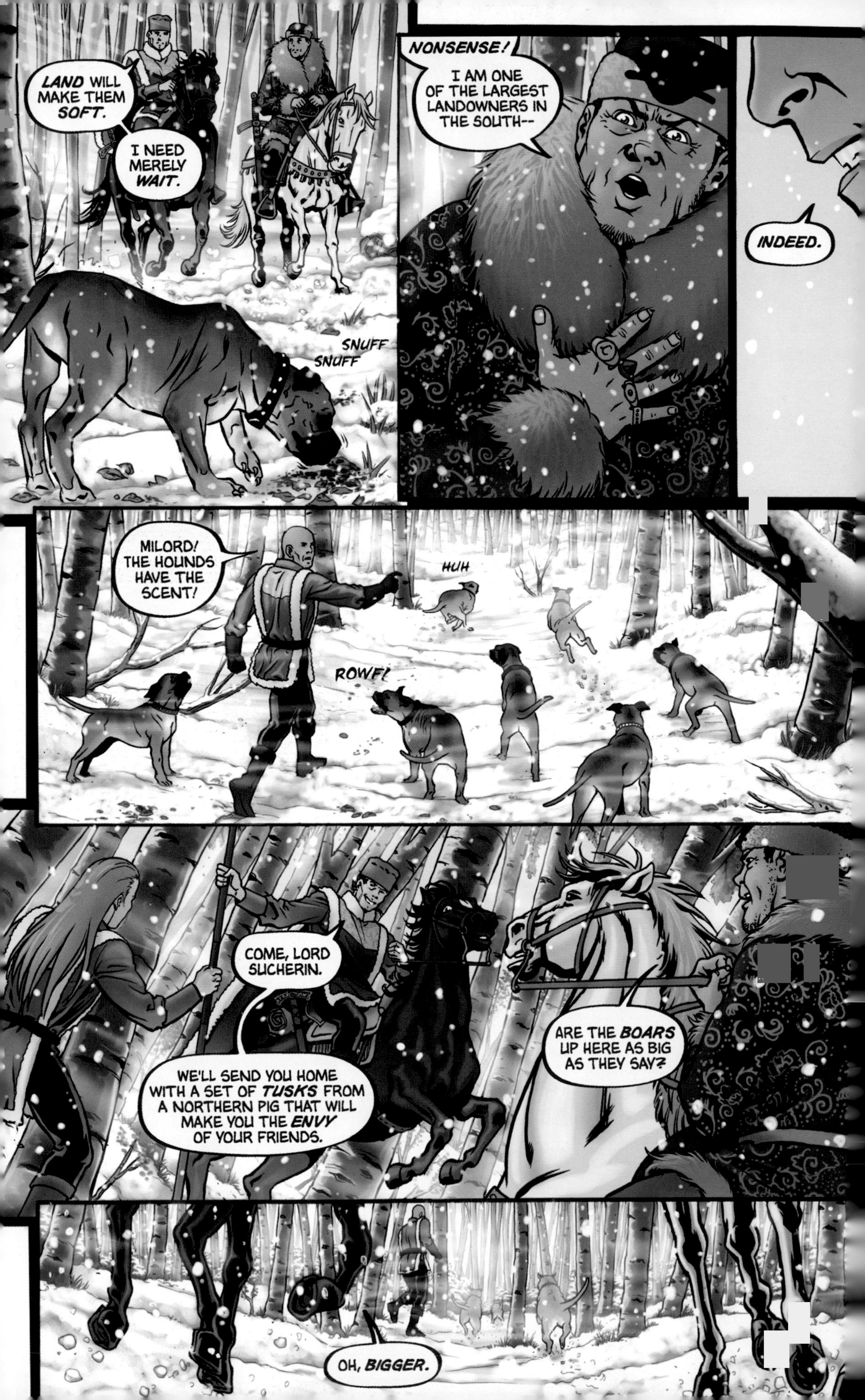
LAND WILL MAKE THEM SOFT.
I NEED MERELY WAIT.
SNUFF
SNUFF
NONSENSE!
I AM ONE OF THE LARGEST LANDOWNERS IN THE SOUTH--
INDEED.
MILORD! THE HOUNDS HAVE THE SCENT!
HUH
ROWF!
COME, LORD SUCHERIN.
WE'LL SEND YOU HOME WITH A SET OF TUSKS FROM A NORTHERN PIG THAT WILL MAKE YOU THE ENVY OF YOUR FRIENDS.
ARE THE BOARS UP HERE AS BIG AS THEY SAY?
OH, BIGGER.

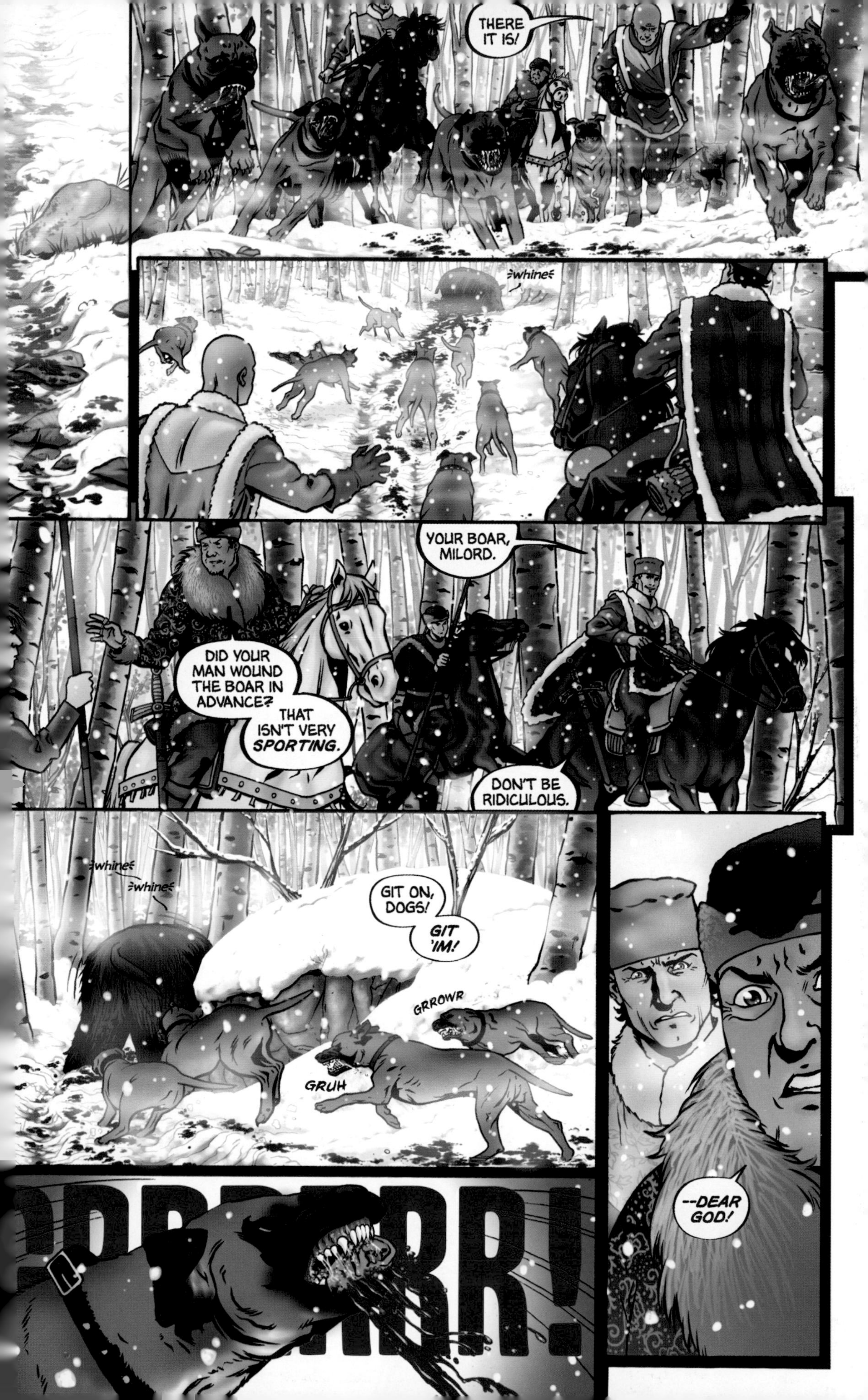
THERE IT IS!
whine
YOUR BOAR, MILORD.
DID YOUR MAN WOUND THE BOAR IN ADVANCE?
THAT ISN'T VERY SPORTING.
DON'T BE RIDICULOUS.
whine
whine
GIT ON, DOGS!
GIT 'IM!
GRRROWR
GRUH
--DEAR GOD!

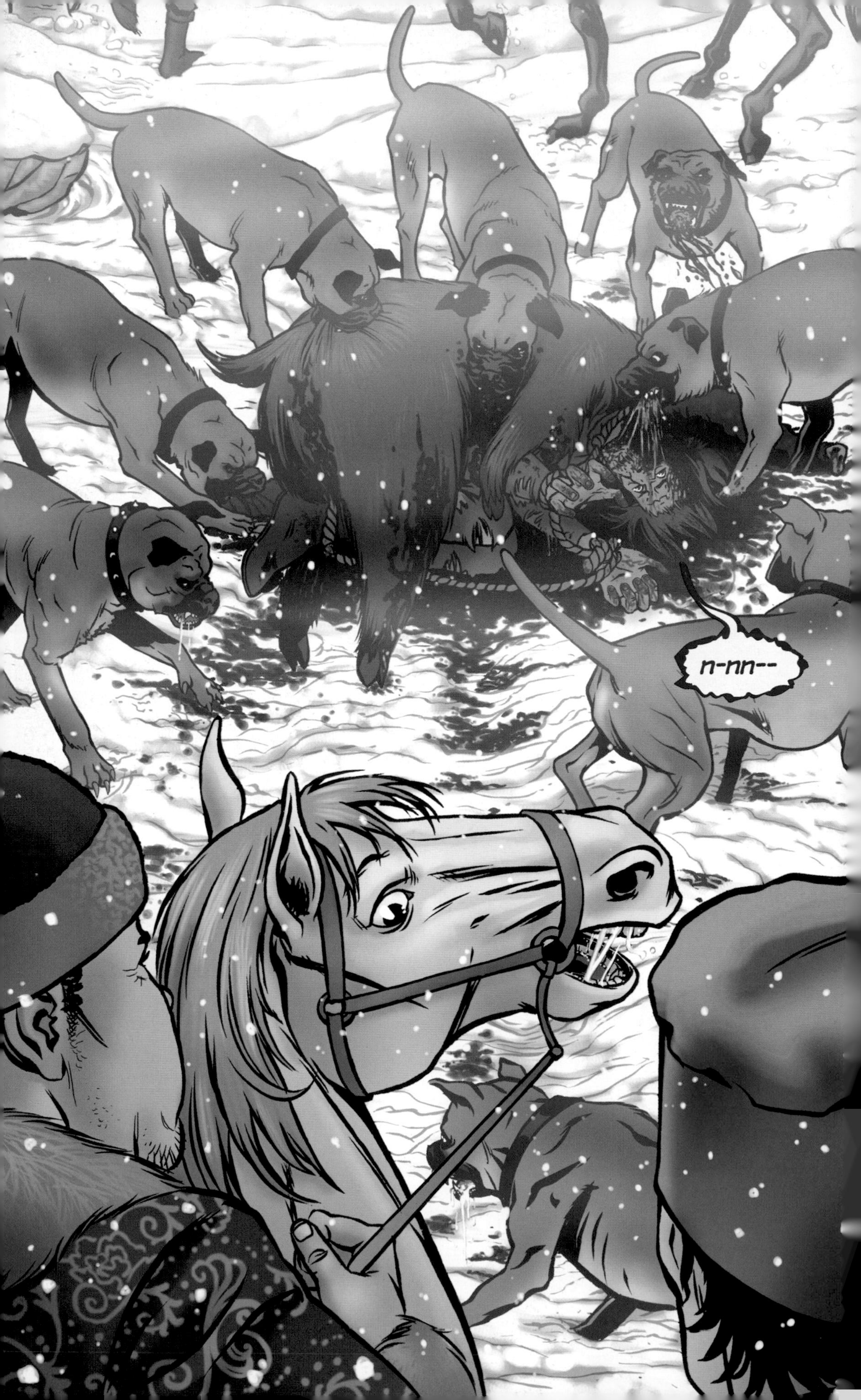
n-nn--

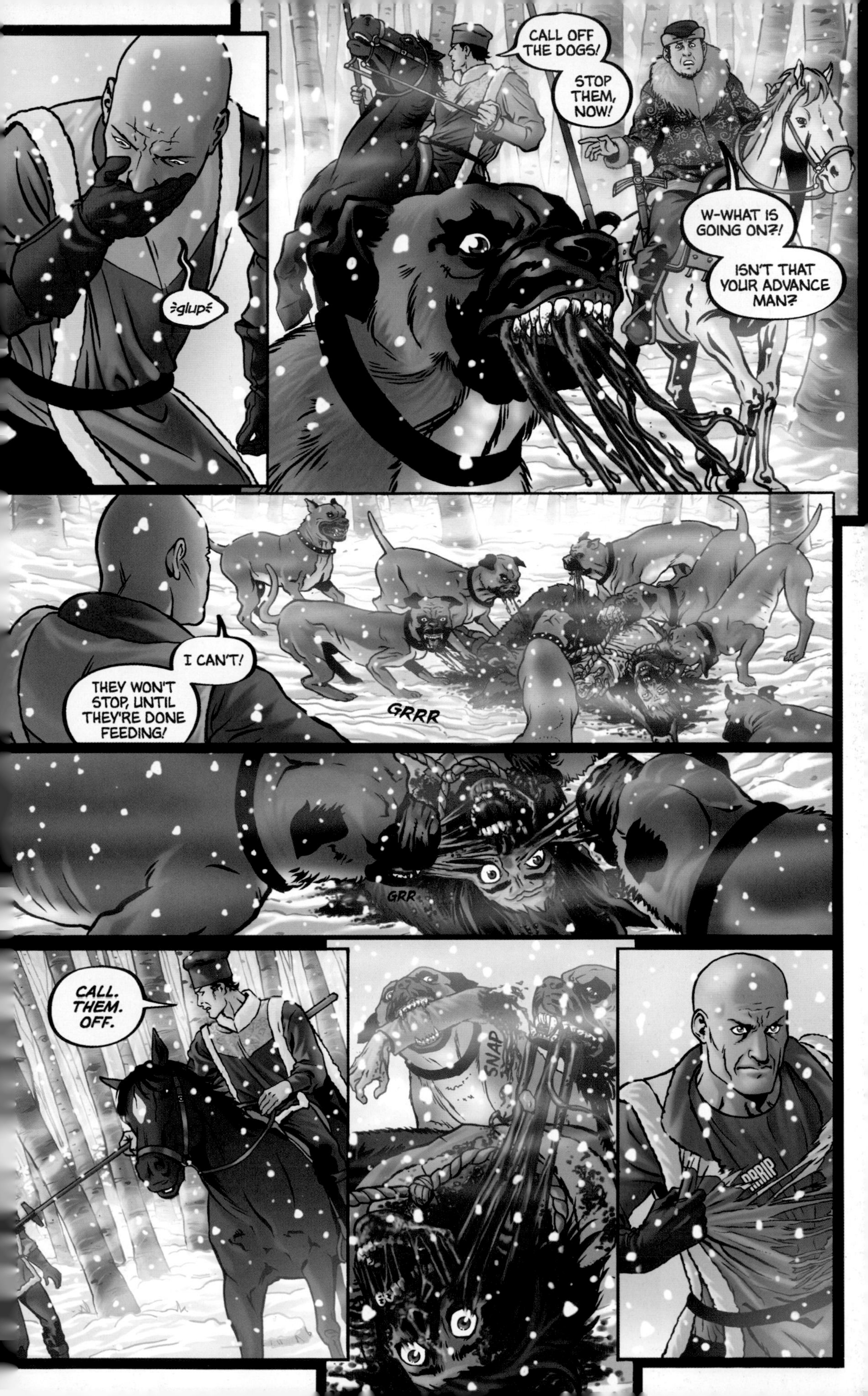

≈glup≈
CALL OFF THE DOGS!
STOP THEM, NOW!
W-WHAT IS GOING ON?!
ISN'T THAT YOUR ADVANCE MAN?
I CAN'T!
THEY WON'T STOP, UNTIL THEY'RE DONE FEEDING!
GRRR
GRR
CALL. THEM. OFF.
SNAP
RRRIP

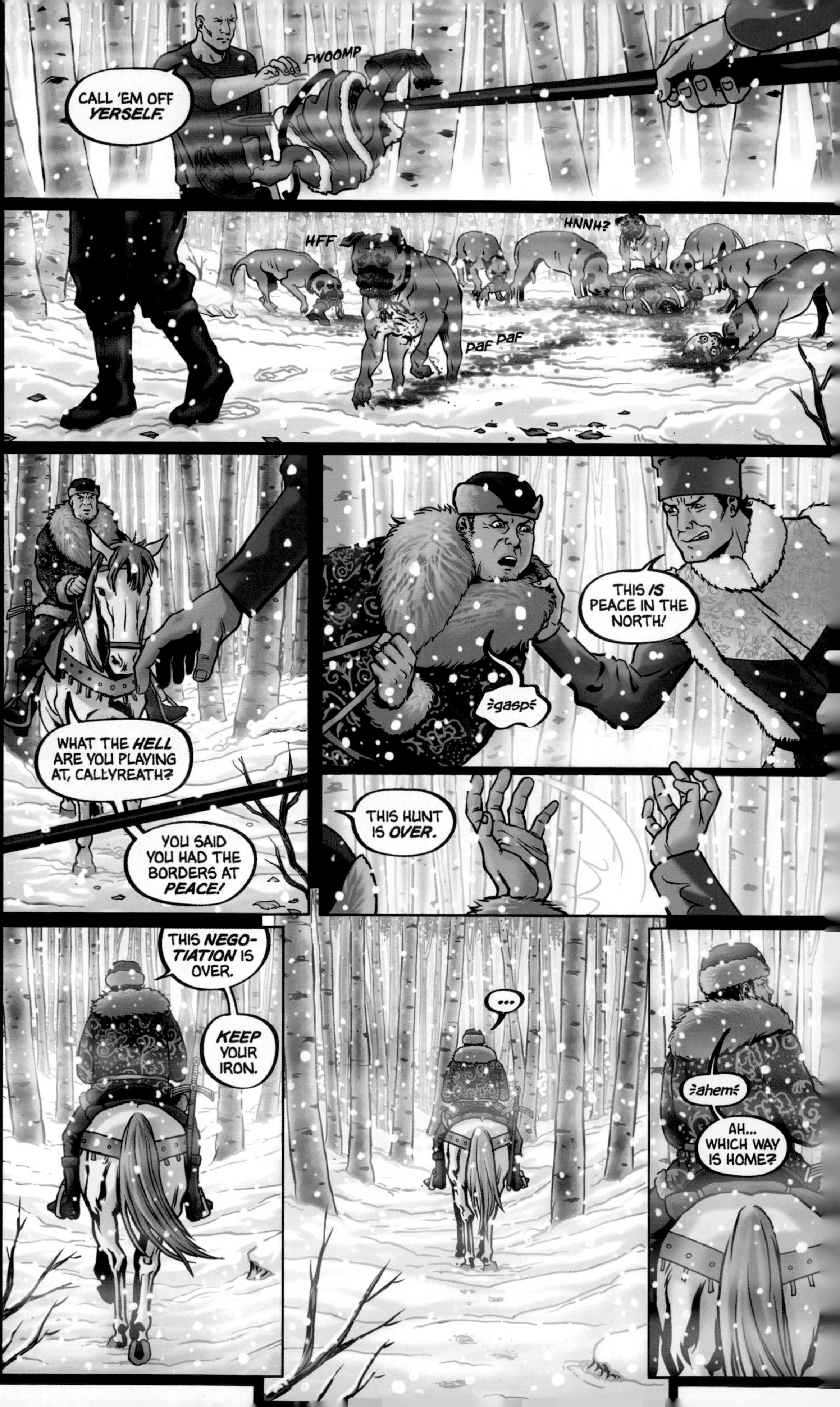
CALL 'EM OFF YERSELF.
FWOOMP
HFF
HNNH?
paf paf
WHAT THE HELL ARE YOU PLAYING AT, CALLYREATH?
YOU SAID YOU HAD THE BORDERS AT PEACE!
THIS IS PEACE IN THE NORTH!
gasp
THIS HUNT IS OVER.
THIS NEGO-TIATION IS OVER.
KEEP YOUR IRON.
...
ahem
AH... WHICH WAY IS HOME?

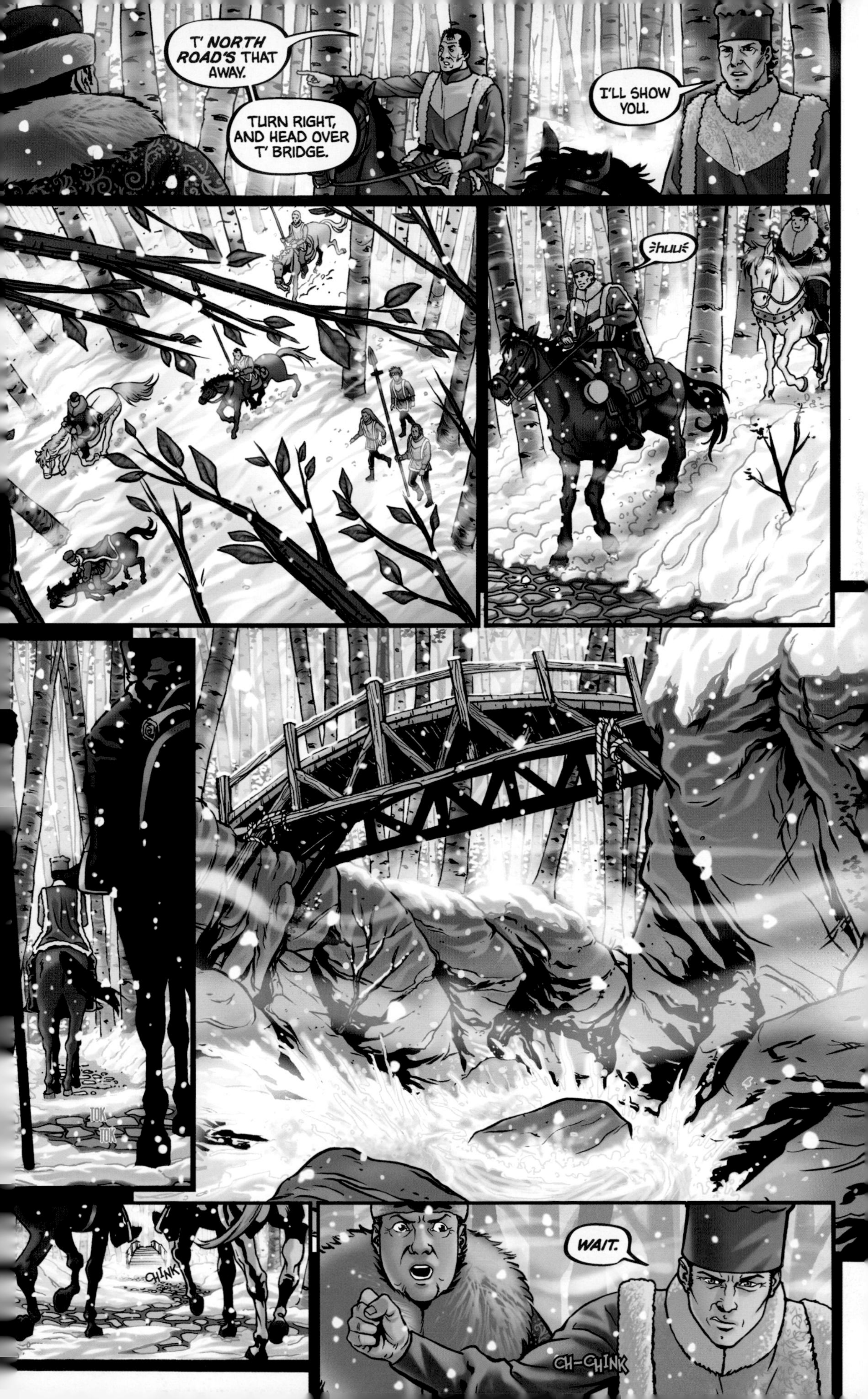
T' NORTH ROAD'S THAT AWAY.
TURN RIGHT, AND HEAD OVER T' BRIDGE.
I'LL SHOW YOU.
HUU
TOK TOK
CHINK
WAIT.
CH-CHINK

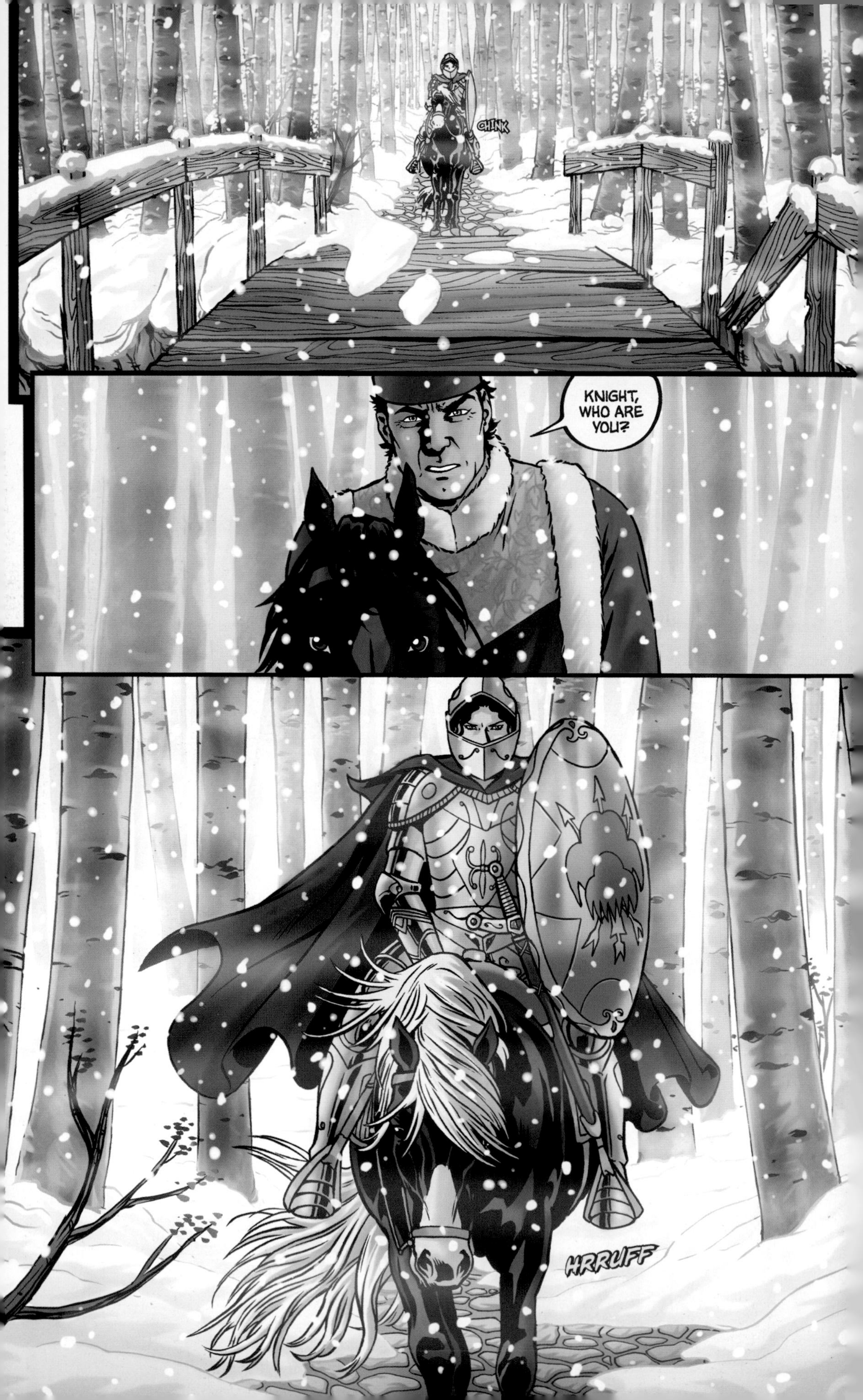
CHINK
KNIGHT, WHO ARE YOU?
HRRUFF

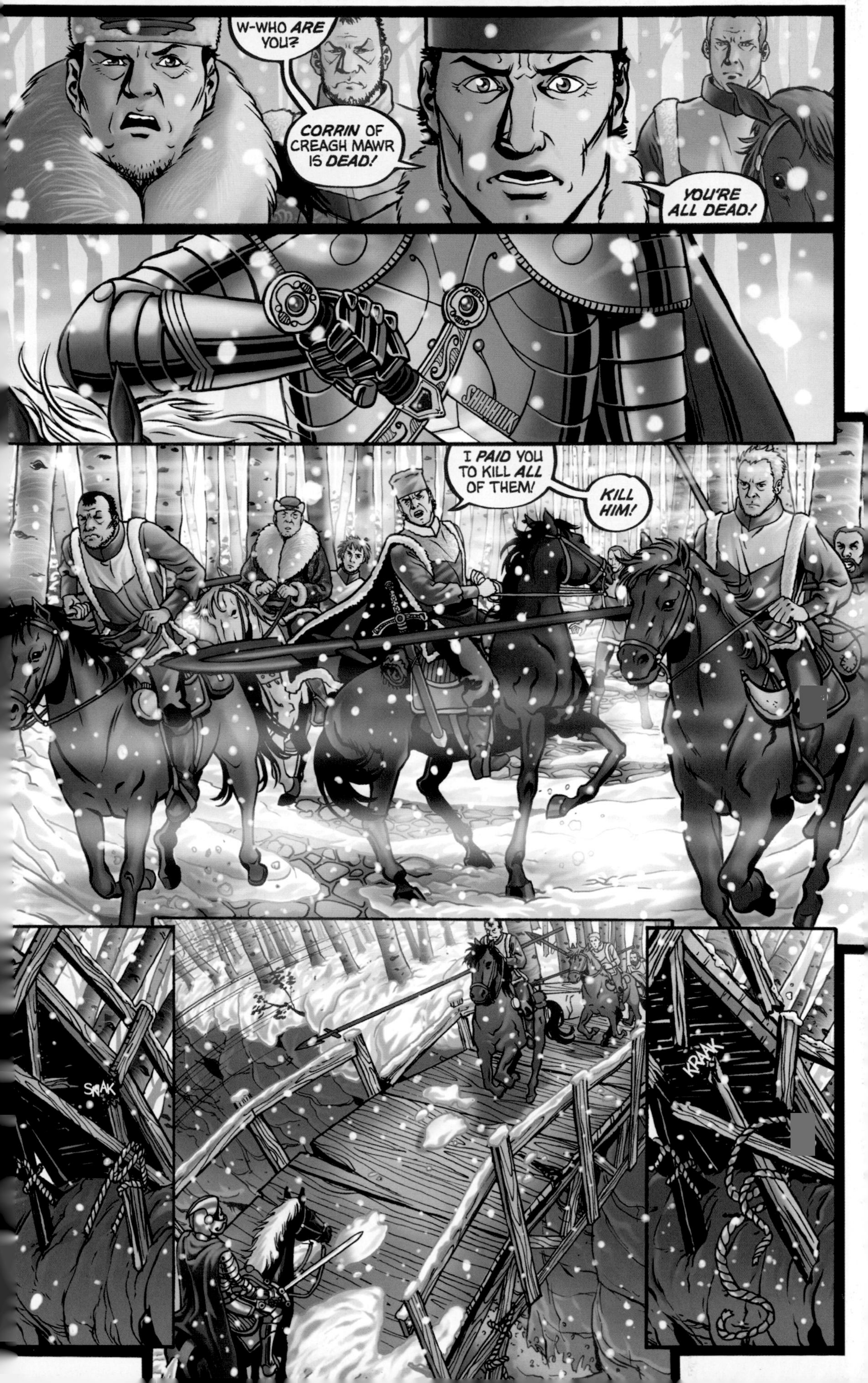
W-WHO ARE YOU?
CORRIN OF CREAGH MAWR IS DEAD!
YOU'RE ALL DEAD!
SHHHHK
I PAID YOU TO KILL ALL OF THEM!
KILL HIM!
SKRAK
KRAAK

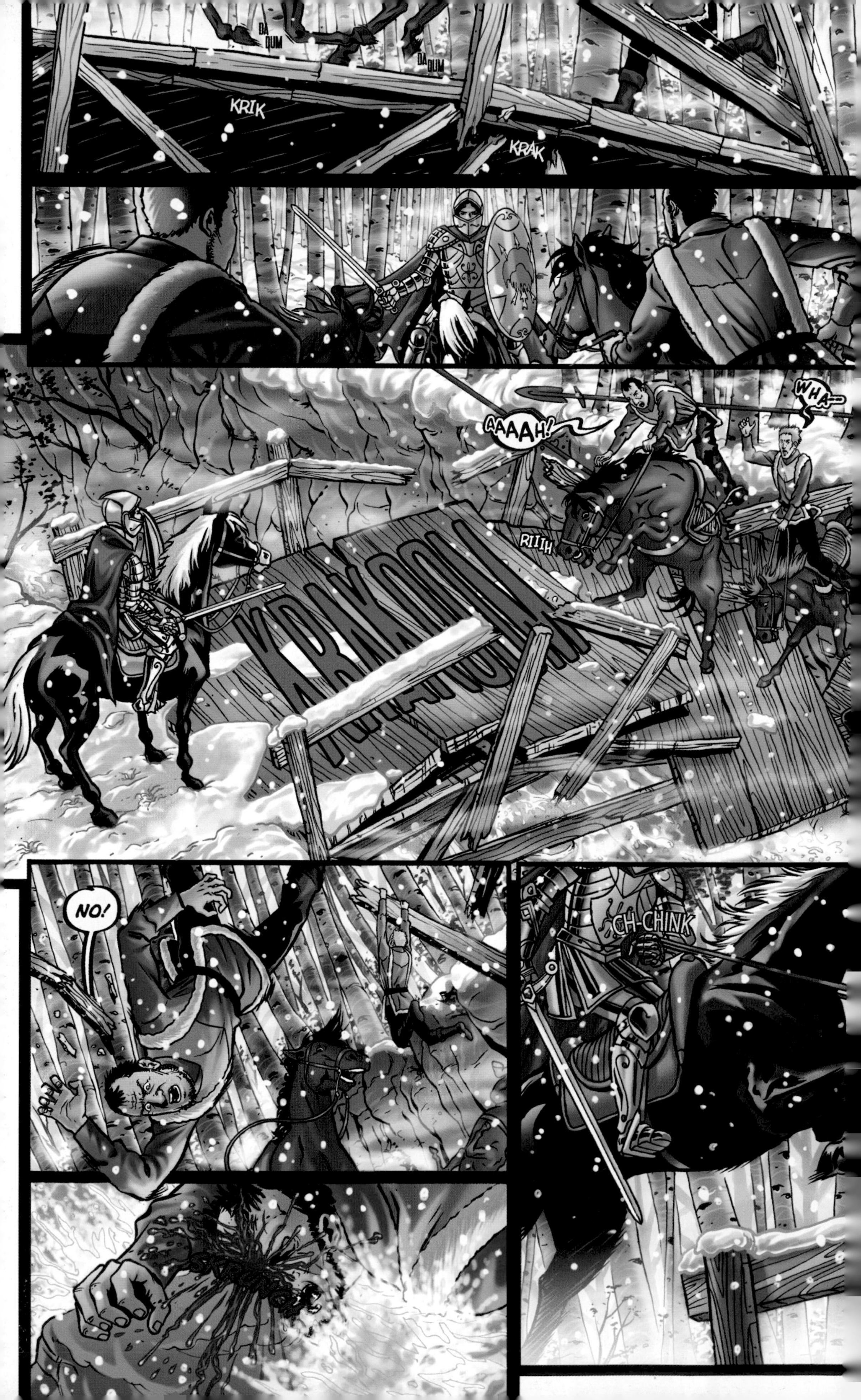

DA DUM
DA DUM
KRIK
KRAK
AAAAH!
WHA--
RIIIH
KRAKOOM
NO!
CH-CHINK

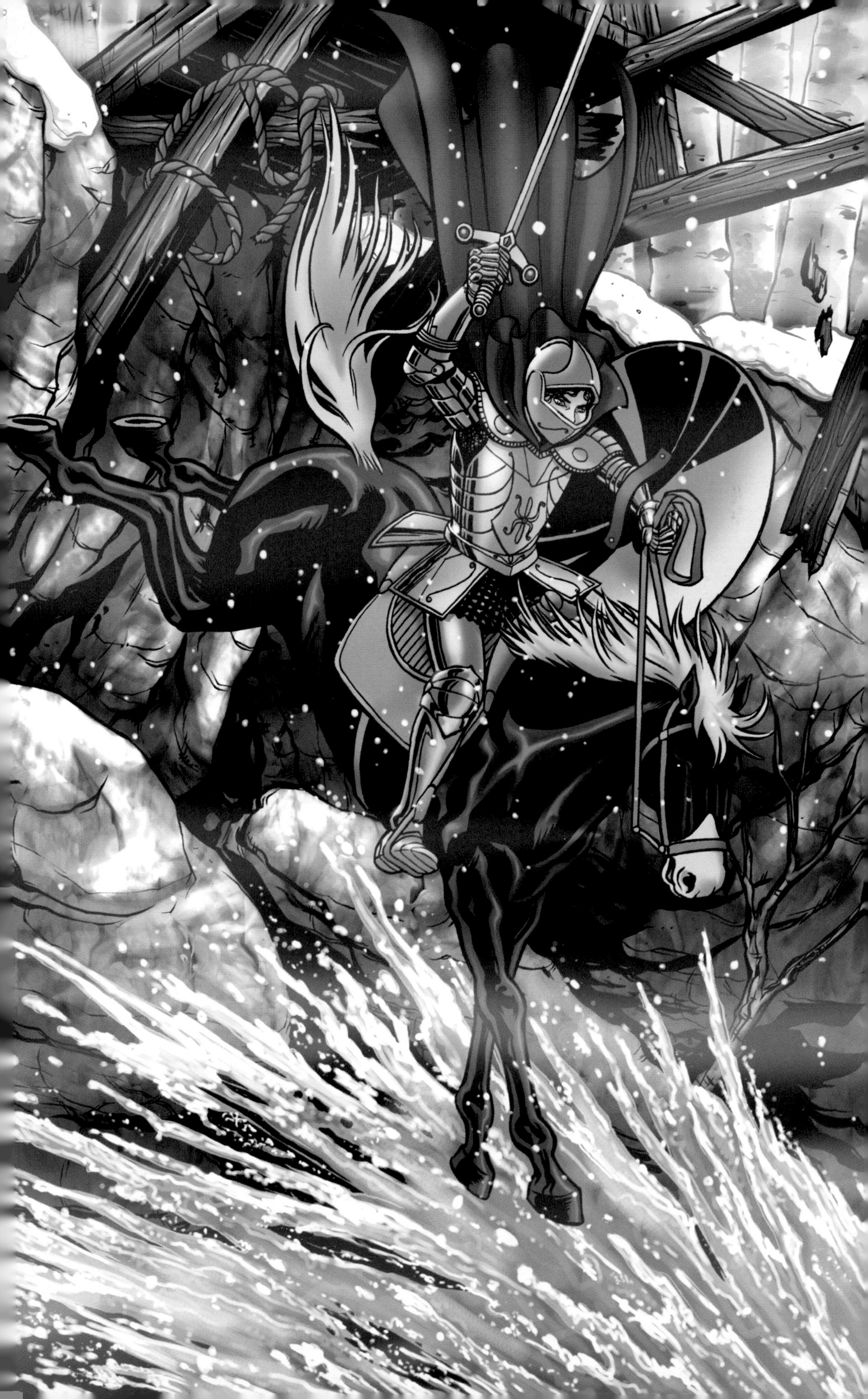

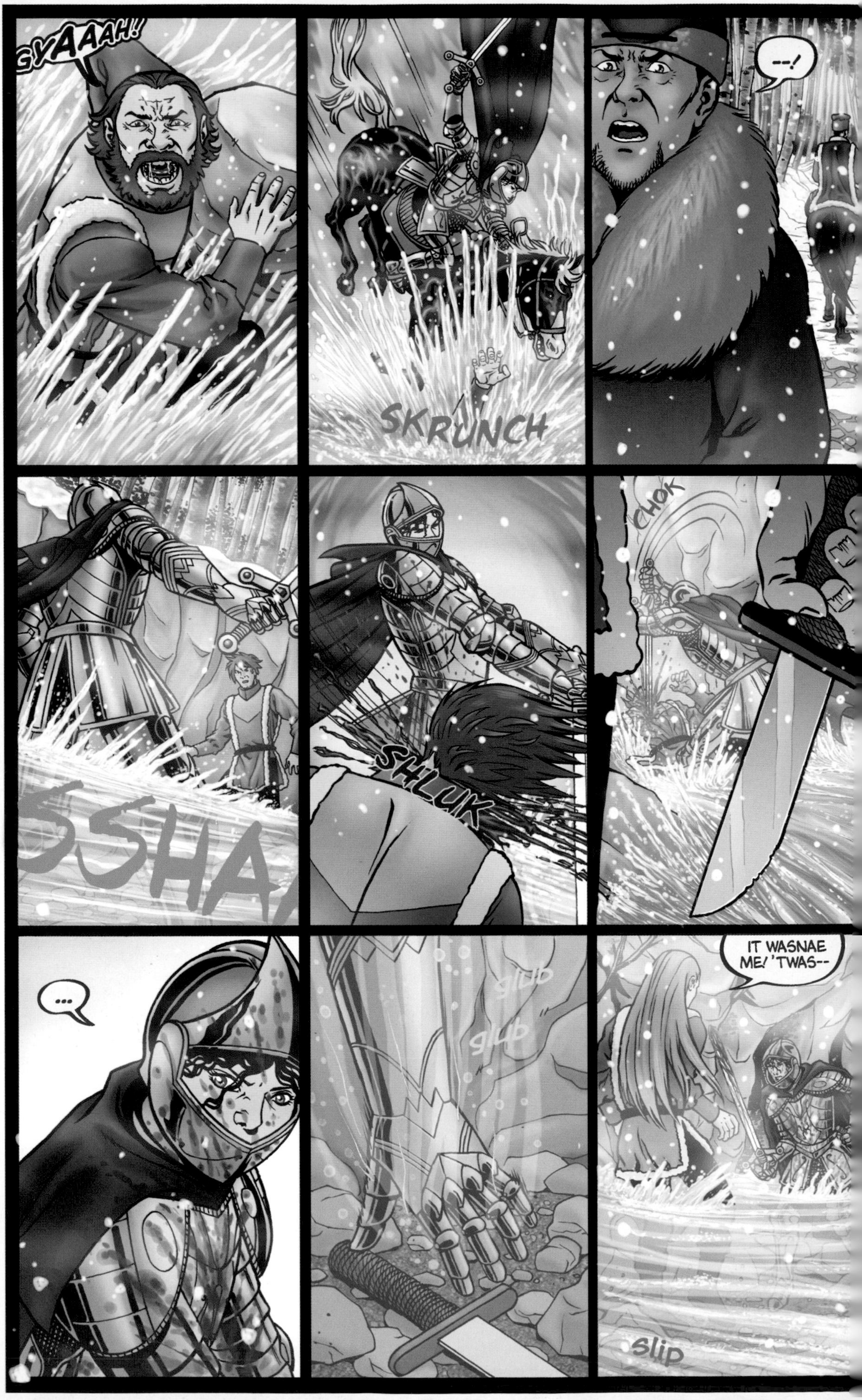
GYAAAH!
SKRUNCH
--!
SSHA
SHLUK
CHOK
...
glub
glub
IT WASNAE ME! 'TWAS--
slip

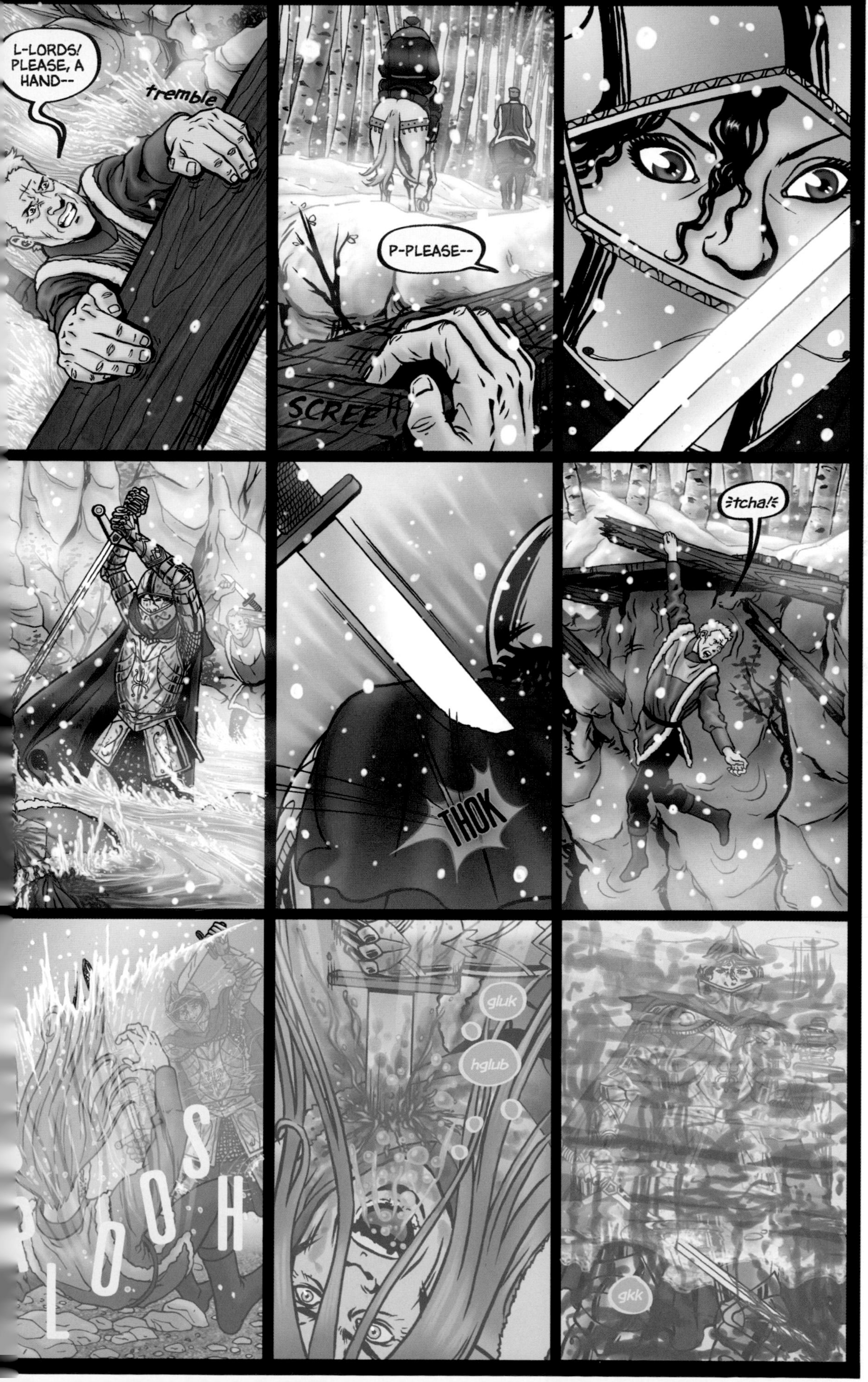
L-LORDS! PLEASE, A HAND--
tremble
P-PLEASE--
SCREE
THOK
tcha!
PLOOSH
gluk
hglub
gkk

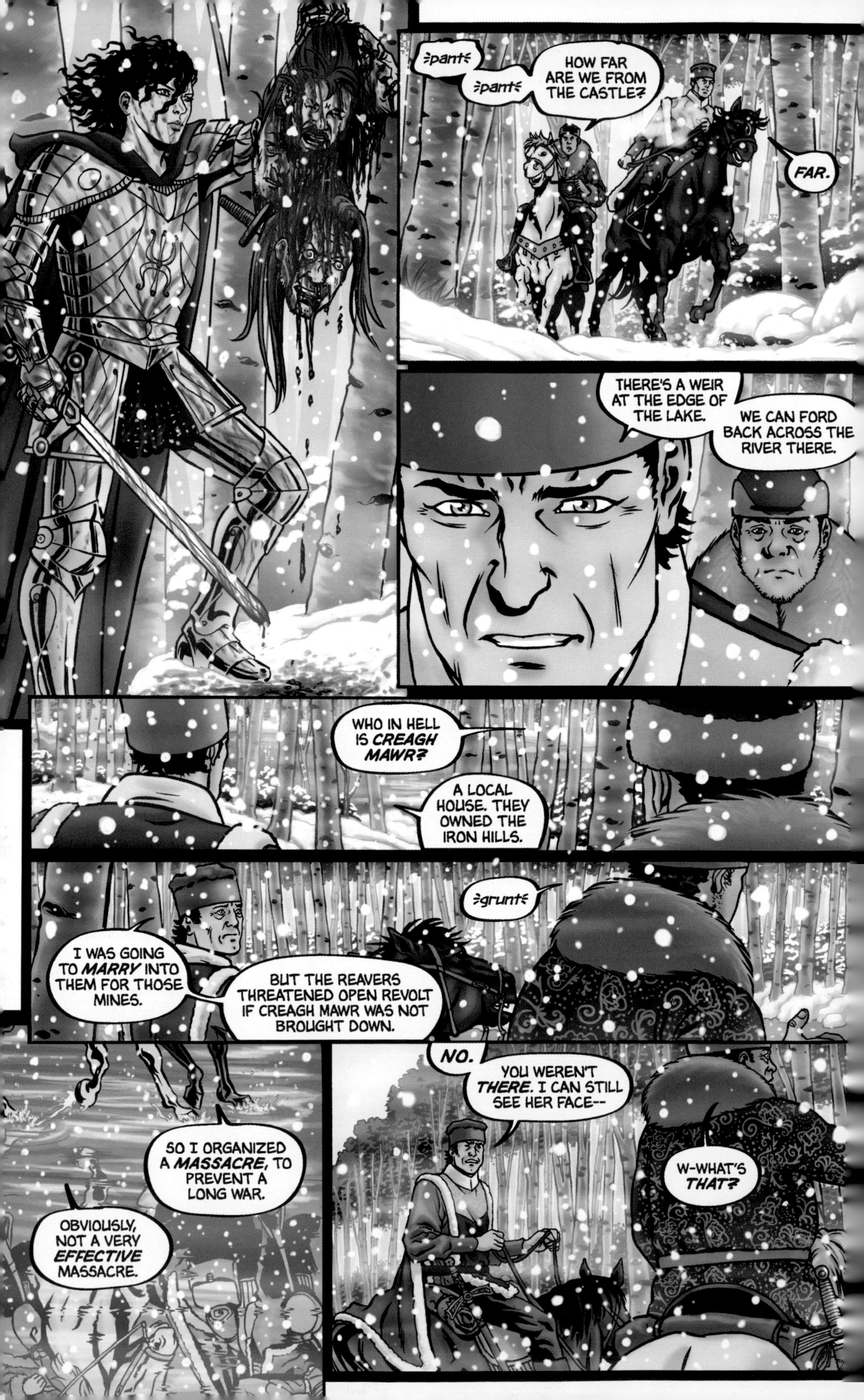

pant
pant
HOW FAR ARE WE FROM THE CASTLE?
FAR.
THERE'S A WEIR AT THE EDGE OF THE LAKE.
WE CAN FORD BACK ACROSS THE RIVER THERE.
WHO IN HELL IS CREAGH MAWR?
A LOCAL HOUSE. THEY OWNED THE IRON HILLS.
grunt
I WAS GOING TO MARRY INTO THEM FOR THOSE MINES.
BUT THE REAVERS THREATENED OPEN REVOLT IF CREAGH MAWR WAS NOT BROUGHT DOWN.
SO I ORGANIZED A MASSACRE, TO PREVENT A LONG WAR.
OBVIOUSLY, NOT A VERY EFFECTIVE MASSACRE.
NO.
YOU WEREN'T THERE. I CAN STILL SEE HER FACE--
W-WHAT'S THAT?

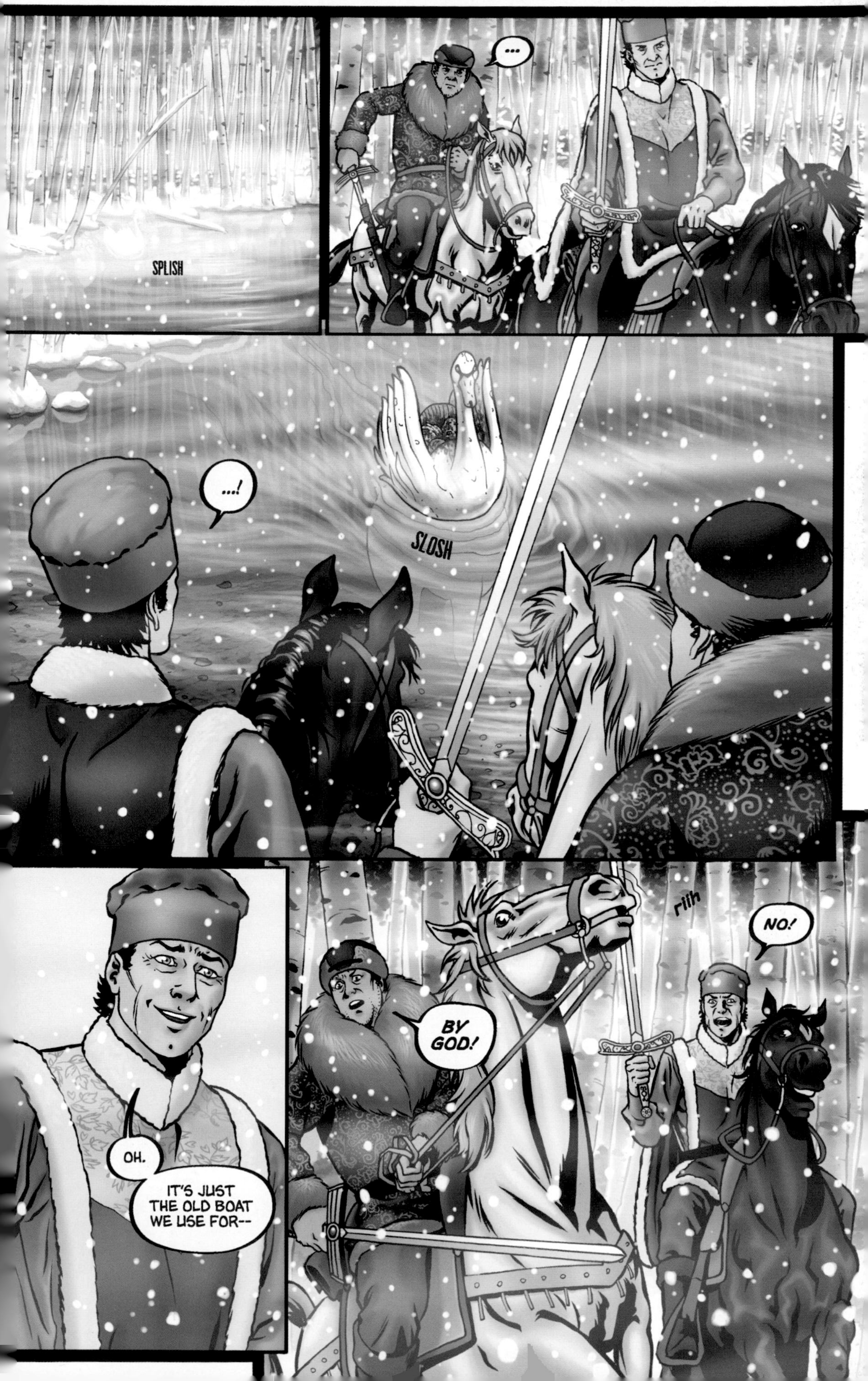
SPLISH
...
...!
SLOSH
OH.
IT'S JUST THE OLD BOAT WE USE FOR--
BY GOD!
riih
NO!

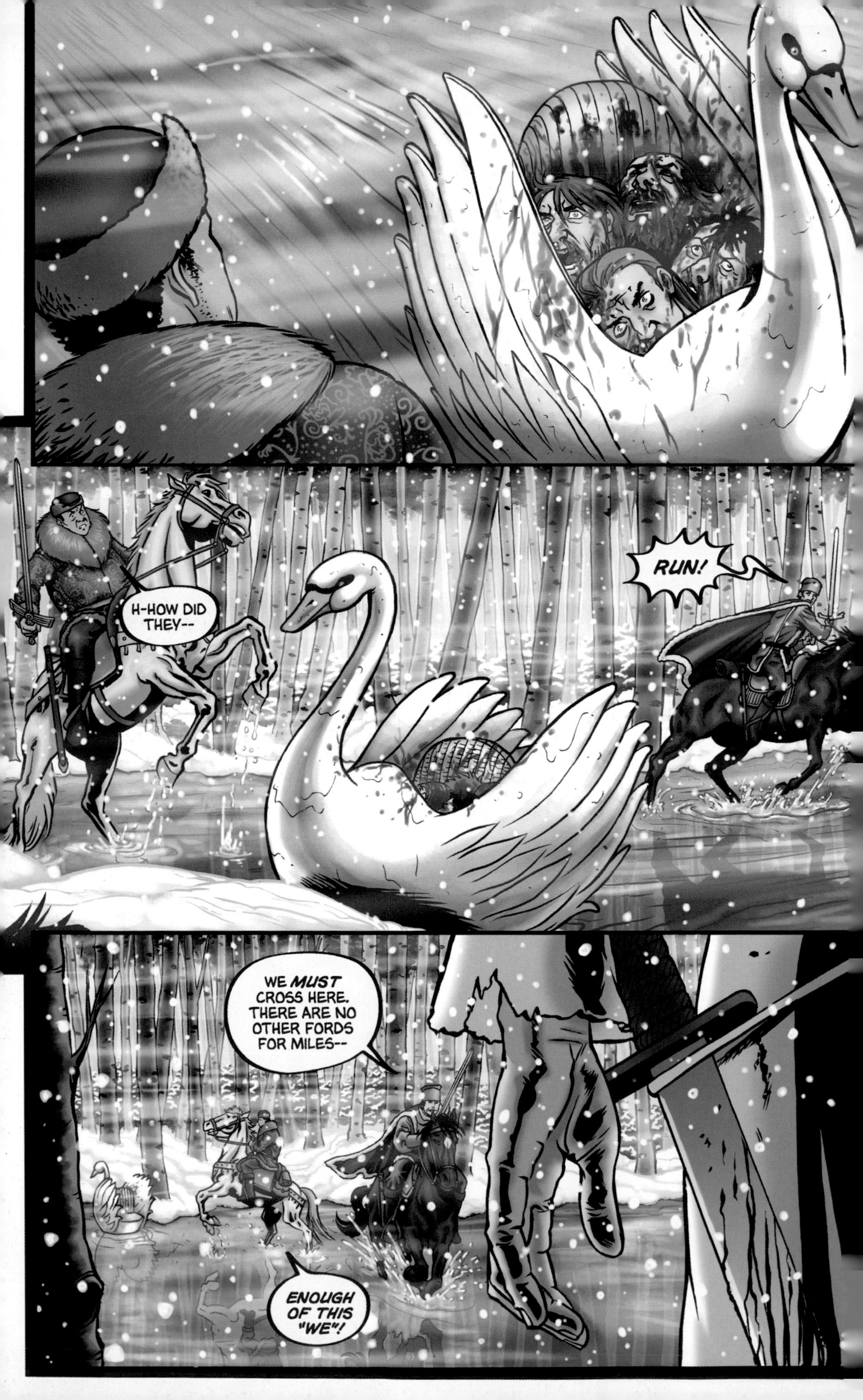
H-HOW DID THEY--
RUN!
WE MUST CROSS HERE. THERE ARE NO OTHER FORDS FOR MILES--
ENOUGH OF THIS "WE"!

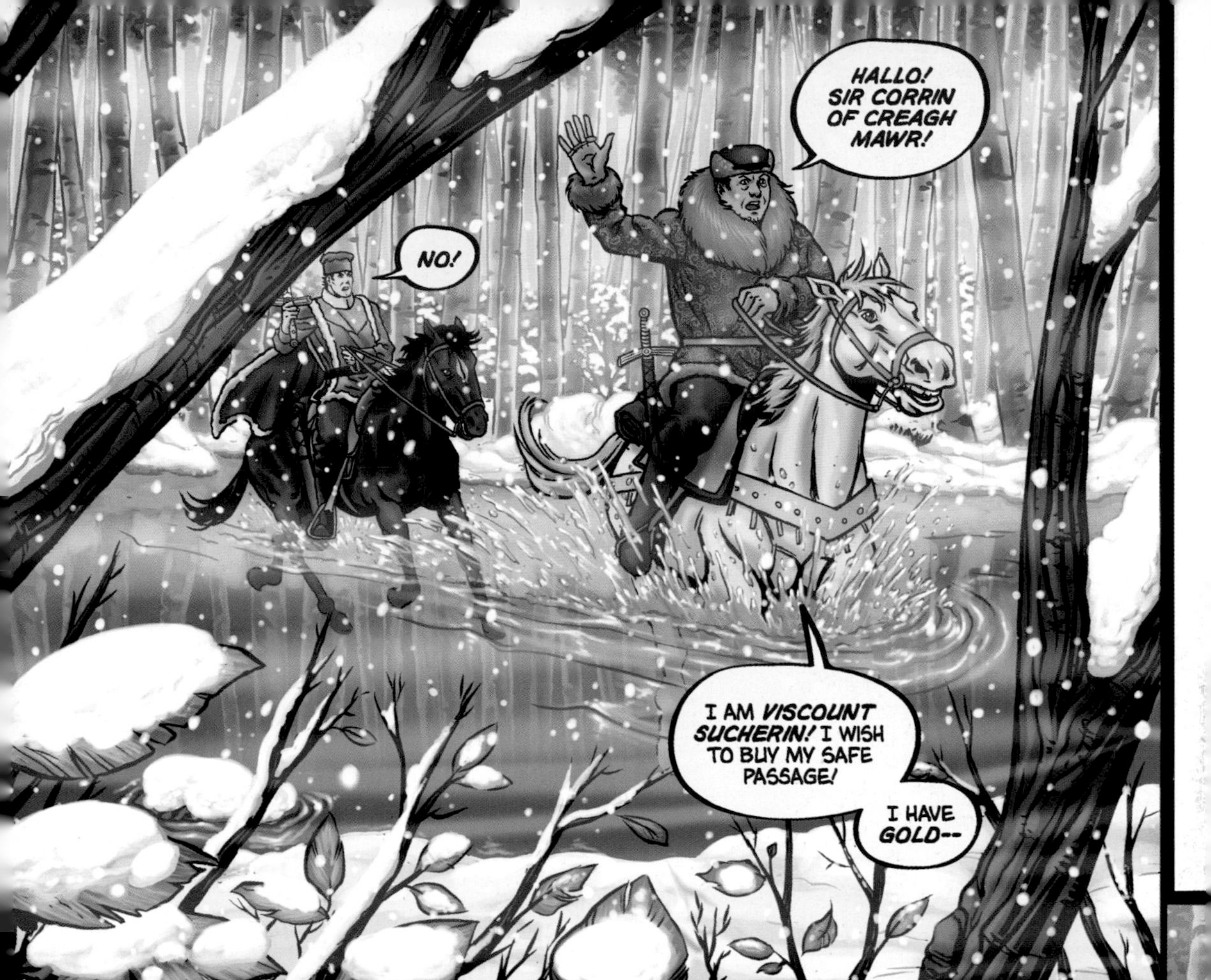
HALLO! SIR CORRIN OF CREAGH MAWR!
NO!
I AM VISCOUNT SUCHERIN! I WISH TO BUY MY SAFE PASSAGE!
I HAVE GOLD--

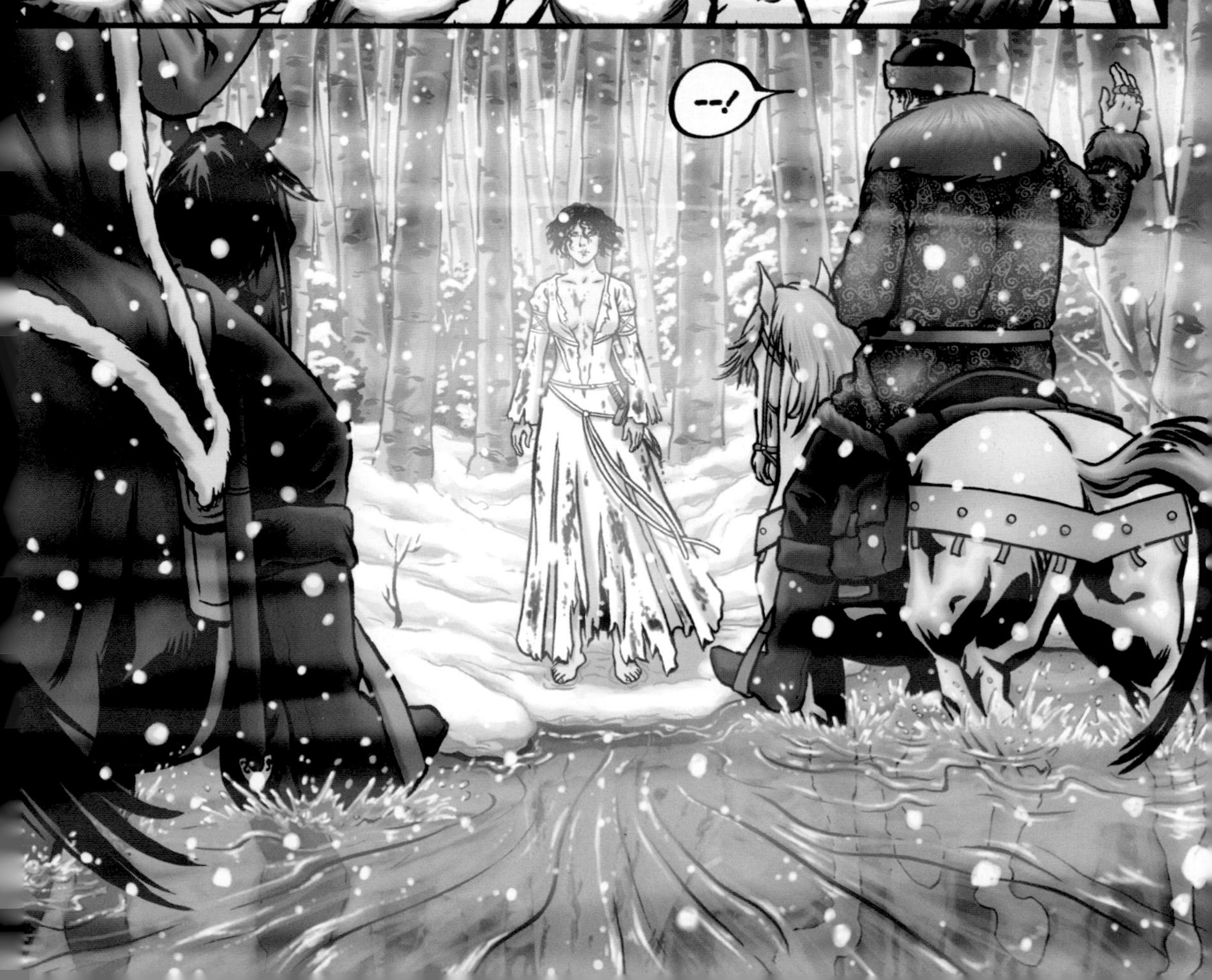
--!

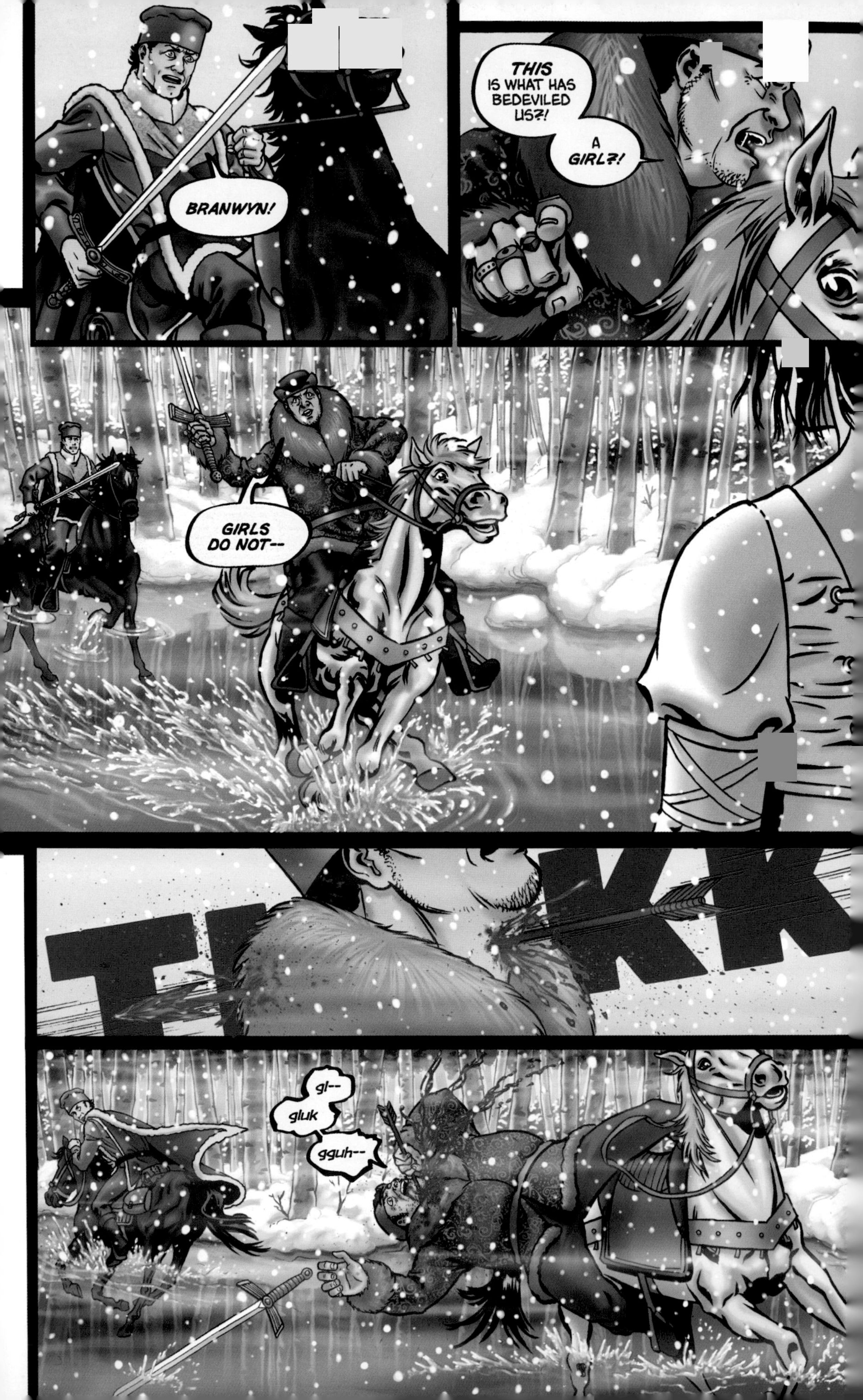
BRANWYN!
THIS IS WHAT HAS BEDEVILED US?!
A GIRL?!
GIRLS DO NOT--
gl--
gluk
gguh--

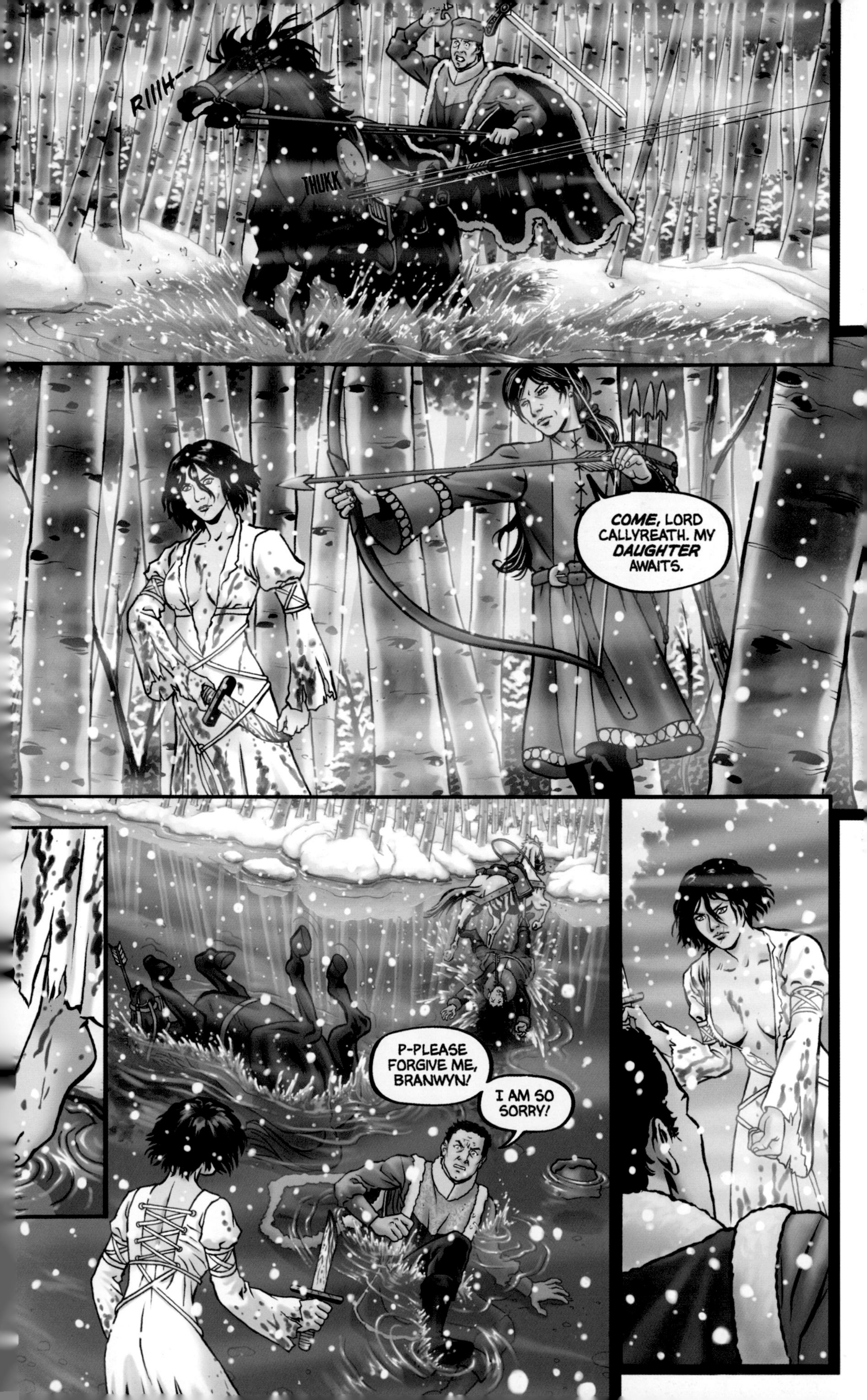
RIIIH--
THUKK
COME, LORD CALLYREATH. MY DAUGHTER AWAITS.
P-PLEASE FORGIVE ME, BRANWYN!
I AM SO SORRY!

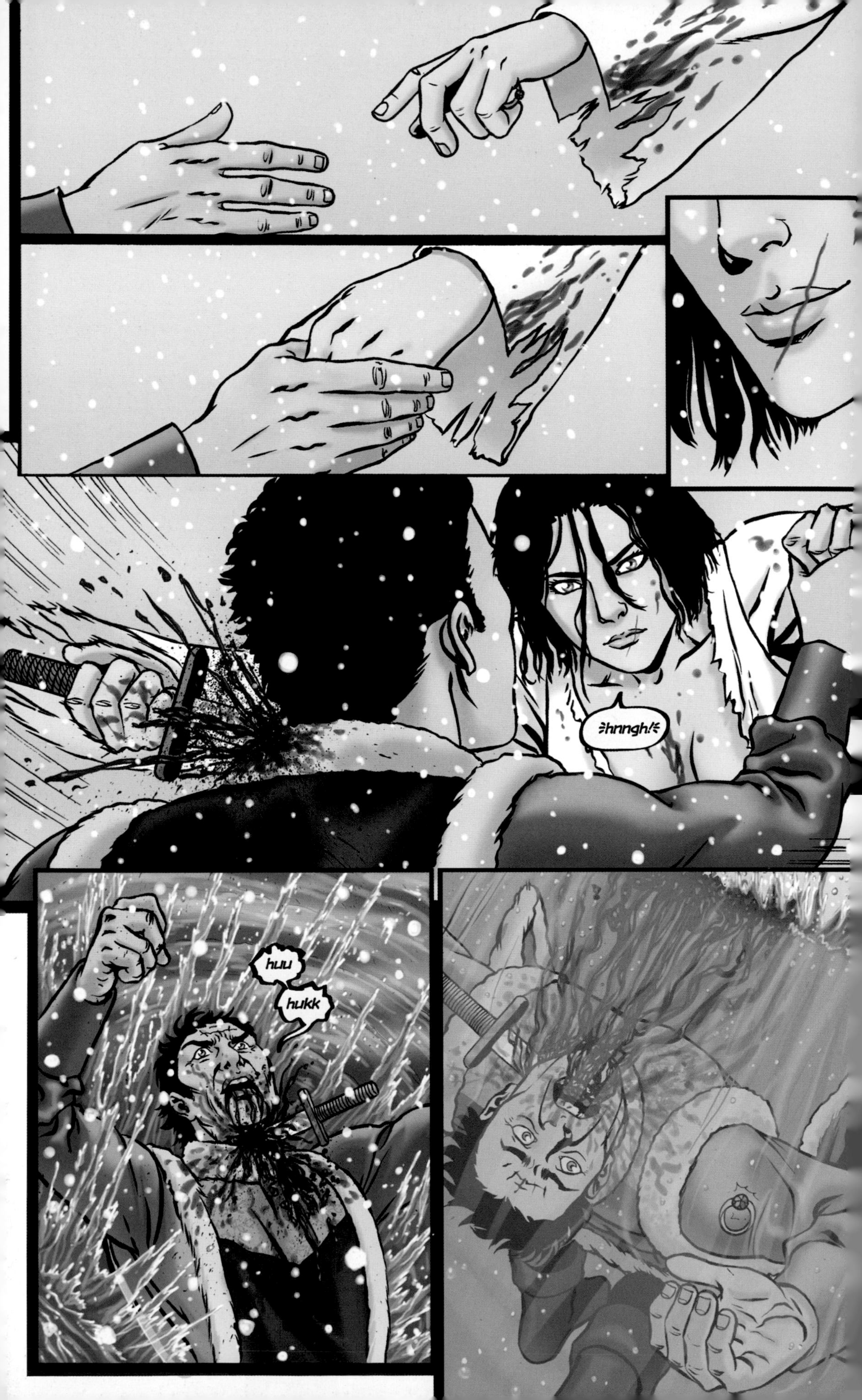
hnngh!
huu
hukk

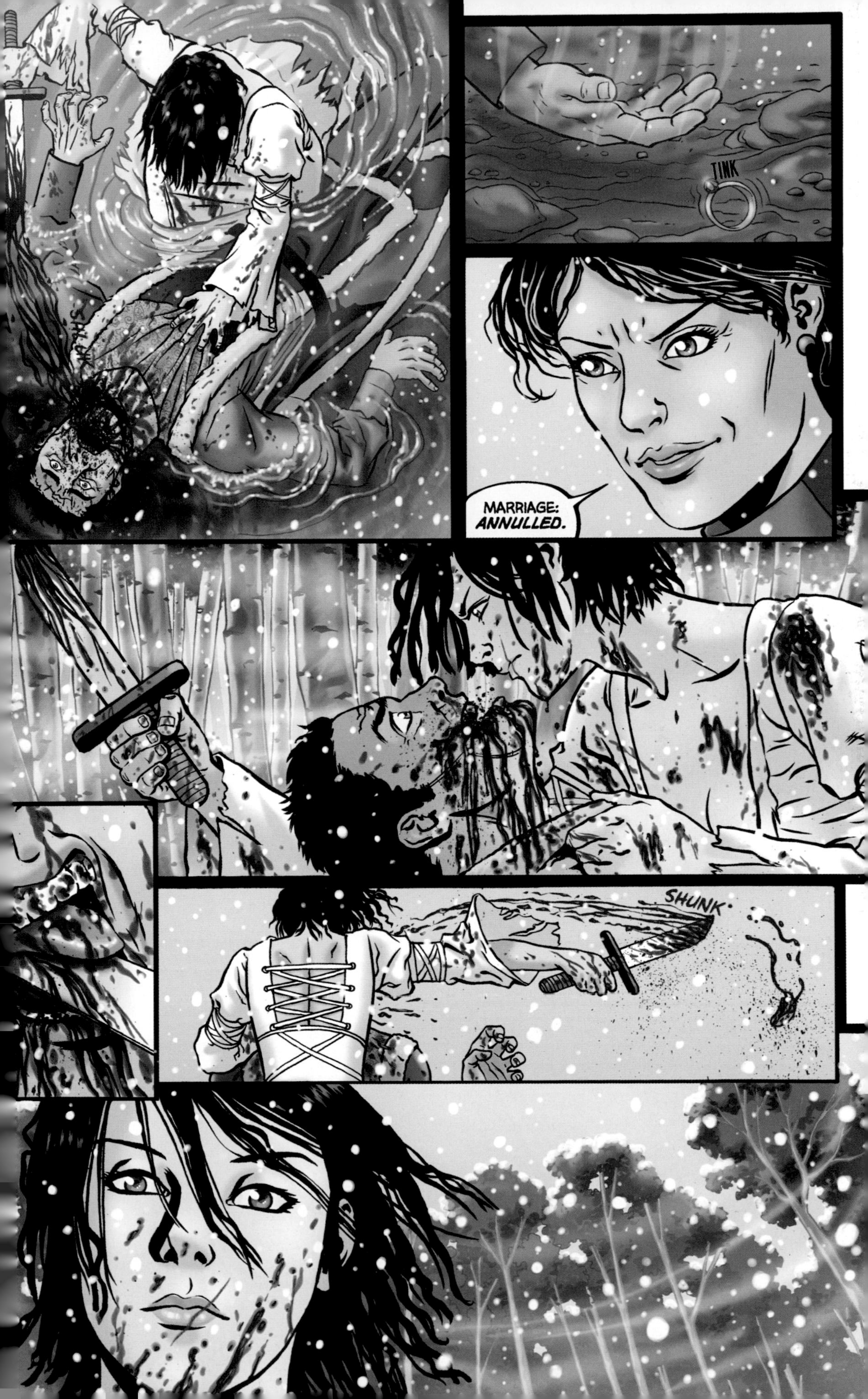
TINK
MARRIAGE:
ANNULLED.
SHUNK

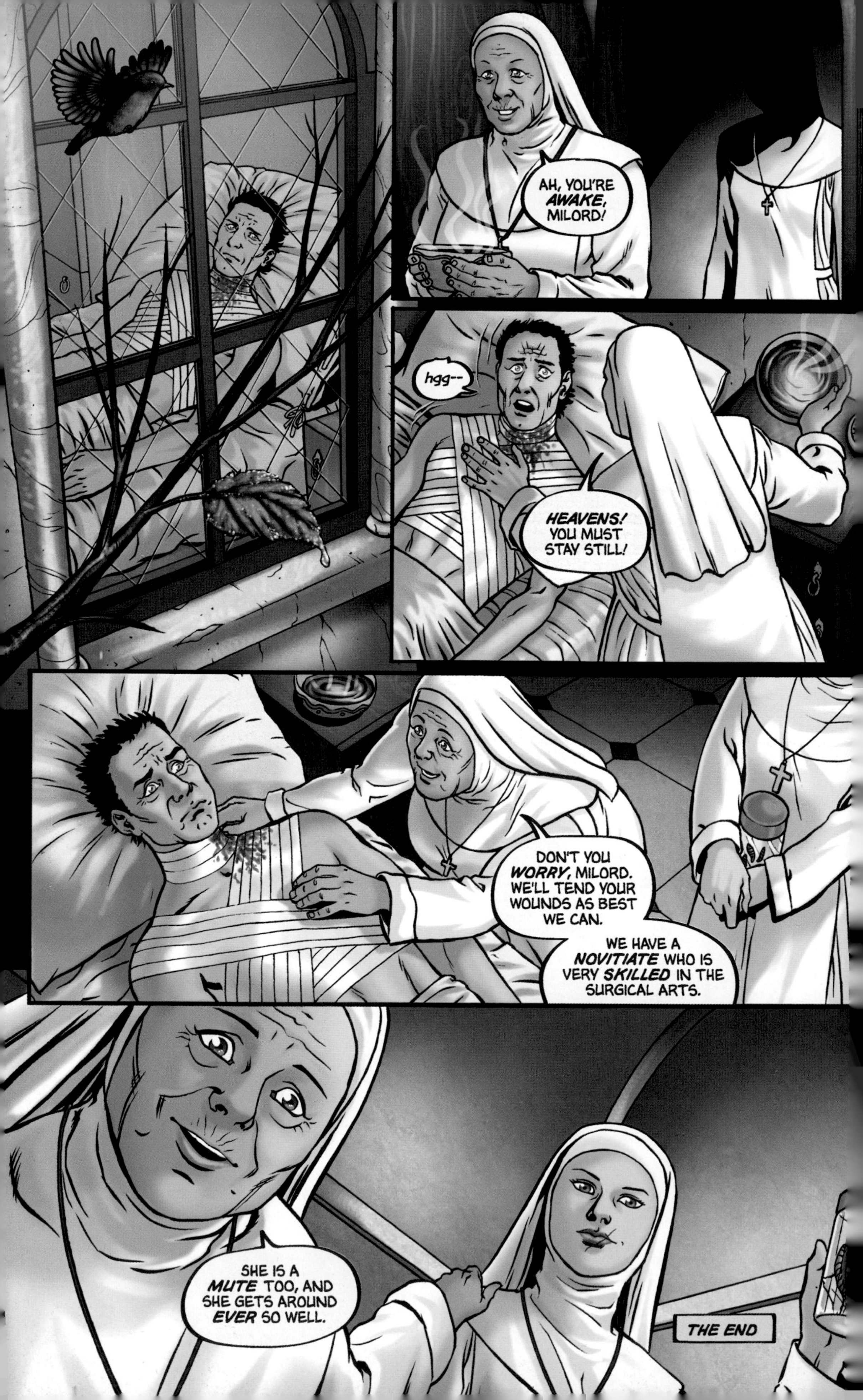
AH, YOU'RE AWAKE, MILORD!
hgg--
HEAVENS! YOU MUST STAY STILL!
DON'T YOU WORRY, MILORD. WE'LL TEND YOUR WOUNDS AS BEST WE CAN.
WE HAVE A NOVITIATE WHO IS VERY SKILLED IN THE SURGICAL ARTS.
SHE IS A MUTE TOO, AND SHE GETS AROUND EVER SO WELL.
THE END

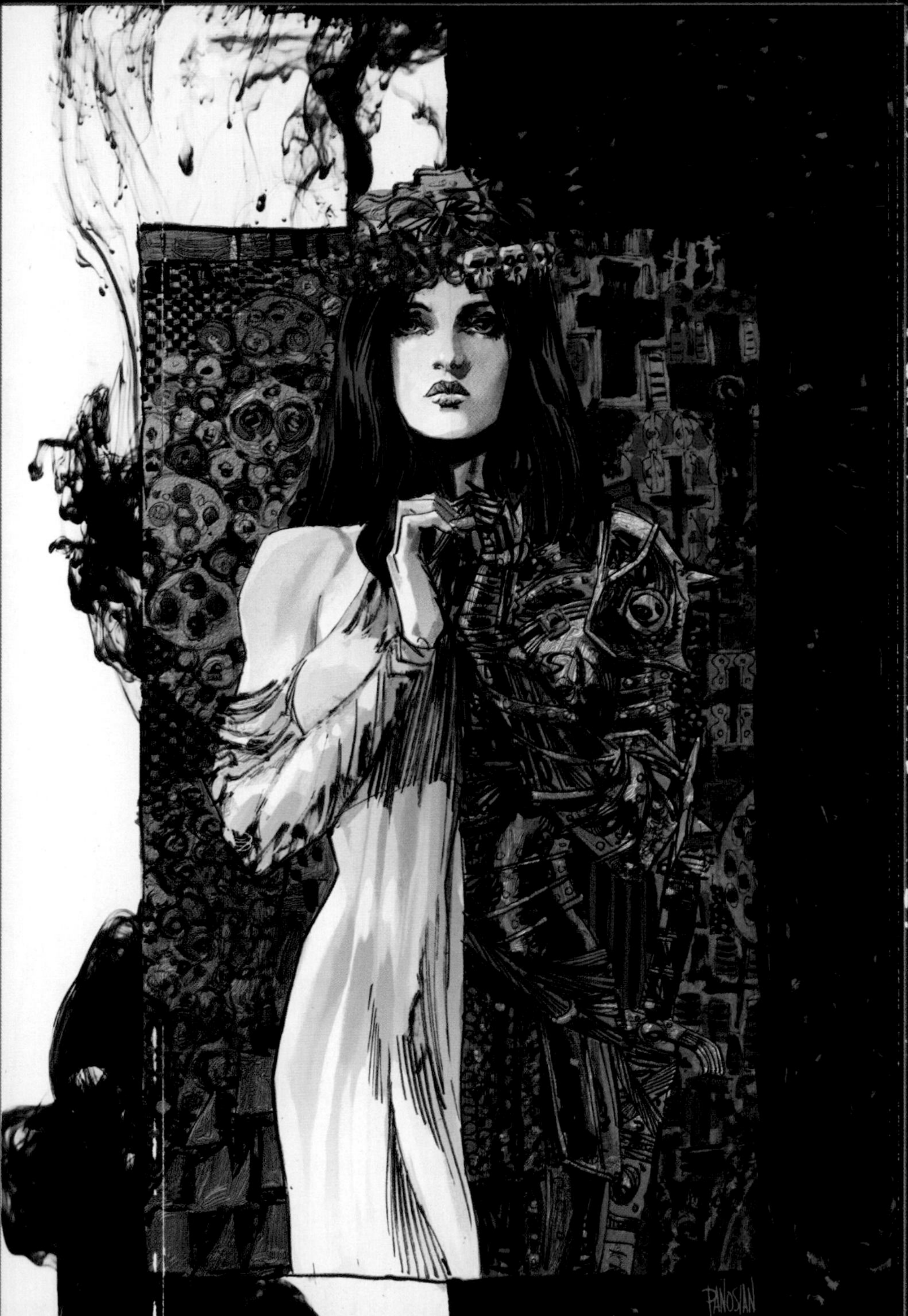
PANOSIAN

DAN PANOSIAN

BRIDE OF BLOOD II

THEY CUT OUT HER TONGUE. NOW THEY'LL NEVER HEAR HER COMING!

FROM THE SADISTS THAT BROUGHT YOU **BEE VIXENS FROM MARS** AND **PRISON SHIP ANTARES**

DARK HORSE COMICS PRESENTS AN ALEX DE CAMPI PRODUCTION "BRIDE OF BLOOD II"

THE BRIDE   THE GROOM   THE HOUNDS and THE REAVERS

FILM EDITOR BRENDAN WRIGHT A.C.E.   ASSISTANT EDITOR IAN TUCKER   PRODUCTION DESIGNER JIMMY PRESLER   CGI ARTIST RYAN JORGENSEN

PRODUCED BY MIKE RICHARDSON   SCREENPLAY BY ALEX DE CAMPI   DIRECTED BY FEDERICA MANFREDI

03•05•14

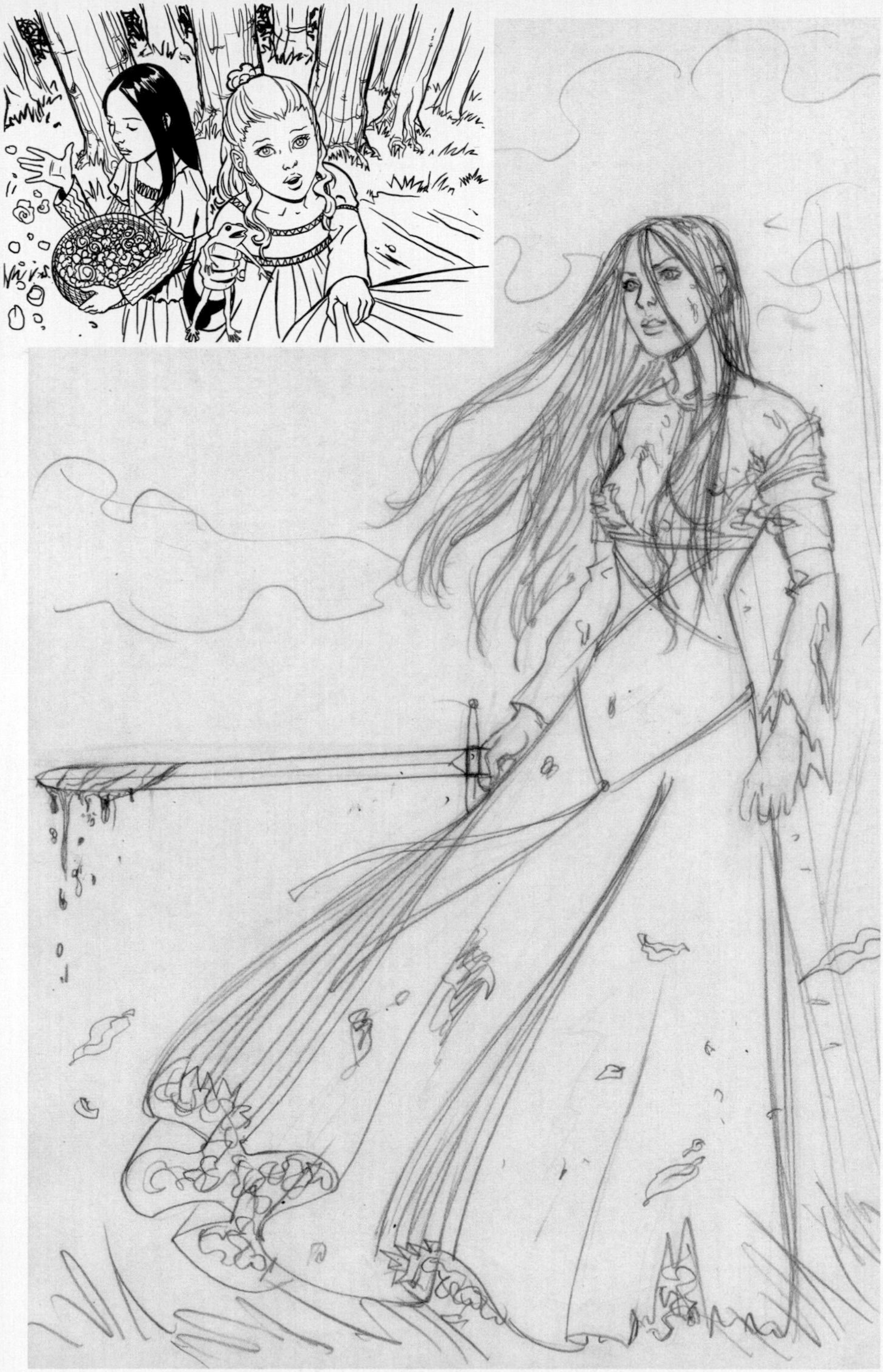

Manfredi's design for Branwyn. Inset: An early ink test.

An assortment of Manfredi's pencils from part 1.

BEHIND THE SCENES

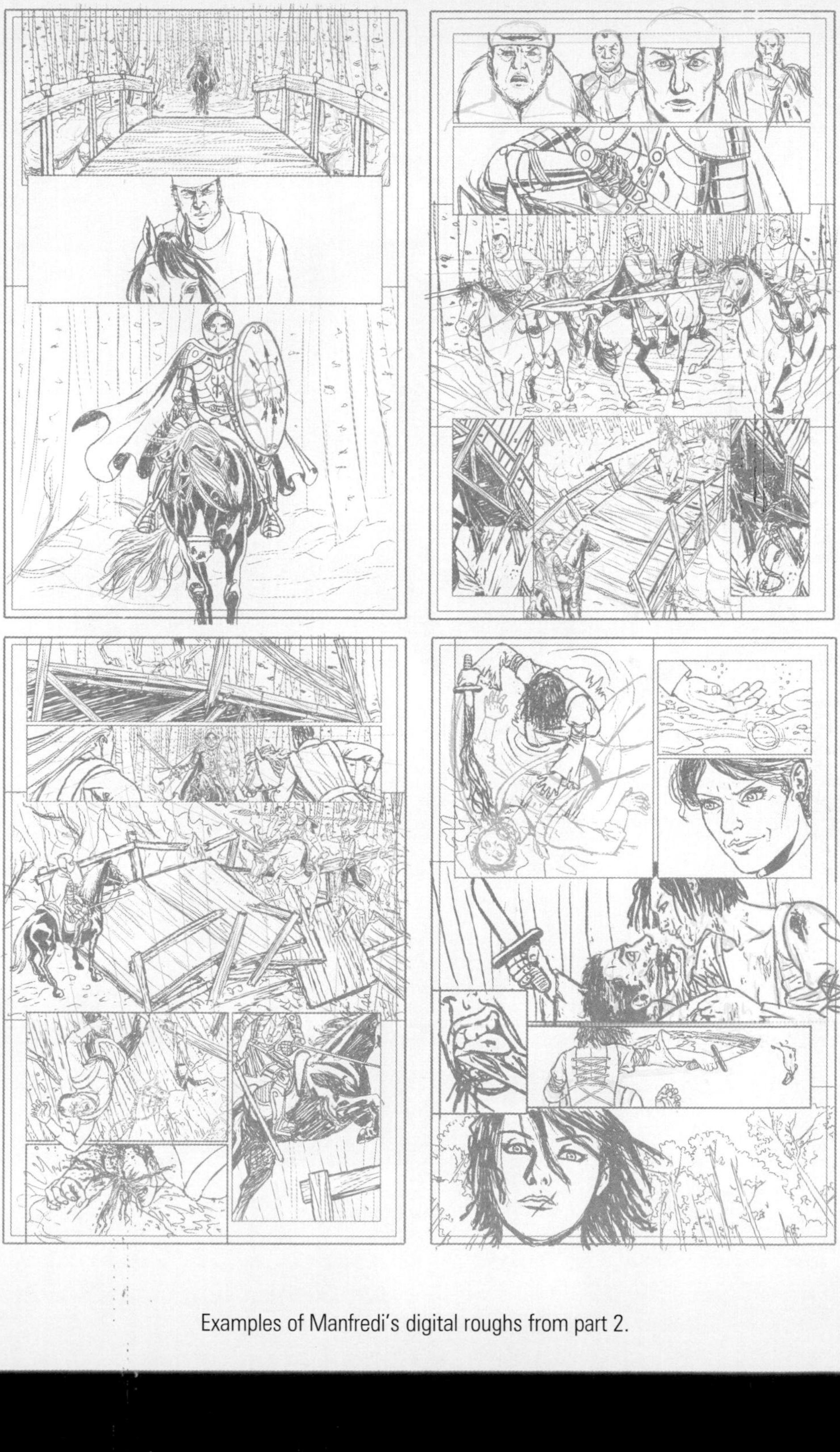

Examples of Manfredi's digital roughs from part 2.

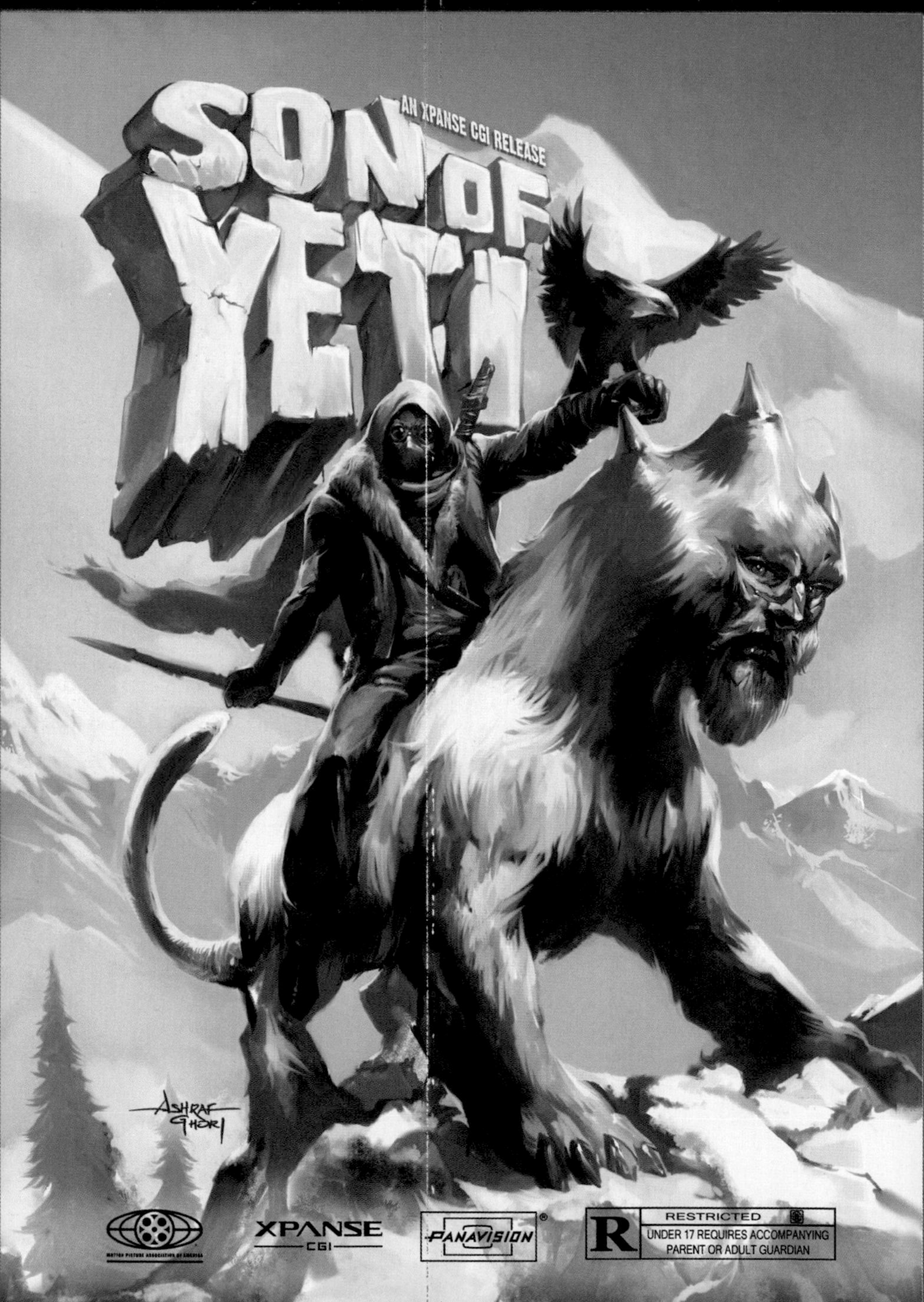
SON OF YETI
AN XPANSE CGI RELEASE
ASHRAF GHORI
XPANSE CGI
PANAVISION
R
RESTRICTED
UNDER 17 REQUIRES ACCOMPANYING PARENT OR ADULT GUARDIAN

ASHRAF GHORI

COMING SOON

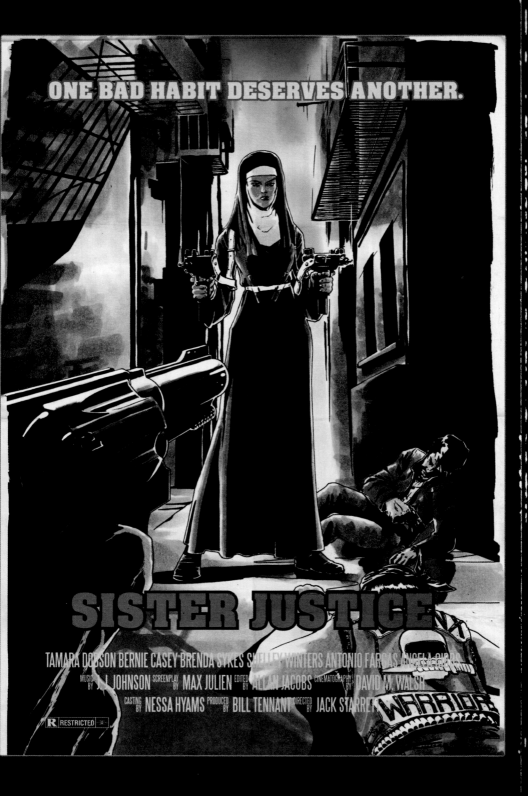

ONE BAD HABIT DESERVES ANOTHER.

SISTER JUSTICE

TAMARA DOBSON BERNIE CASEY BRENDA SYKES SHELLEY WINTERS ANTONIO FARGAS ANGELA GIBBS
MUSIC BY J.J. JOHNSON SCREENPLAY BY MAX JULIEN EDITED BY ALLAN JACOBS CINEMATOGRAPHY BY DAVID M. WALSH
CASTING BY NESSA HYAMS PRODUCED BY BILL TENNANT DIRECTED BY JACK STARRET

R RESTRICTED

ERIC KIM

END O

FLIP BOOK FOR

NEXT FEATURE

F REEL

F REEL

NEXT FEATURE

FLIP BOOK FOR

END O

ALSO BY ALEX DE CAMPI

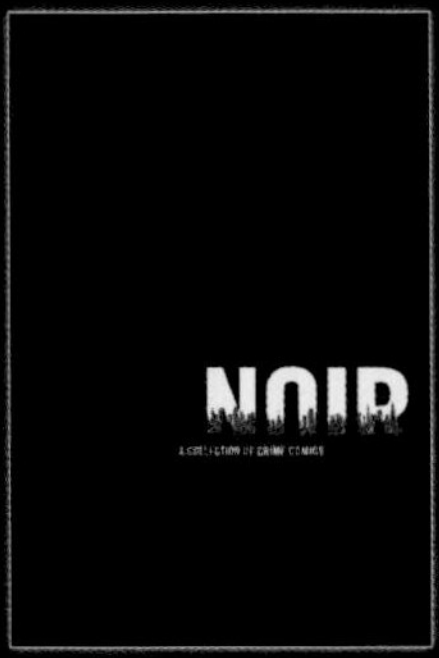
NOIR

NOIR: A COLLECTION OF CRIME COMICS
Brian Azzarello, Ed Brubaker, Sean Phillips, Jeff Lemire, Alex de Campi, David Lapham, Paul Grist, and others
978-1-59582-358-8
$12.99

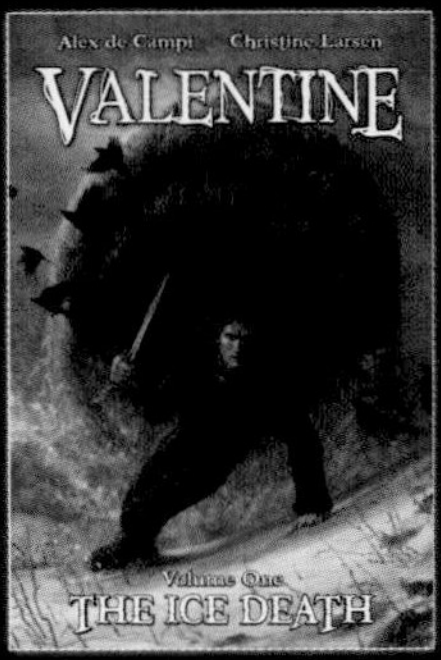
Alex de Campi
Christine Larsen
VALENTINE
Volume One
THE ICE DEATH

VALENTINE VOLUME 1: THE ICE DEATH
Alex de Campi and Christine Larsen
978-1-60706-624-8
$24.99

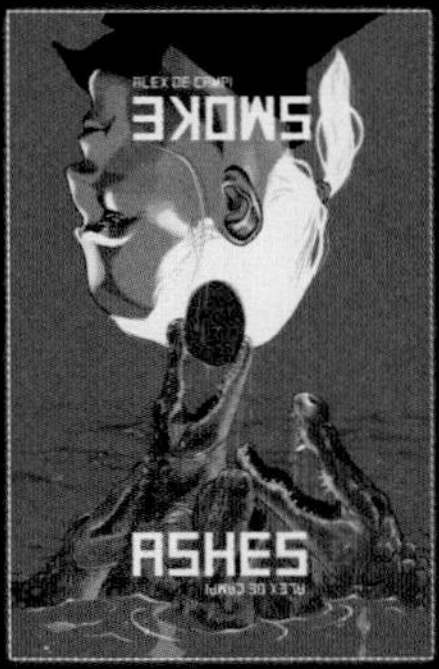
ALEX DE CAMPI
SMOKE
ASHES

SMOKE/ASHES
Alex de Campi, Igor Kordey, Carla Speed McNeil, Bill Sienkiewicz, Richard Pace, Colleen Doran, and Dan McDaid
978-1-61655-169-8
$29.99

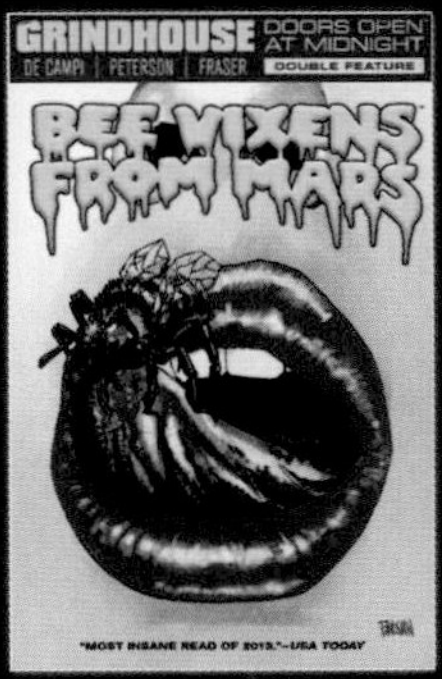
GRINDHOUSE
DOORS OPEN AT MIDNIGHT
DE CAMPI | PETERSON | FRASER
DOUBLE FEATURE
BEE VIXENS FROM MARS

GRINDHOUSE: DOORS OPEN AT MIDNIGHT VOLUME 1—BEE VIXENS FROM MARS & PRISON SHIP ANTARES
Alex de Campi, Chris Peterson, and Simon Fraser
978-1-61655-377-7
$17.99

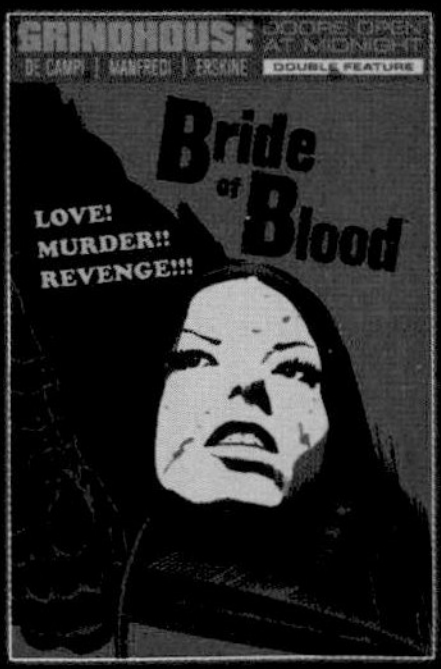
GRINDHOUSE
DOORS OPEN AT MIDNIGHT
DE CAMPI | MANFREDI | ERSKINE
DOUBLE FEATURE
Bride of Blood
LOVE!
MURDER!!
REVENGE!!!

GRINDHOUSE: DOORS OPEN AT MIDNIGHT VOLUME 2—BRIDE OF BLOOD & FLESH FEAST OF THE DEVIL DOLL
Alex de Campi, Federica Manfredi, and Gary Erskine
978-1-61655-378-4
$17.99

COMING SOON

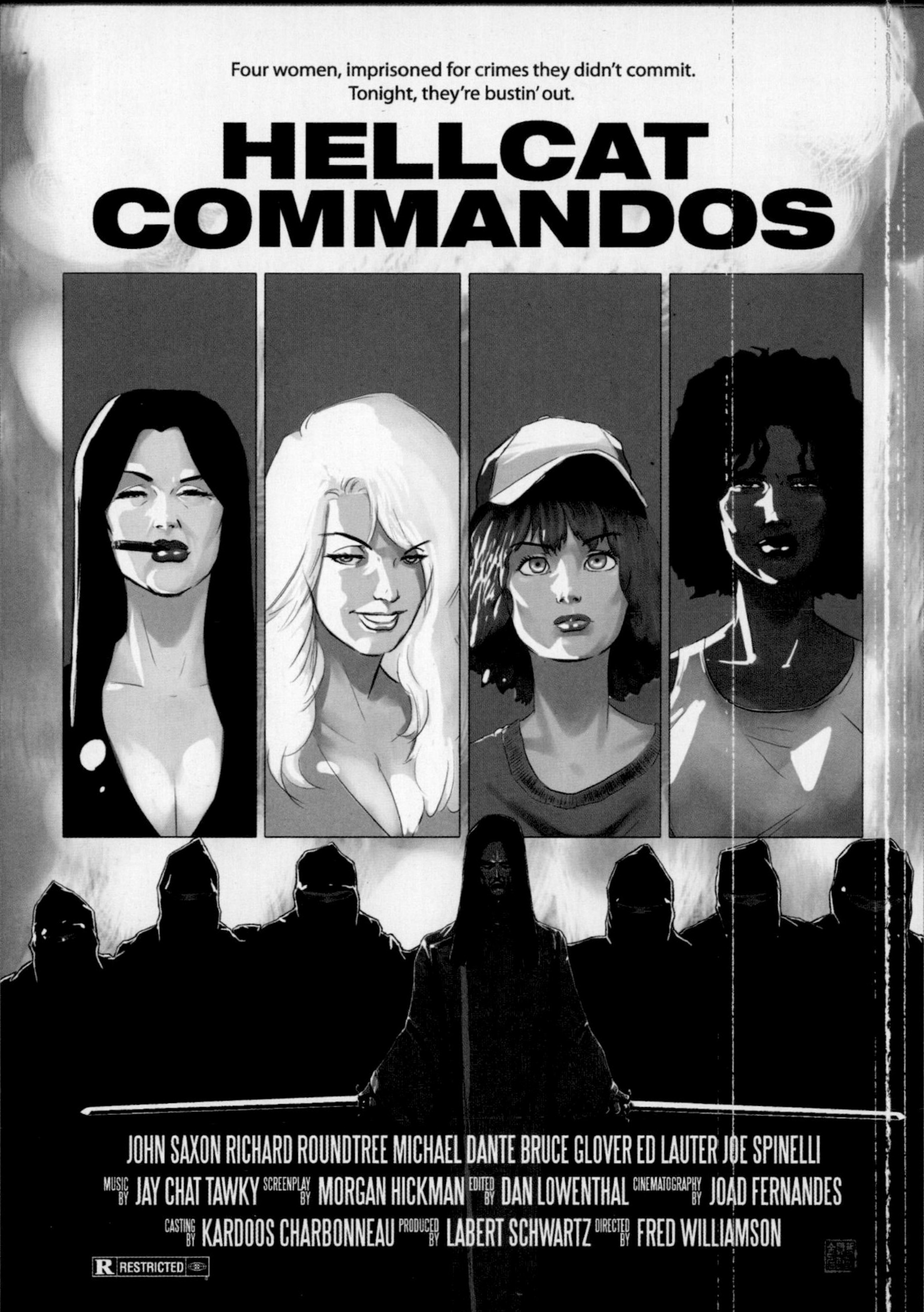
Four women, imprisoned for crimes they didn't commit.
Tonight, they're bustin' out.
HELLCAT COMMANDOS
JOHN SAXON RICHARD ROUNDTREE MICHAEL DANTE BRUCE GLOVER ED LAUTER JOE SPINELLI
MUSIC BY JAY CHAT TAWKY SCREENPLAY BY MORGAN HICKMAN EDITED BY DAN LOWENTHAL CINEMATOGRAPHY BY JOAD FERNANDES
CASTING BY KARDOOS CHARBONNEAU PRODUCED BY LABERT SCHWARTZ DIRECTED BY FRED WILLIAMSON
R RESTRICTED

ERIC KIM

COMING SOON

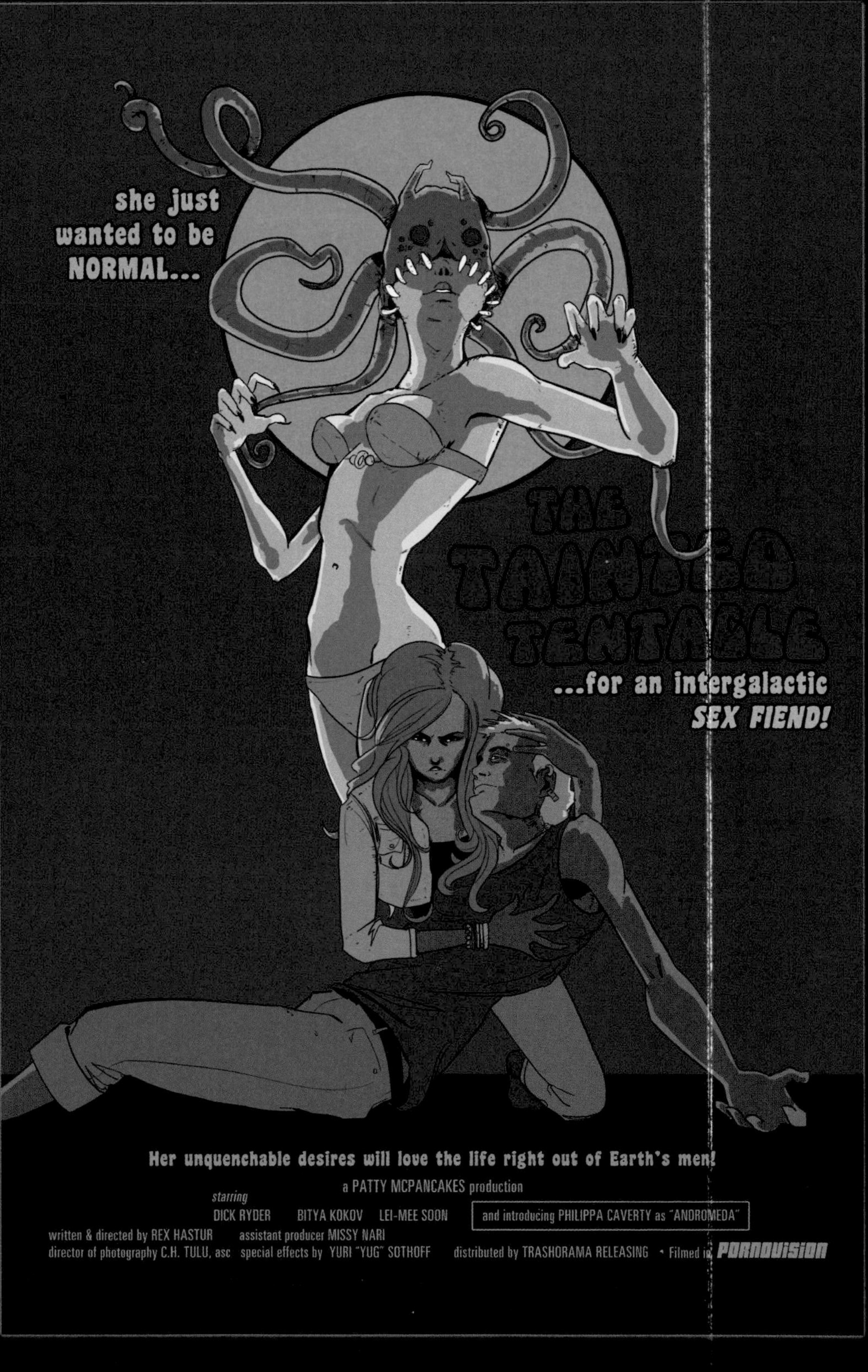

she just wanted to be NORMAL...
THE TAINTED TENTACLE
...for an intergalactic SEX FIEND!
Her unquenchable desires will love the life right out of Earth's men!
a PATTY MCPANCAKES production
starring
DICK RYDER BITYA KOKOV LEI-MEE SOON
and introducing PHILIPPA CAVERTY as "ANDROMEDA"
written & directed by REX HASTUR assistant producer MISSY NARI
director of photography C.H. TULU, asc special effects by YURI "YUG" SOTHOFF distributed by TRASHORAMA RELEASING • Filmed in PORNOVISION

PATTY McPANCAKES

COMING SOON

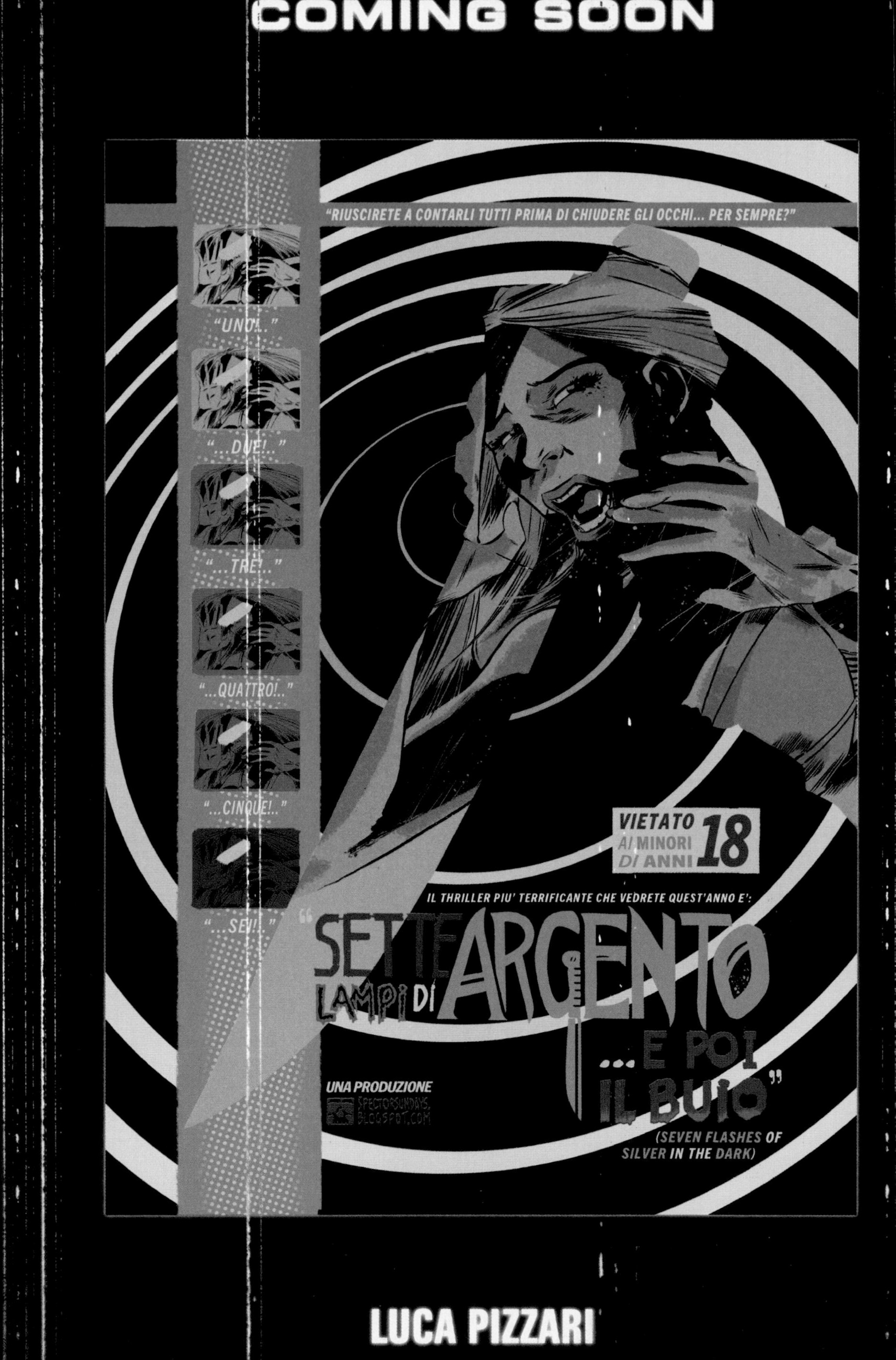
"RIUSCIRETE A CONTARLI TUTTI PRIMA DI CHIUDERE GLI OCCHI... PER SEMPRE?"
"UNO!.."
"...DUE!.."
"...TRE!.."
"...QUATTRO!.."
"...CINQUE!.."
"...SEI!.."
VIETATO AI MINORI DI ANNI 18
IL THRILLER PIU' TERRIFICANTE CHE VEDRETE QUEST'ANNO E':
"SETTE LAMPI DI ARGENTO ...E POI IL BUIO"
(SEVEN FLASHES OF SILVER IN THE DARK)
UNA PRODUZIONE
SPECTORSUNDAYS.BLOGSPOT.COM

LUCA PIZZARI

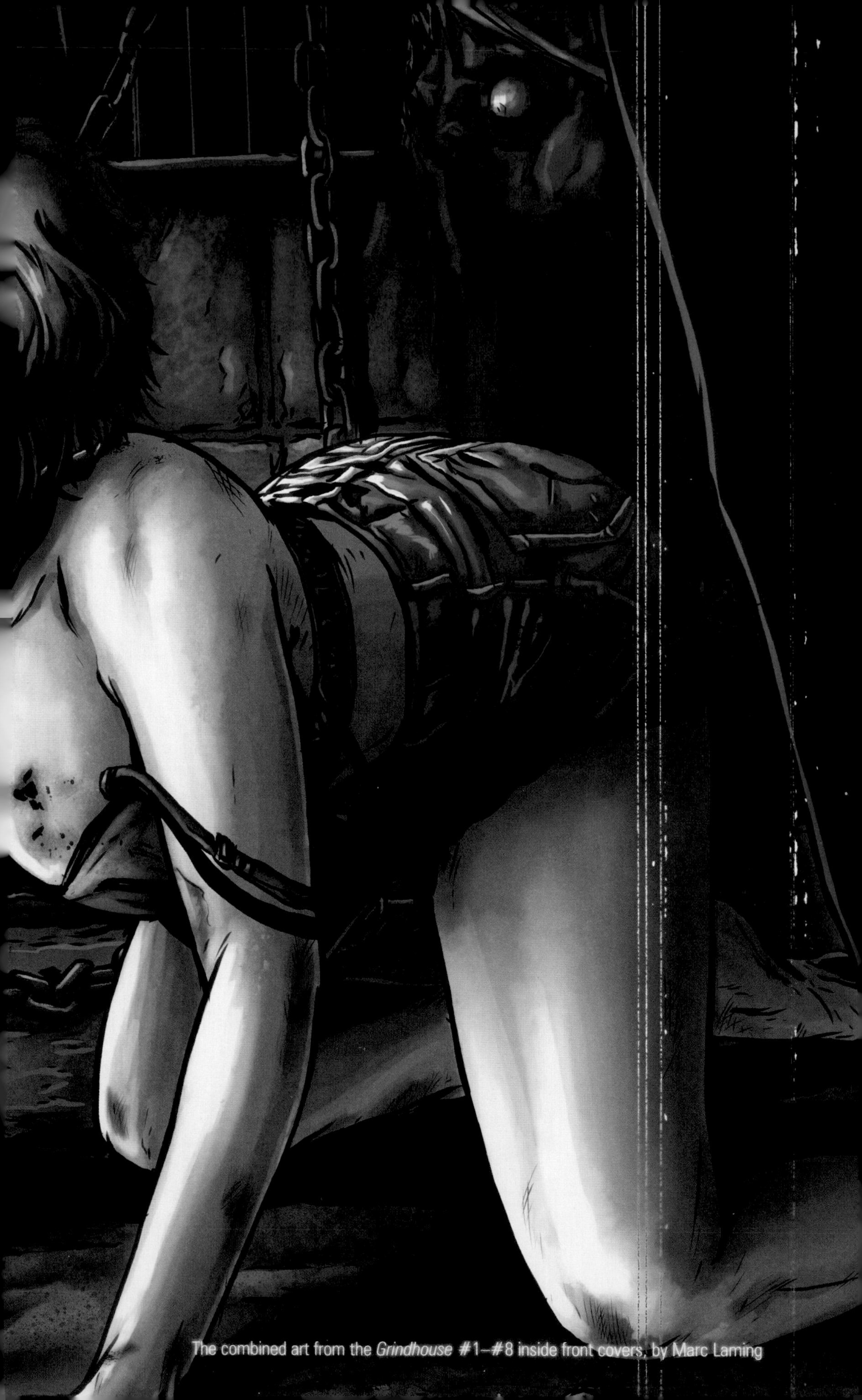

The combined art from the *Grindhouse* #1–#8 inside front covers, by Marc Laming

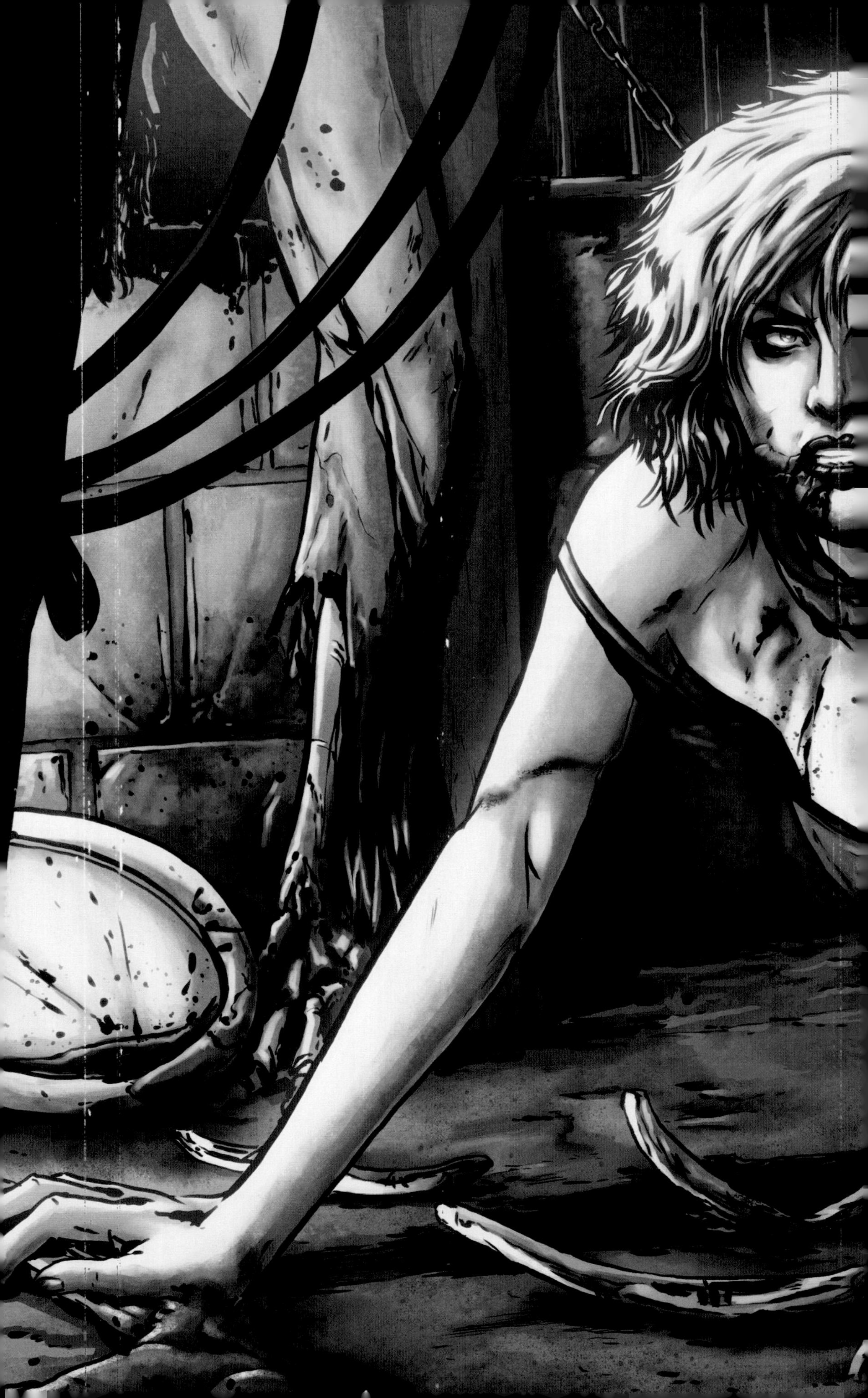

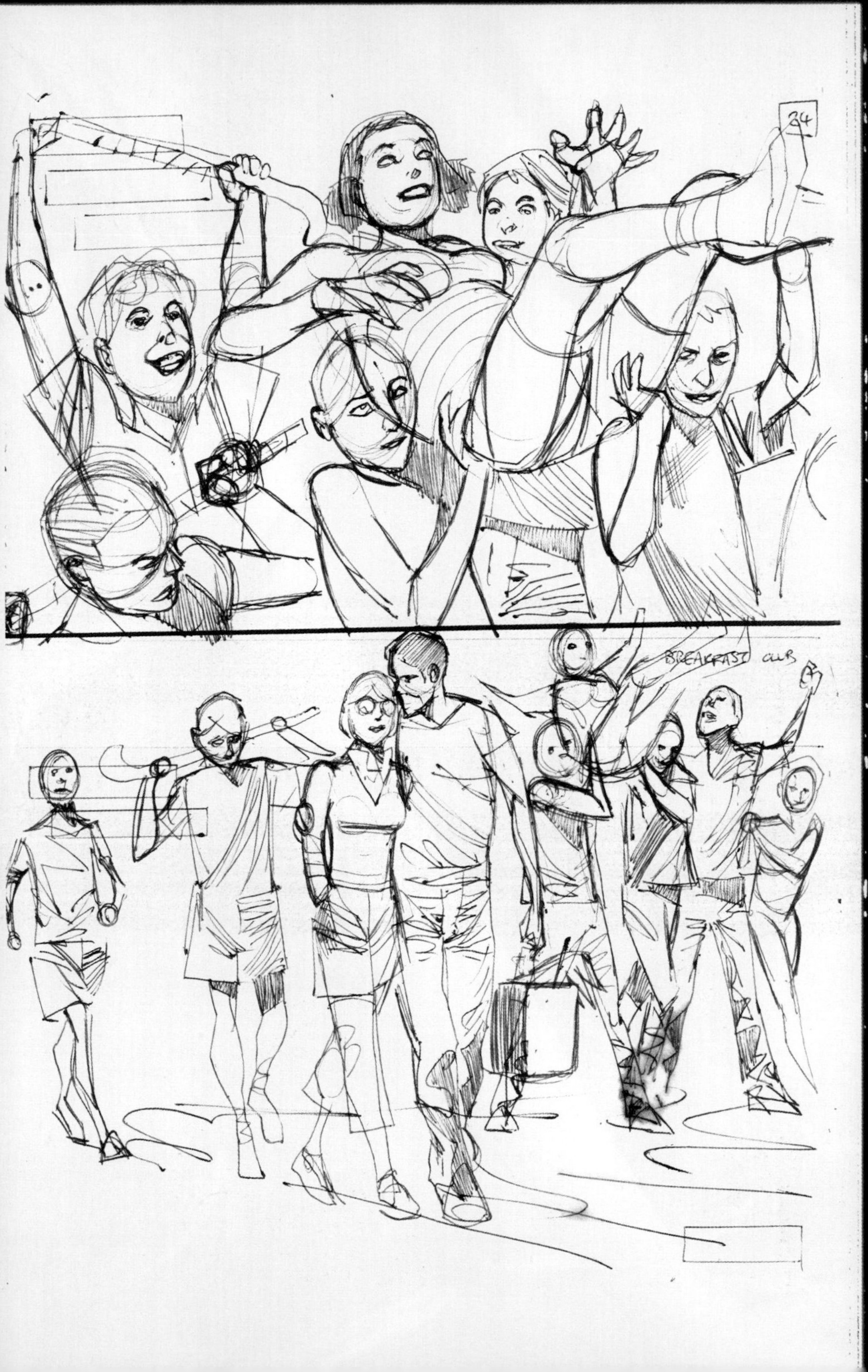
34
BREAKFAST CLUB

BEHIND THE SCENES

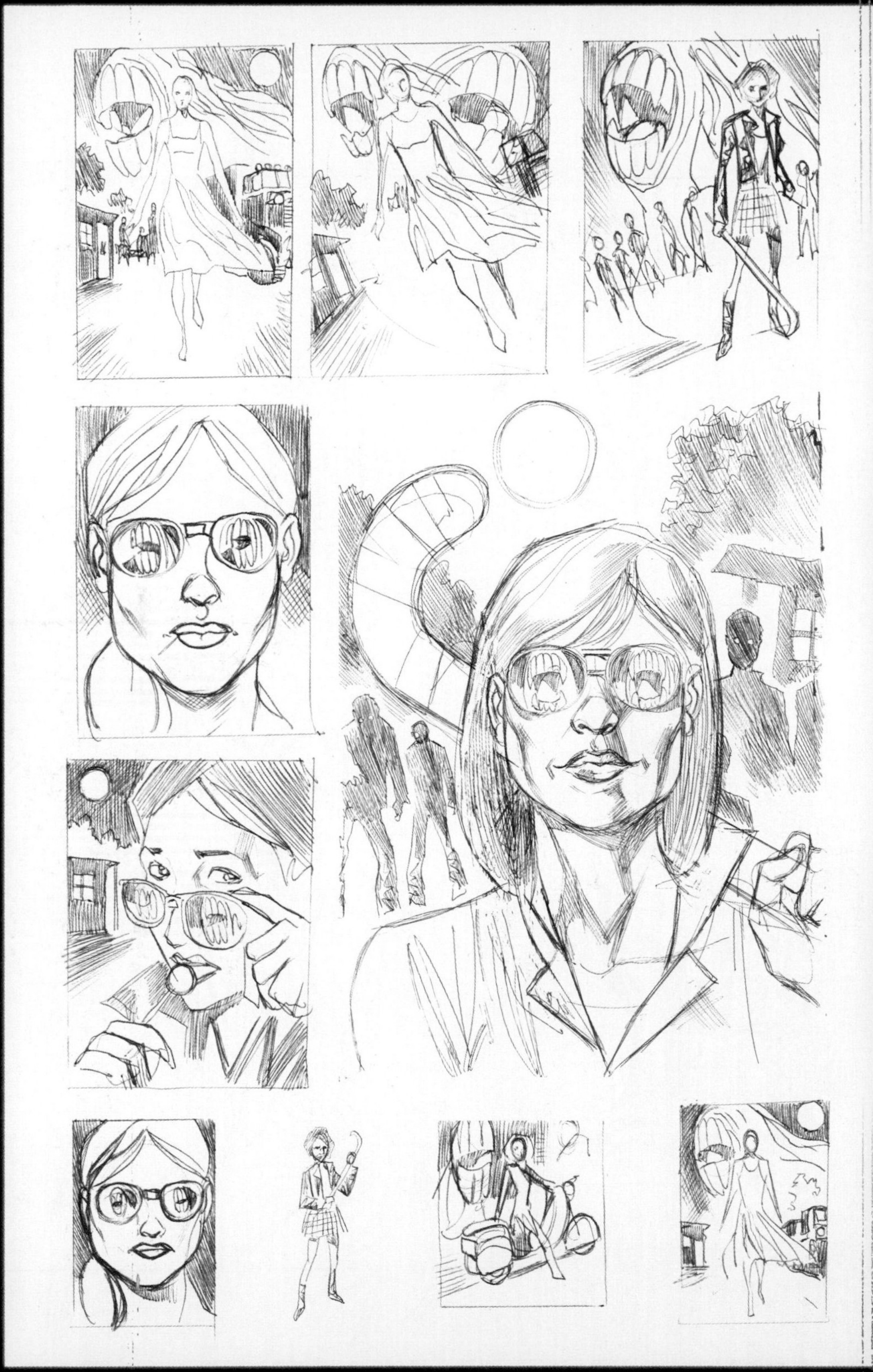

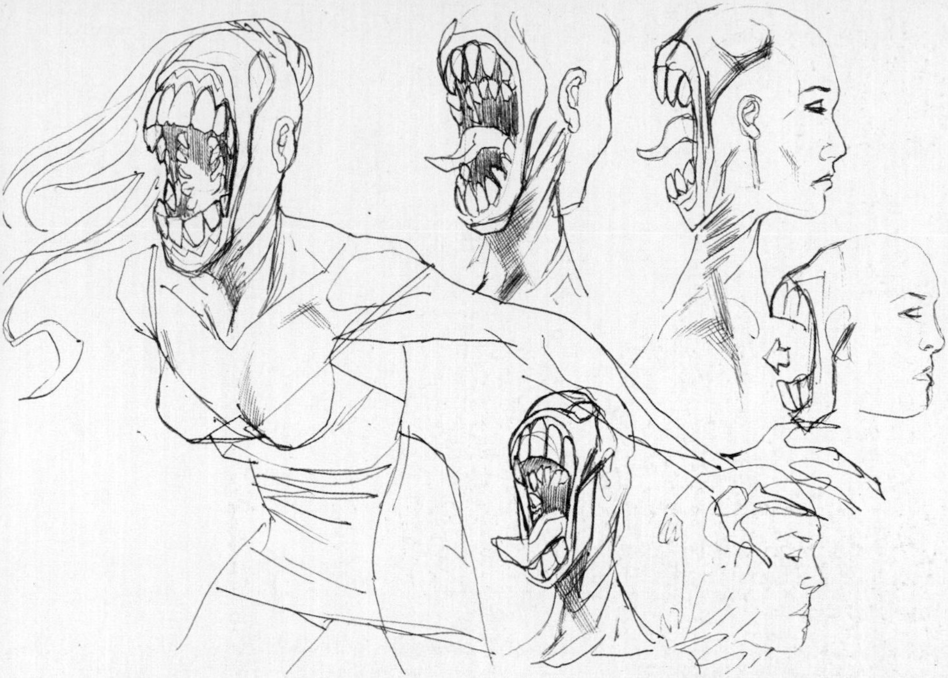

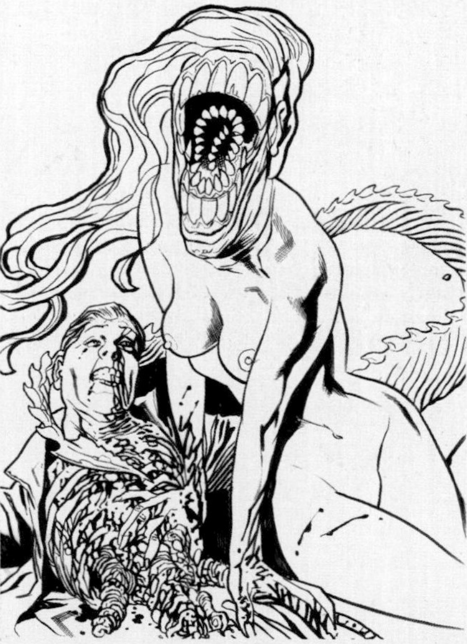

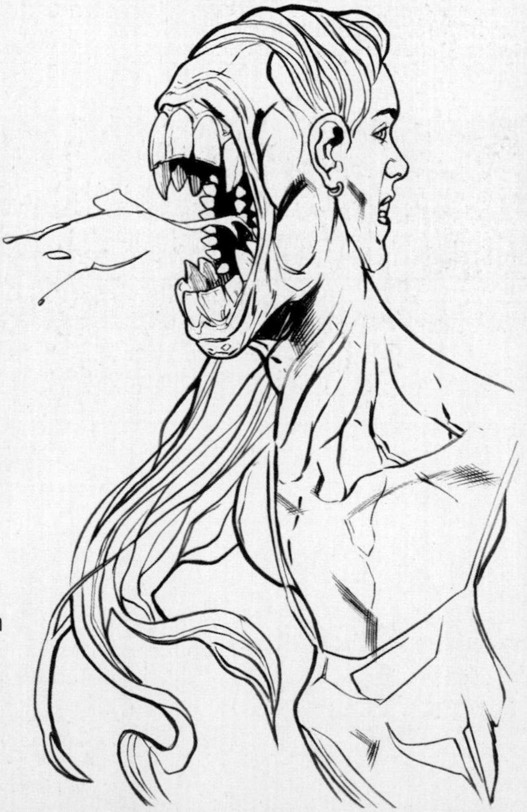

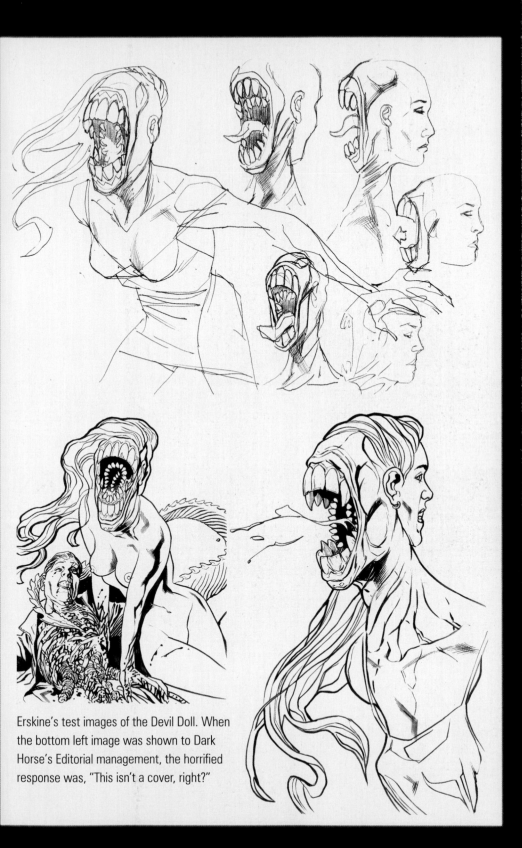

Erskine's test images of the Devil Doll. When the bottom left image was shown to Dark Horse's Editorial management, the horrified response was, "This isn't a cover, right?"

DEVIL DOLL DESIGNS BY GARY ERSKINE

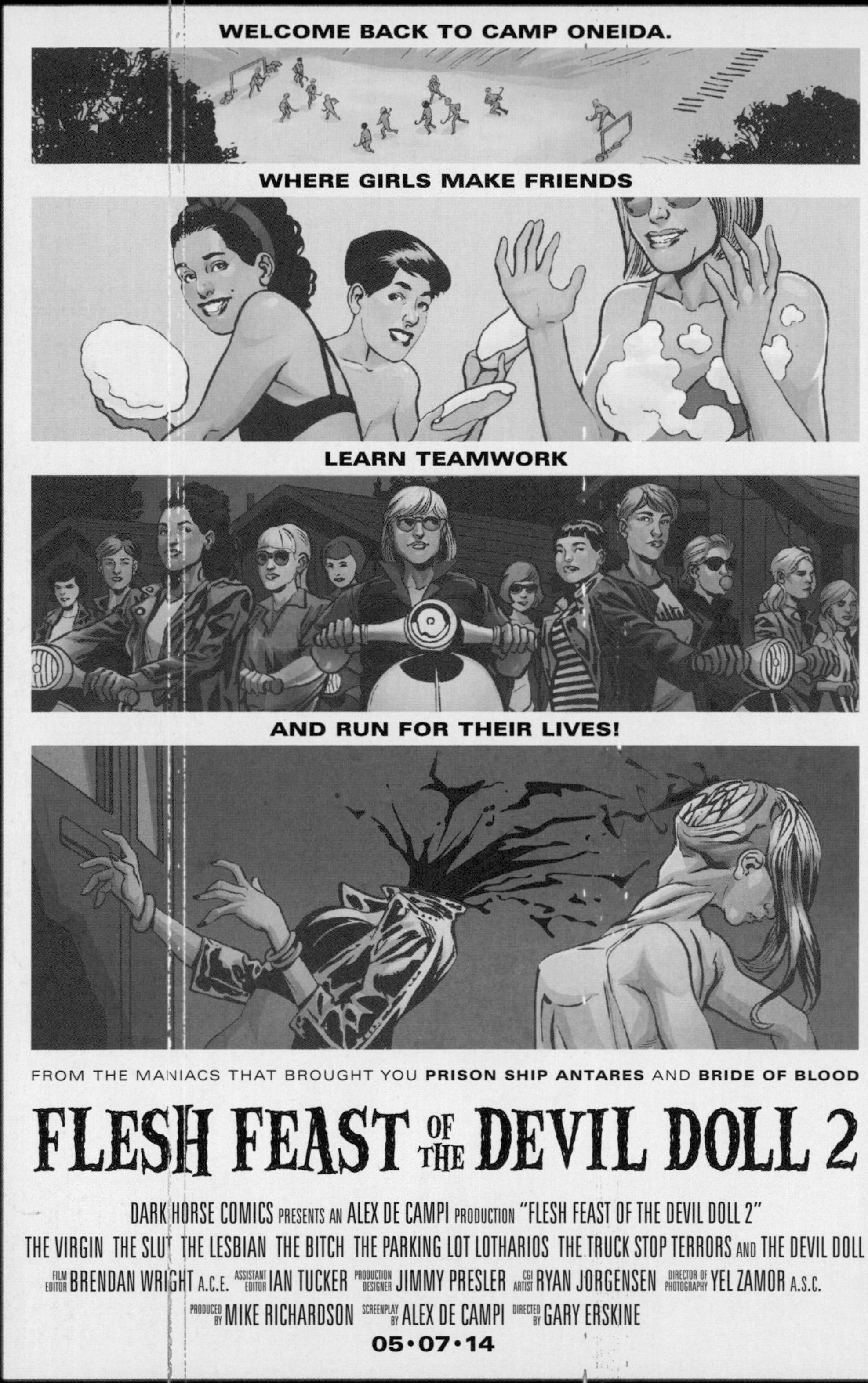
WELCOME BACK TO CAMP ONEIDA.
WHERE GIRLS MAKE FRIENDS
LEARN TEAMWORK
AND RUN FOR THEIR LIVES!
FROM THE MANIACS THAT BROUGHT YOU PRISON SHIP ANTARES AND BRIDE OF BLOOD
FLESH FEAST OF THE DEVIL DOLL 2
DARK HORSE COMICS PRESENTS AN ALEX DE CAMPI PRODUCTION "FLESH FEAST OF THE DEVIL DOLL 2"
THE VIRGIN THE SLUT THE LESBIAN THE BITCH THE PARKING LOT LOTHARIOS THE TRUCK STOP TERRORS AND THE DEVIL DOLL
FILM EDITOR BRENDAN WRIGHT A.C.E. ASSISTANT EDITOR IAN TUCKER PRODUCTION DESIGNER JIMMY PRESLER CGI ARTIST RYAN JORGENSEN DIRECTOR OF PHOTOGRAPHY YEL ZAMOR A.S.C.
PRODUCED BY MIKE RICHARDSON SCREENPLAY BY ALEX DE CAMPI DIRECTED BY GARY ERSKINE
05•07•14

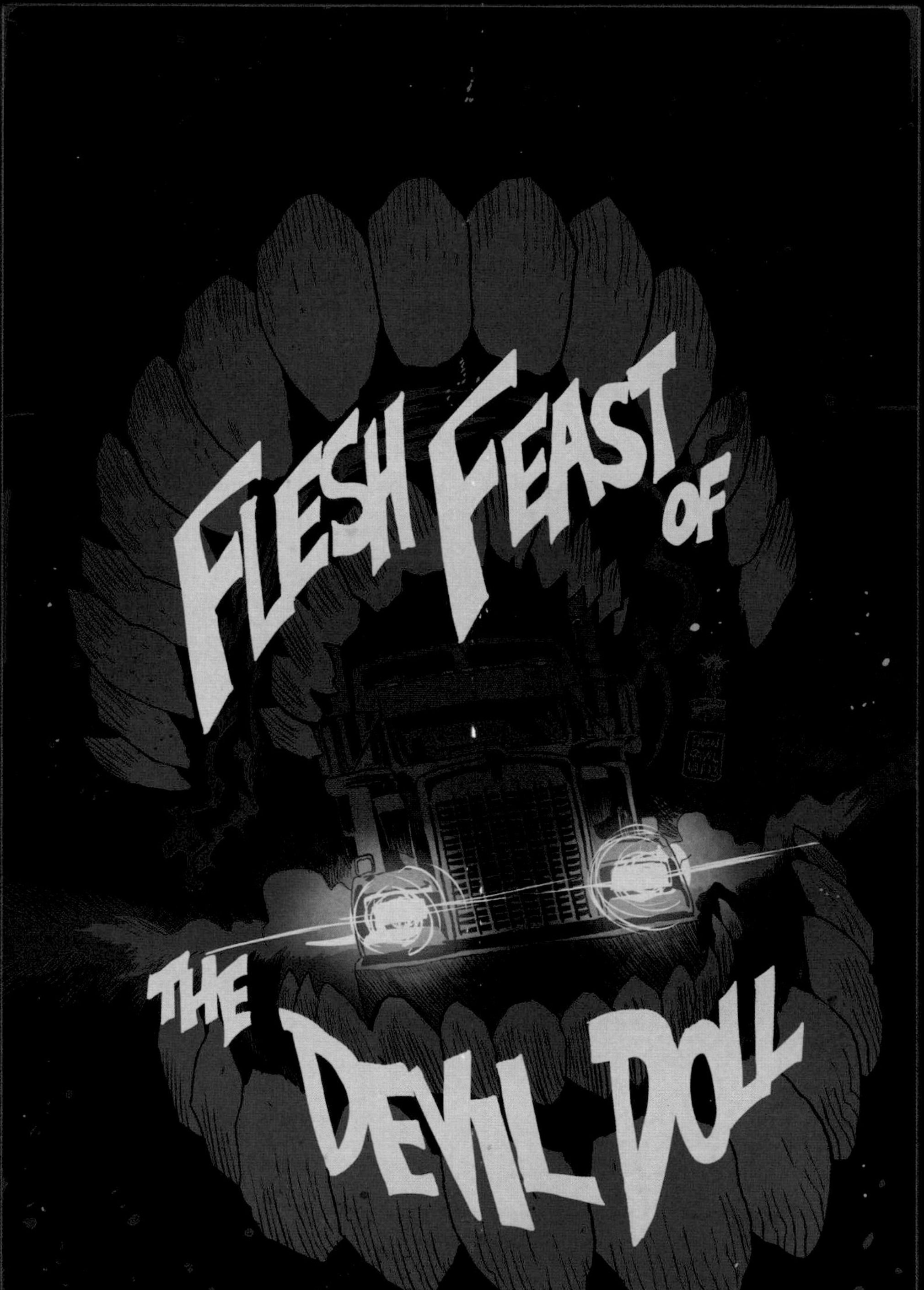
FLESH FEAST OF
THE DEVIL DOLL

FRANCESCO FRANCAVILLA

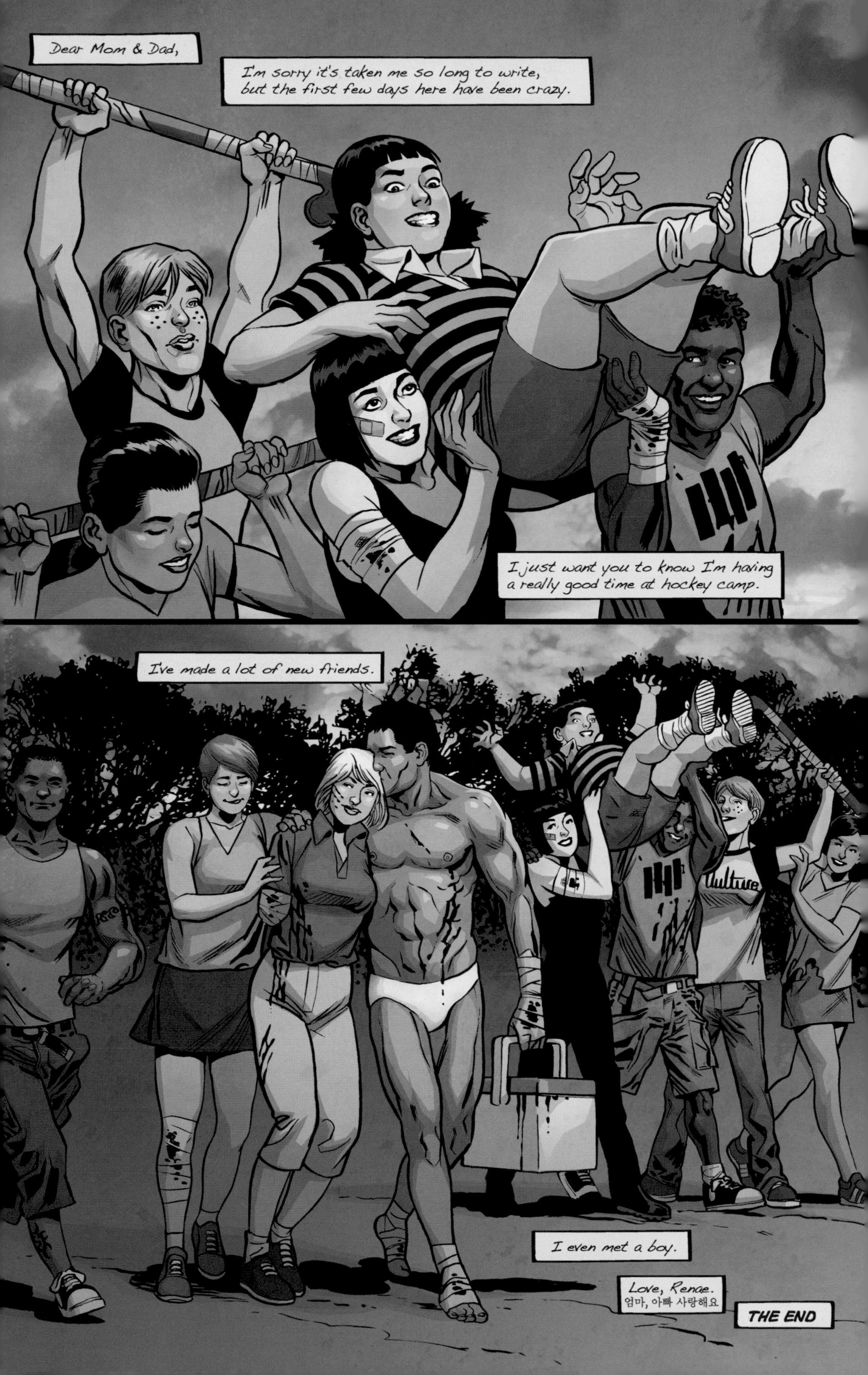
Dear Mom & Dad,
I'm sorry it's taken me so long to write, but the first few days here have been crazy.
I just want you to know I'm having a really good time at hockey camp.
I've made a lot of new friends.
I even met a boy.
Love, Renae.
엄마, 아빠 사랑해요
THE END

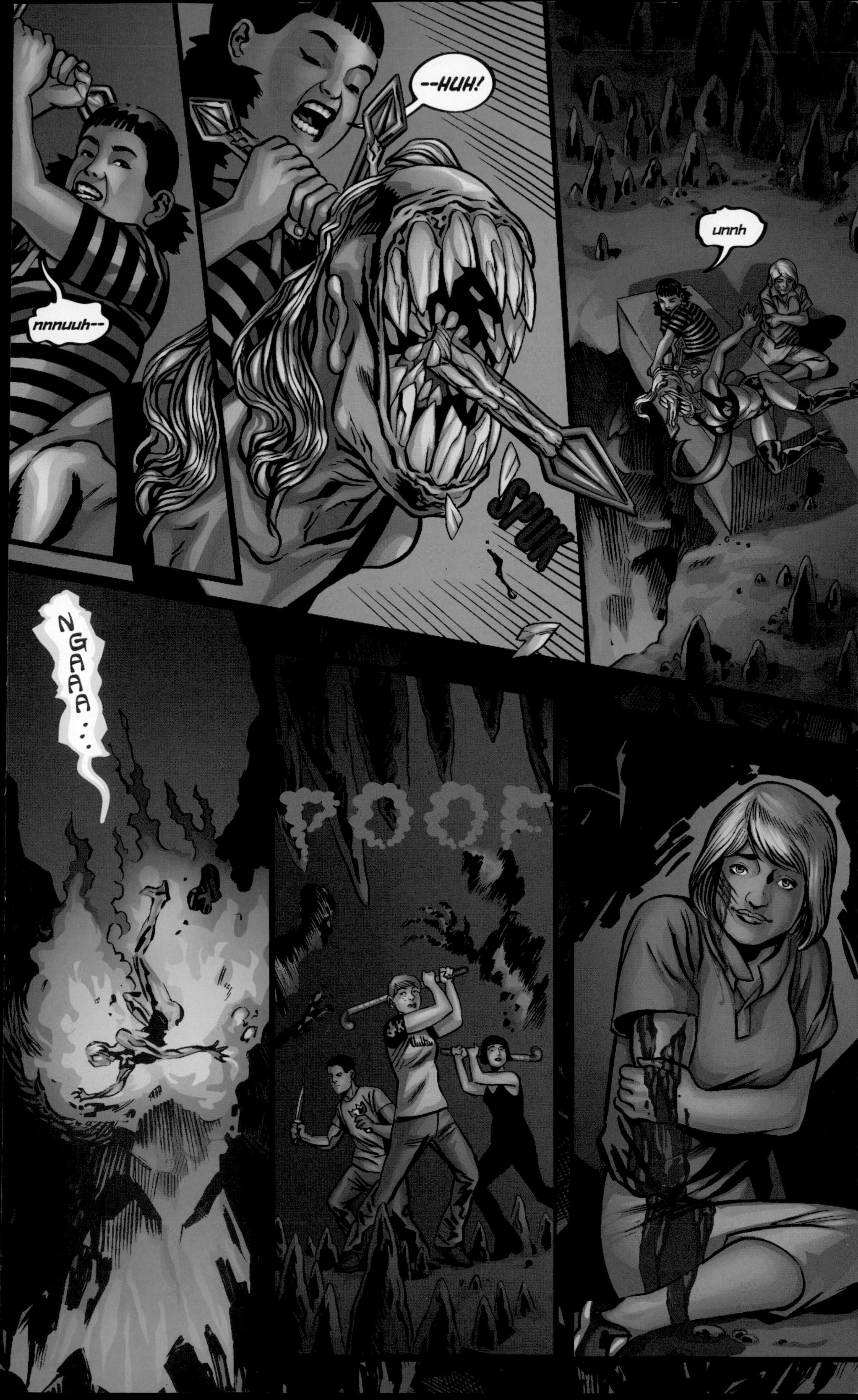
nnnuuh--
--HUH!
SPUK
unnh
NGAAA...
POOF

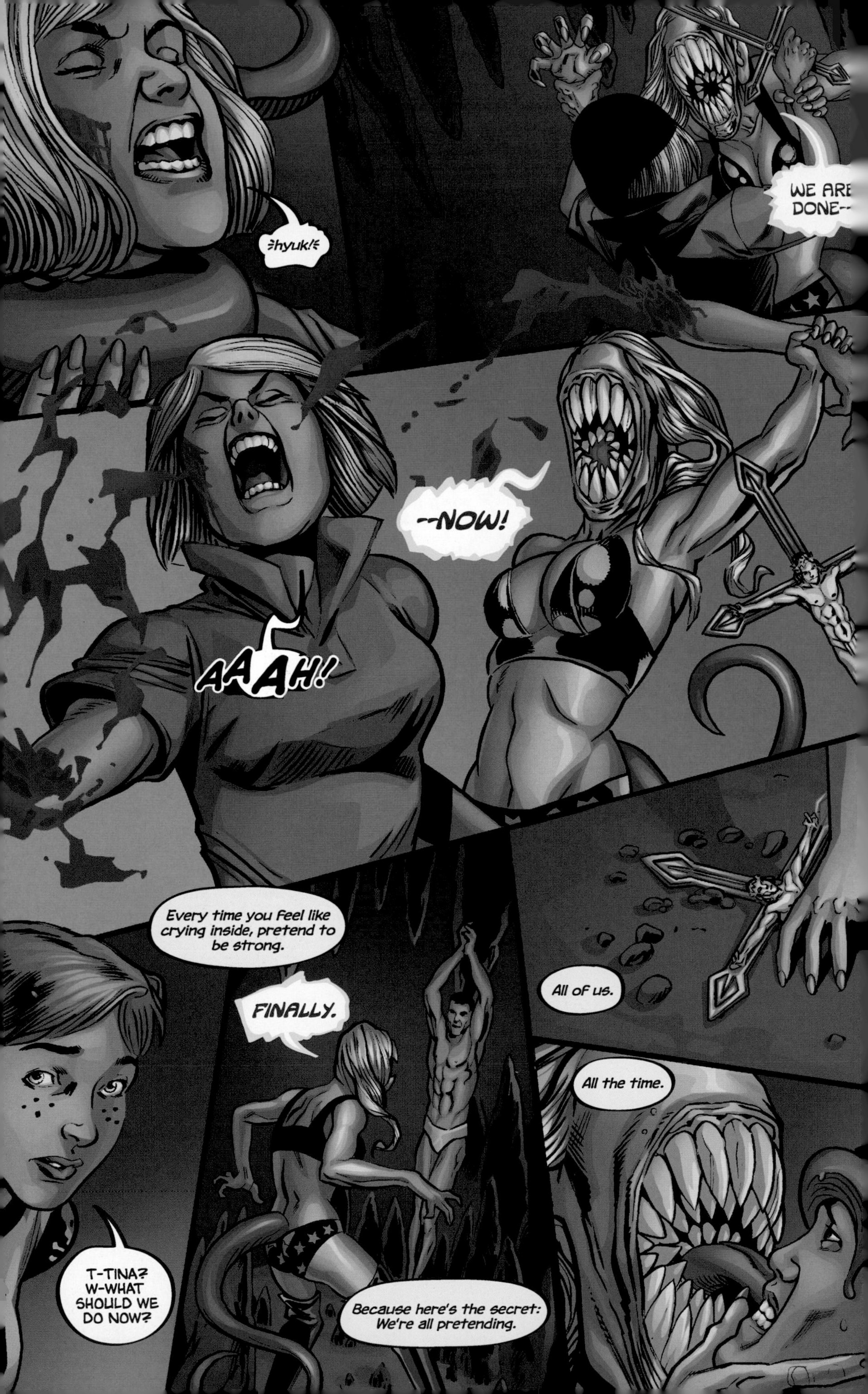

hyuk!
WE ARE DONE--
--NOW!
AAAH!
Every time you feel like crying inside, pretend to be strong.
FINALLY.
T-TINA? W-WHAT SHOULD WE DO NOW?
Because here's the secret: We're all pretending.
All of us.
All the time.

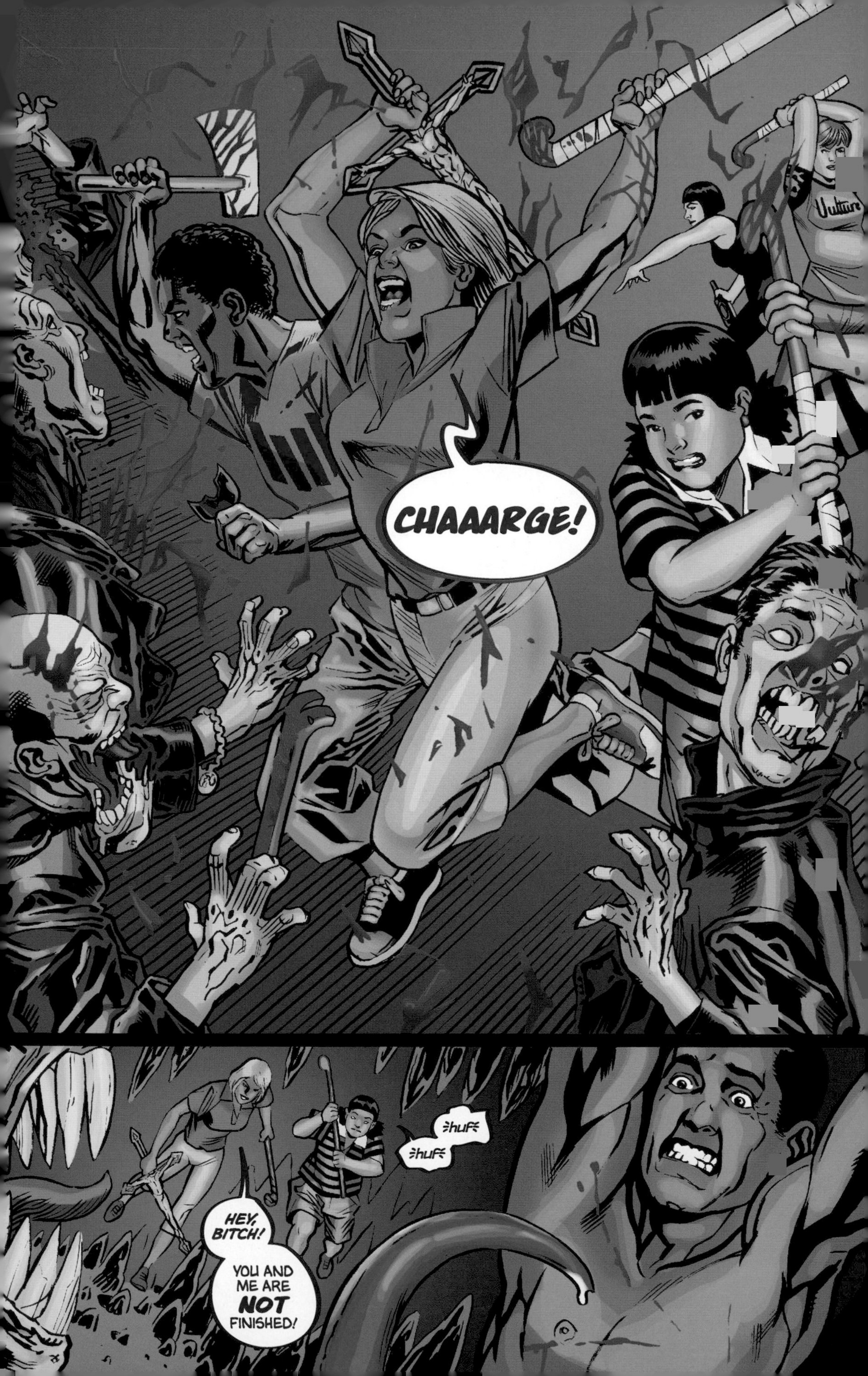
Vulture
CHAAARGE!
huf
huf
HEY, BITCH!
YOU AND ME ARE NOT FINISHED!

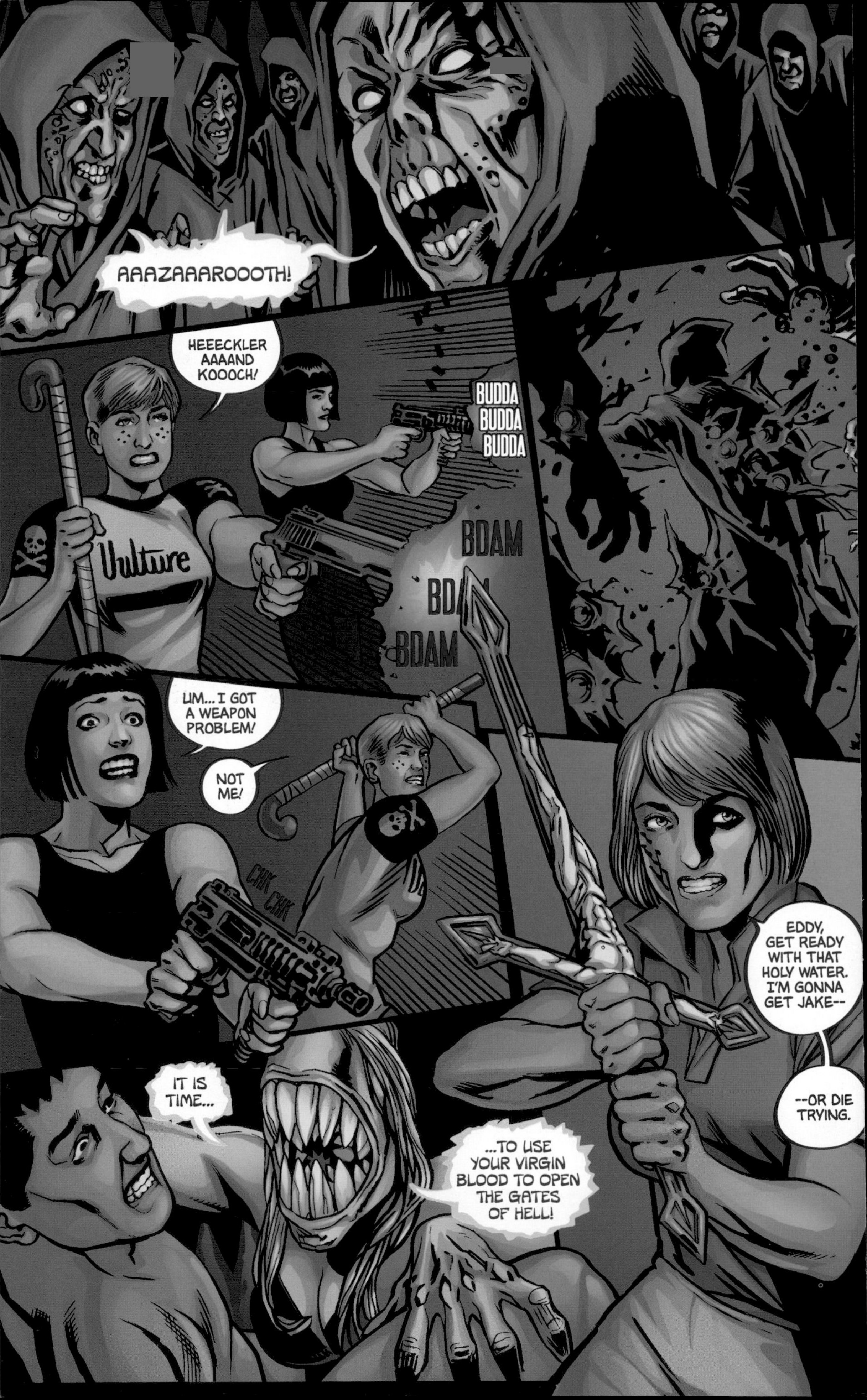
AAAZAAAROOOTH!
HEEECKLER AAAAND KOOOCH!
BUDDA BUDDA BUDDA
BDAM
BDAM
BDAM
UM... I GOT A WEAPON PROBLEM!
NOT ME!
CHK CHK
EDDY, GET READY WITH THAT HOLY WATER. I'M GONNA GET JAKE--
--OR DIE TRYING.
IT IS TIME...
...TO USE YOUR VIRGIN BLOOD TO OPEN THE GATES OF HELL!

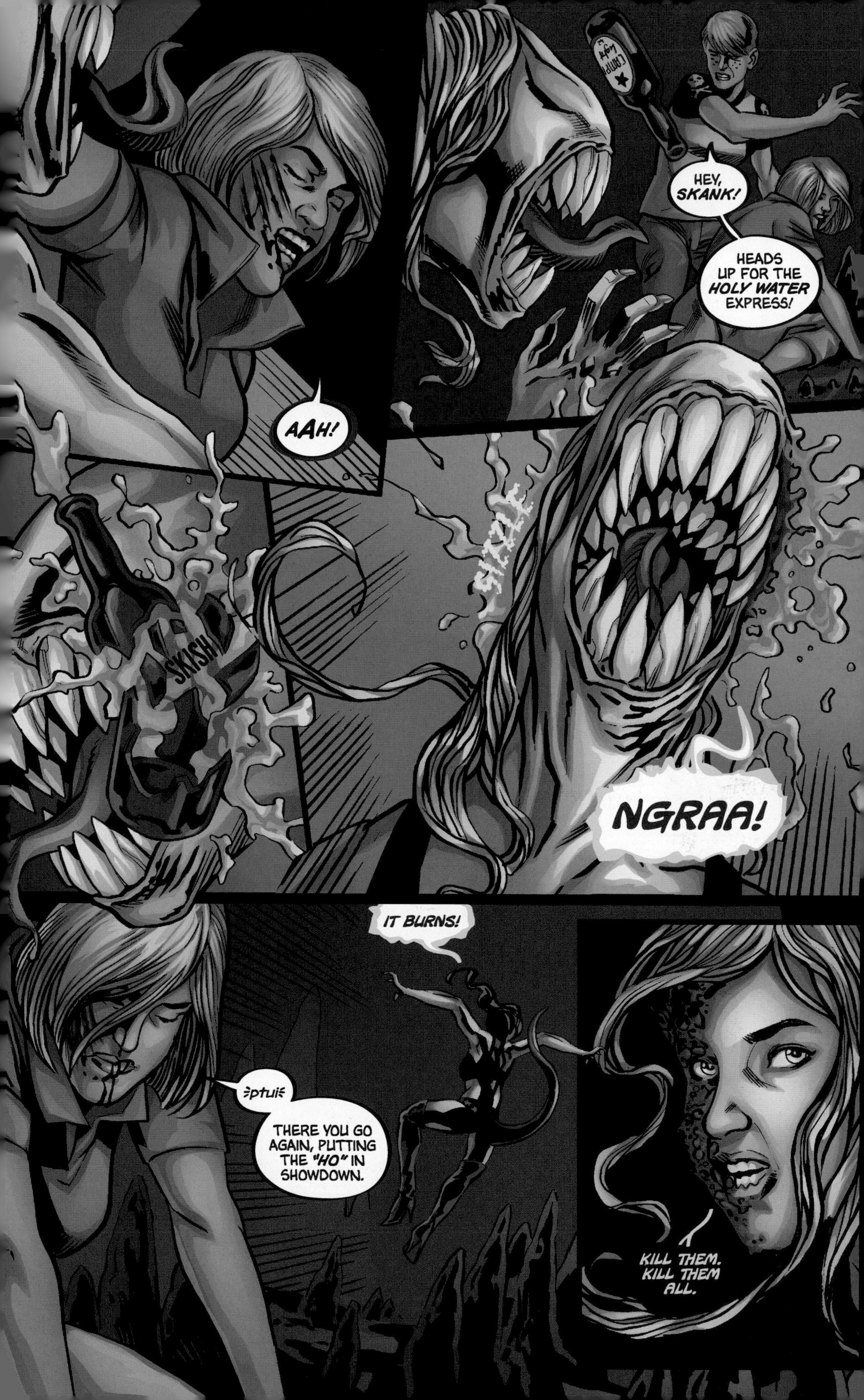
AAH!
HEY, SKANK!
HEADS UP FOR THE HOLY WATER EXPRESS!
SKISH
SIZZLE
NGRAA!
IT BURNS!
ptui
THERE YOU GO AGAIN, PUTTING THE "HO" IN SHOWDOWN.
KILL THEM. KILL THEM ALL.

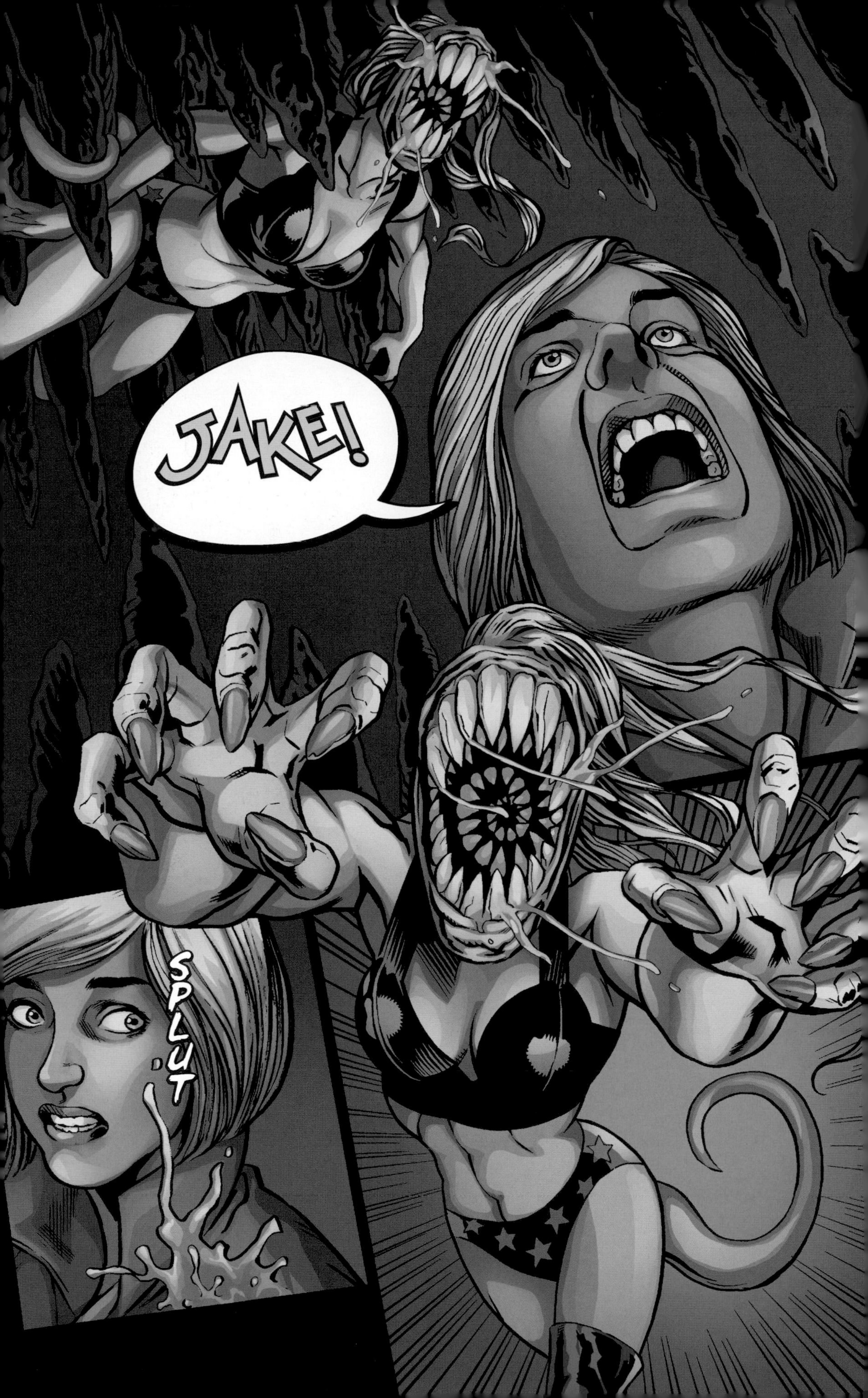

JAKE!
SPLUT

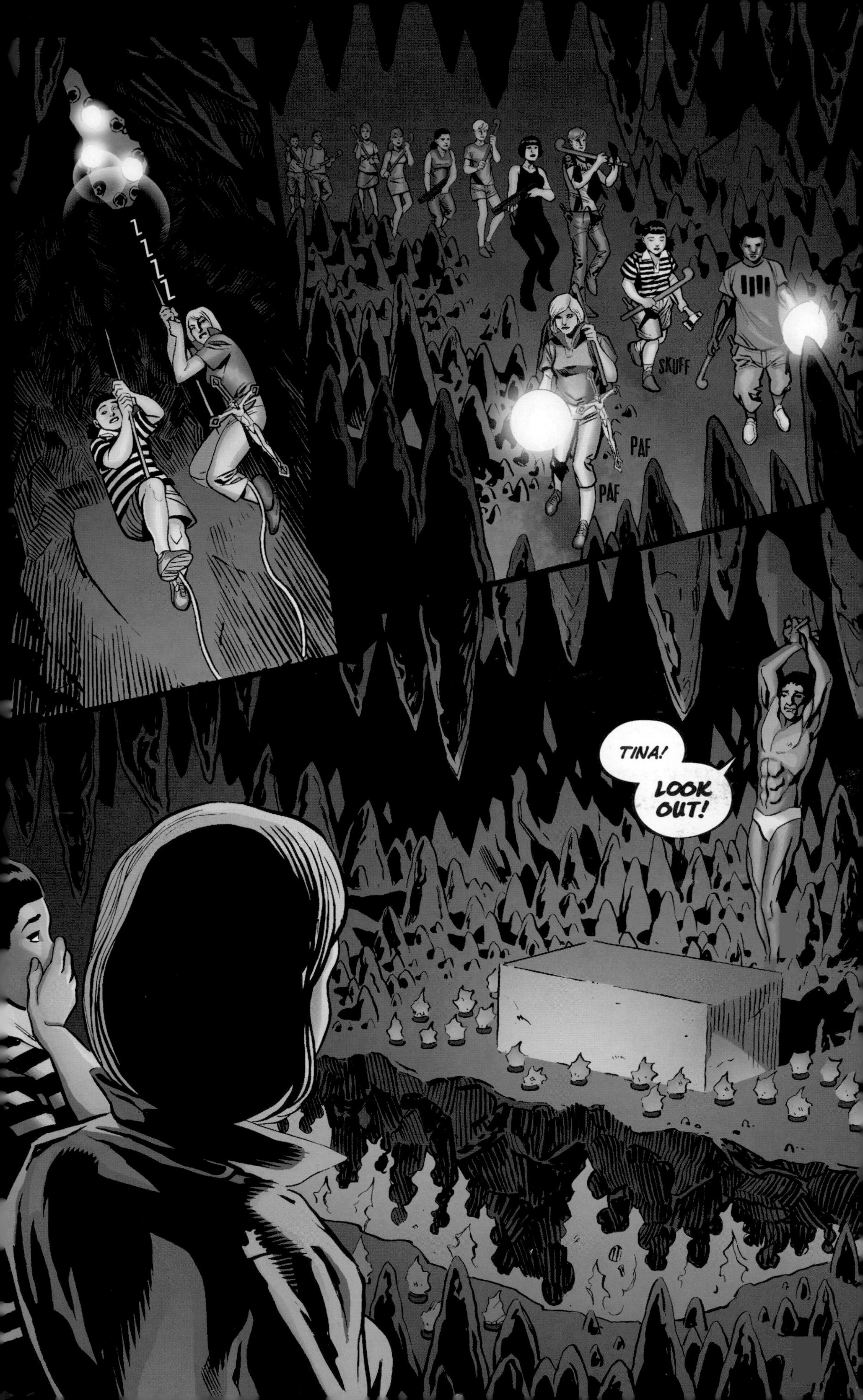
ZZZZZ
SKUFF
PAF
PAF
TINA!
LOOK OUT!

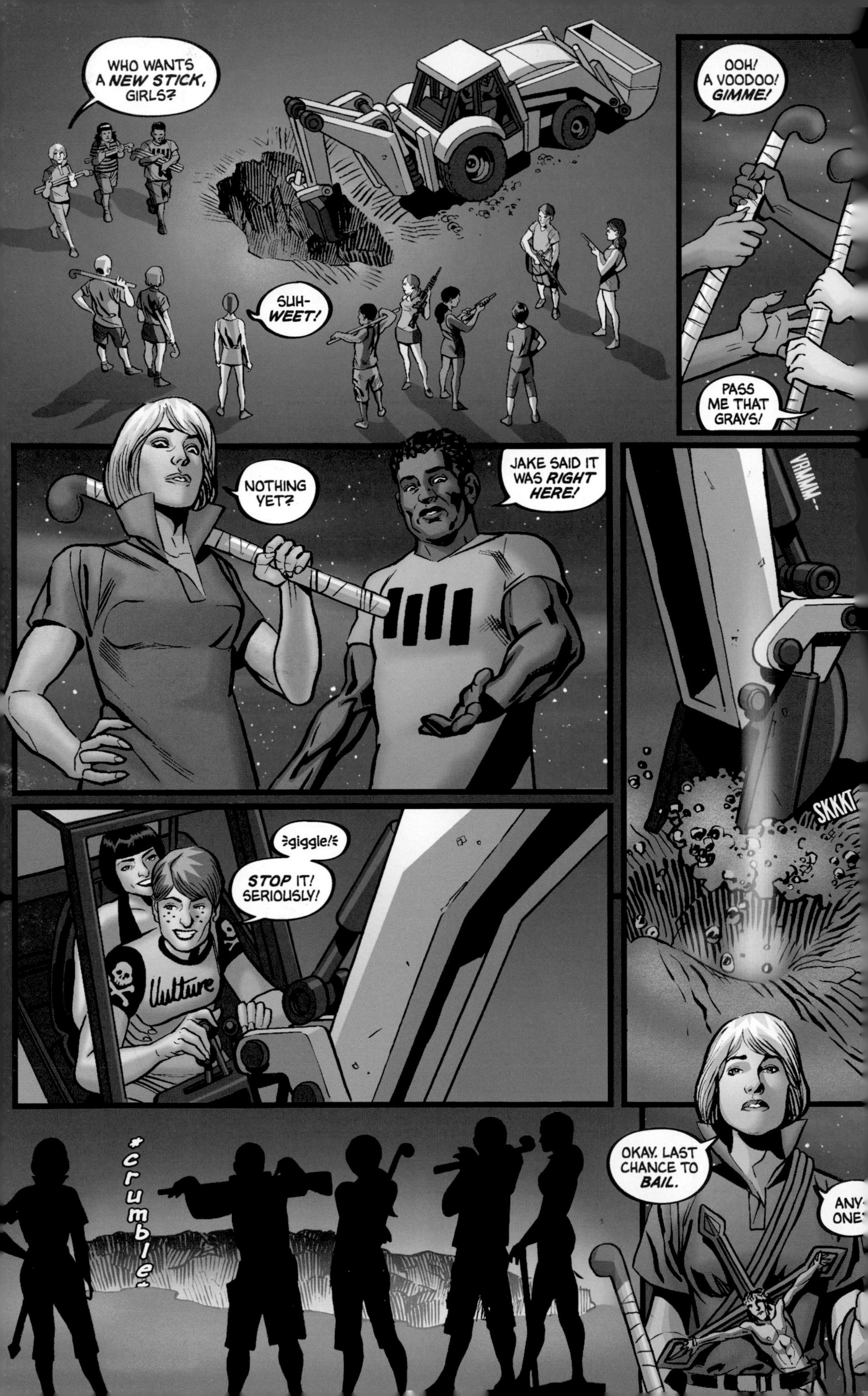
WHO WANTS A NEW STICK, GIRLS?
SUH-WEET!
OOH! A VOODOO! GIMME!
PASS ME THAT GRAYS!
NOTHING YET?
JAKE SAID IT WAS RIGHT HERE!
VRMMM-
SKKKT
giggle!
STOP IT! SERIOUSLY!
crumble
OKAY. LAST CHANCE TO BAIL.
ANY-ONE

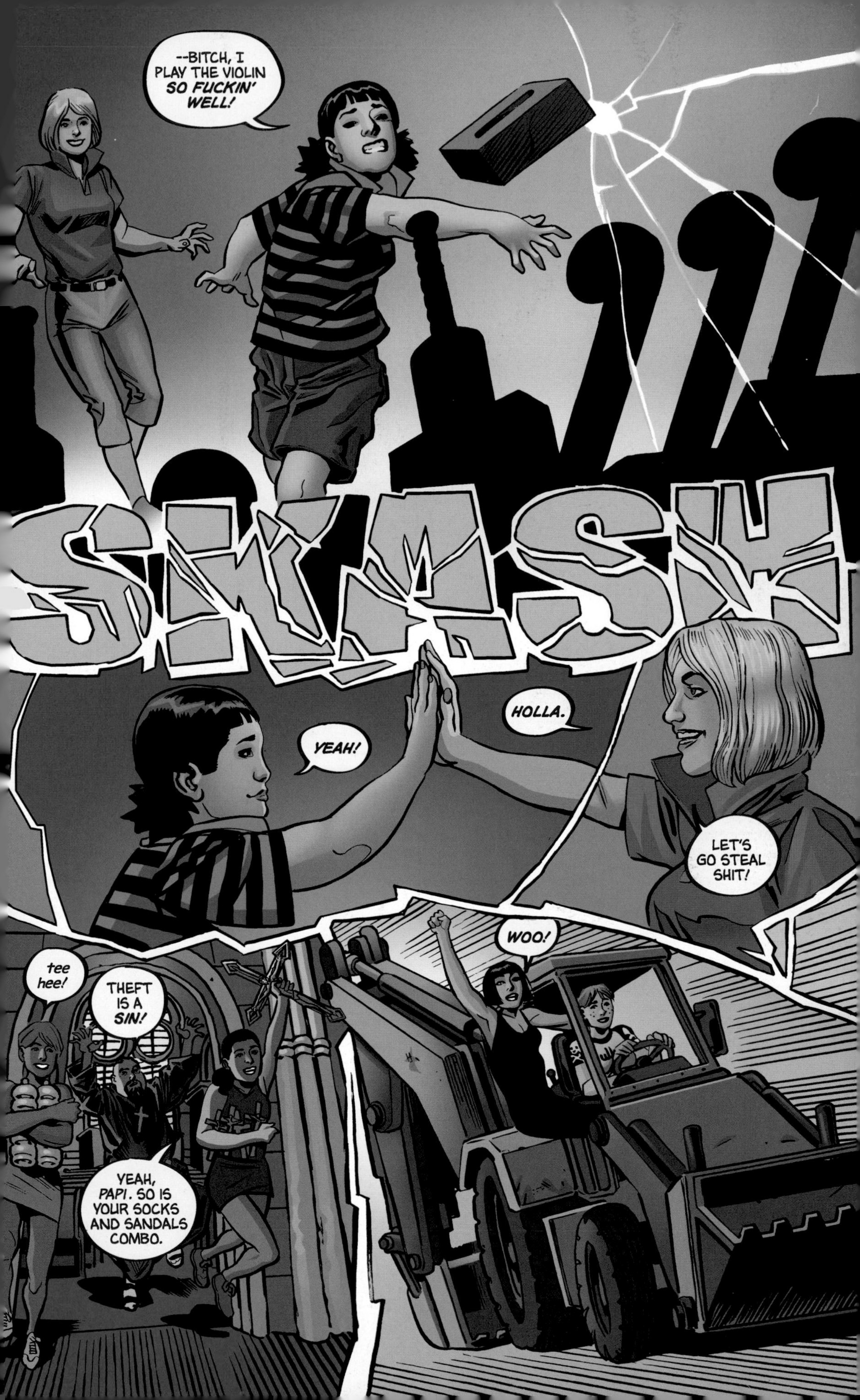
--BITCH, I PLAY THE VIOLIN SO FUCKIN' WELL!
SMASH
YEAH!
HOLLA.
LET'S GO STEAL SHIT!
tee hee!
THEFT IS A SIN!
YEAH, PAPI. SO IS YOUR SOCKS AND SANDALS COMBO.
WOO!

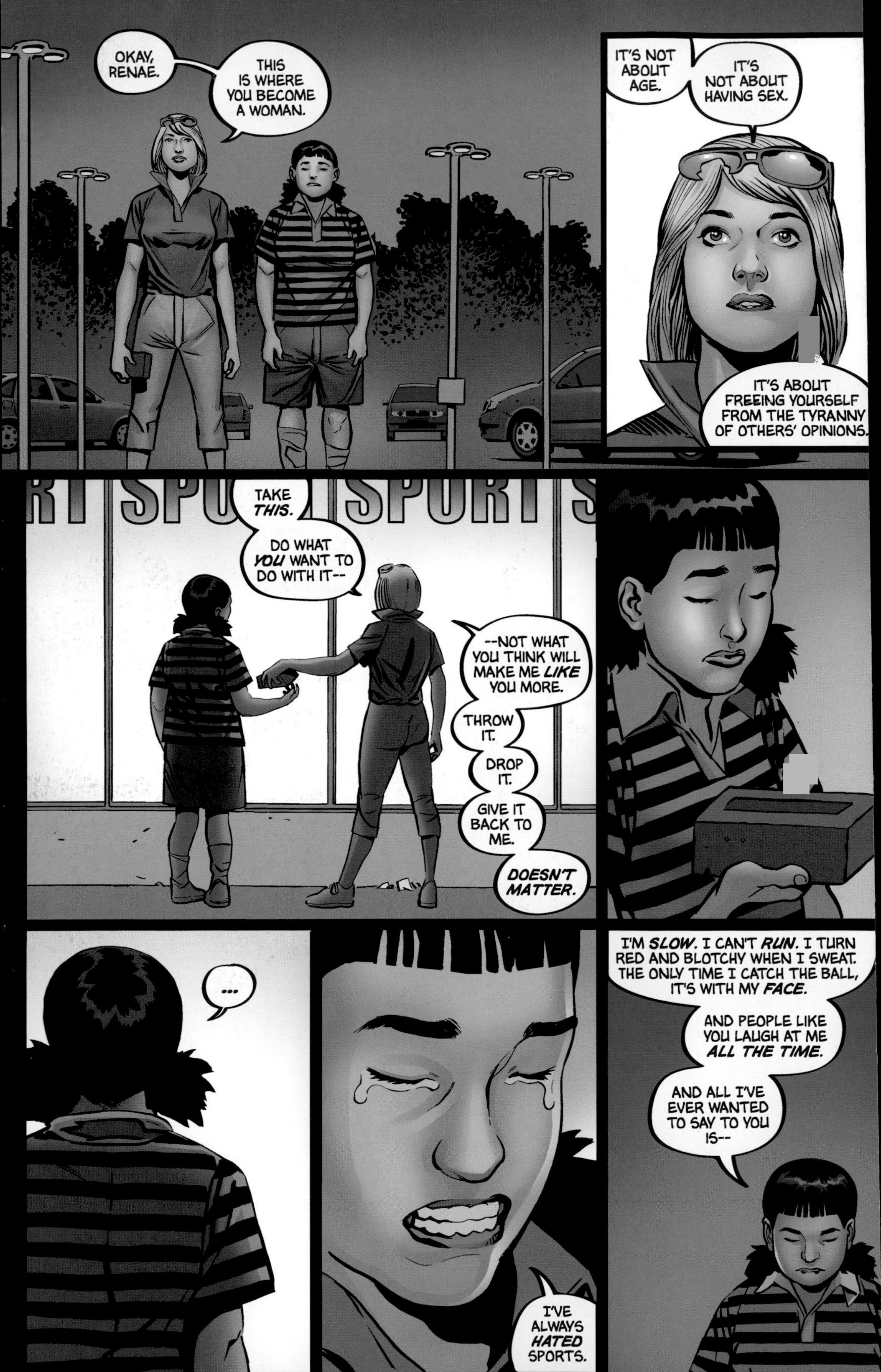

OKAY, RENAE.
THIS IS WHERE YOU BECOME A WOMAN.
IT'S NOT ABOUT AGE.
IT'S NOT ABOUT HAVING SEX.
IT'S ABOUT FREEING YOURSELF FROM THE TYRANNY OF OTHERS' OPINIONS.
SPORT SPORT
TAKE *THIS.*
DO WHAT *YOU* WANT TO DO WITH IT--
--NOT WHAT YOU THINK WILL MAKE ME *LIKE* YOU MORE.
THROW IT.
DROP IT.
GIVE IT BACK TO ME.
DOESN'T MATTER.
...
I'VE ALWAYS *HATED* SPORTS.
I'M *SLOW*. I CAN'T *RUN*. I TURN RED AND BLOTCHY WHEN I SWEAT. THE ONLY TIME I CATCH THE BALL, IT'S WITH MY *FACE.*
AND PEOPLE LIKE YOU LAUGH AT ME *ALL THE TIME.*
AND ALL I'VE EVER WANTED TO SAY TO YOU IS--

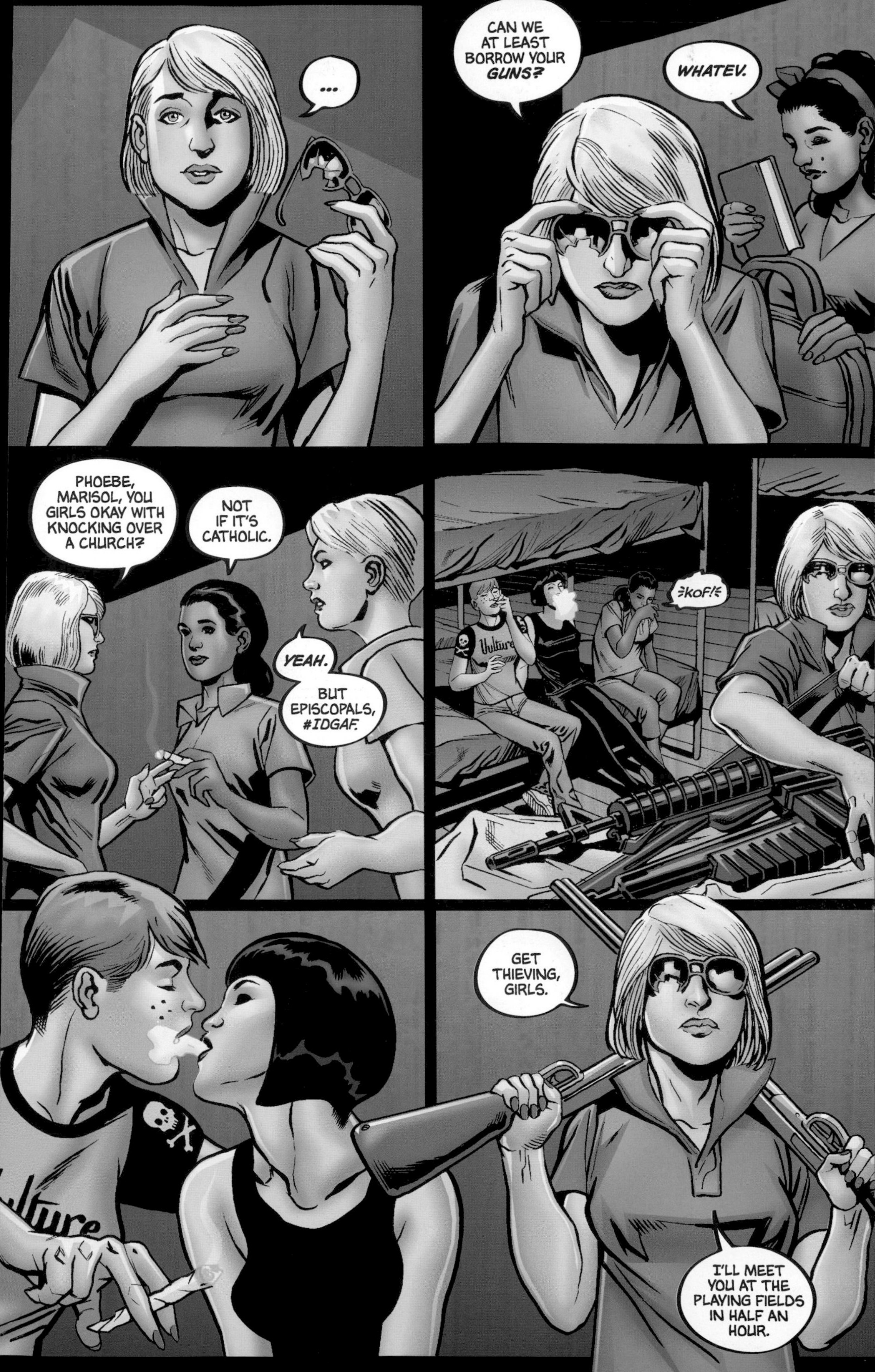
...
CAN WE AT LEAST BORROW YOUR GUNS?
WHATEV.
PHOEBE, MARISOL, YOU GIRLS OKAY WITH KNOCKING OVER A CHURCH?
NOT IF IT'S CATHOLIC.
YEAH.
BUT EPISCOPALS, #IDGAF.
KOF!
Vulture
GET THIEVING, GIRLS.
I'LL MEET YOU AT THE PLAYING FIELDS IN HALF AN HOUR.

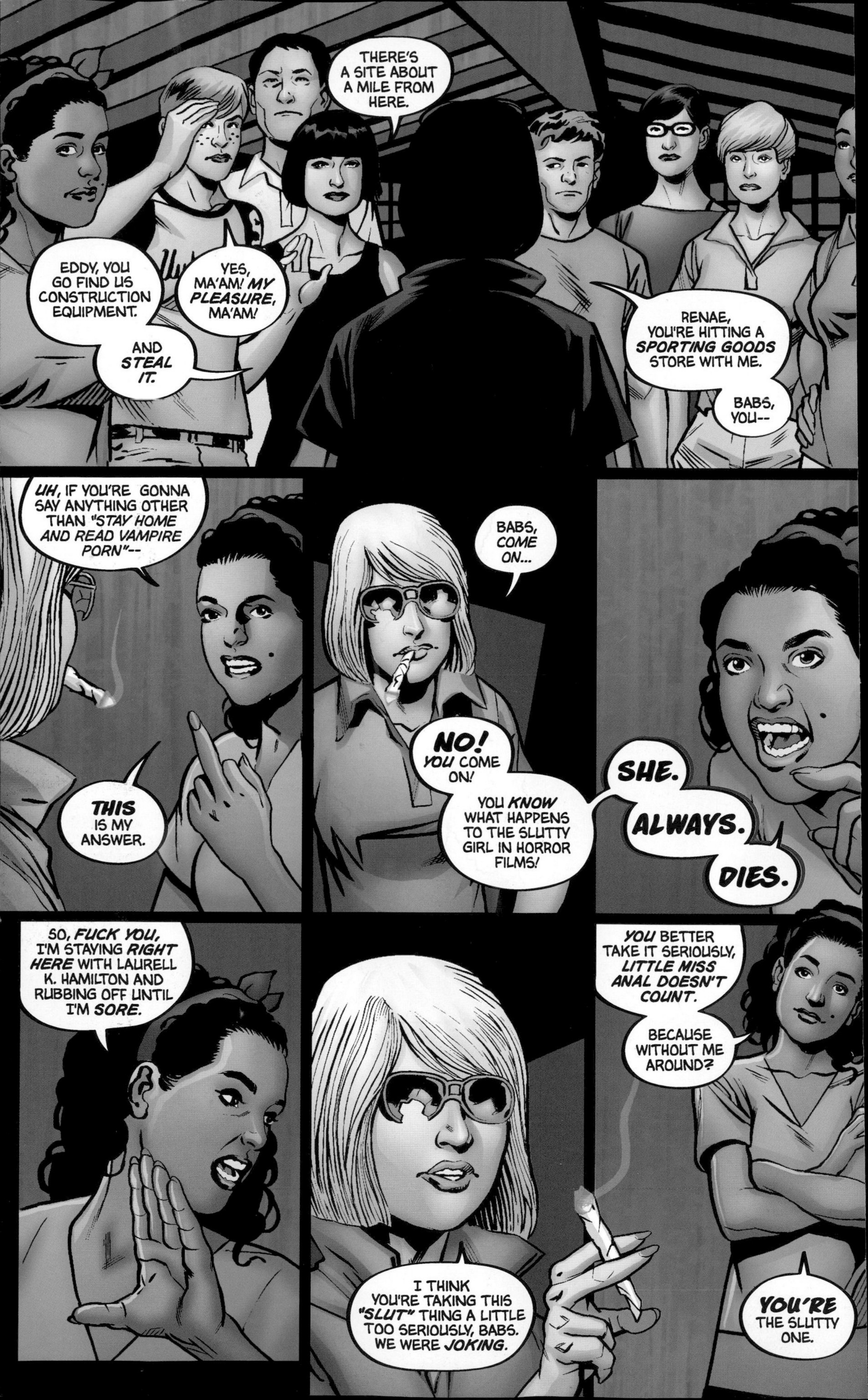
THERE'S A SITE ABOUT A MILE FROM HERE.
EDDY, YOU GO FIND US CONSTRUCTION EQUIPMENT.
AND STEAL IT.
YES, MA'AM! MY PLEASURE, MA'AM!
RENAE, YOU'RE HITTING A SPORTING GOODS STORE WITH ME.
BABS, YOU--
UH, IF YOU'RE GONNA SAY ANYTHING OTHER THAN "STAY HOME AND READ VAMPIRE PORN"--
THIS IS MY ANSWER.
BABS, COME ON...
NO! YOU COME ON!
YOU KNOW WHAT HAPPENS TO THE SLUTTY GIRL IN HORROR FILMS!
SHE.
ALWAYS.
DIES.
SO, FUCK YOU, I'M STAYING RIGHT HERE WITH LAURELL K. HAMILTON AND RUBBING OFF UNTIL I'M SORE.
I THINK YOU'RE TAKING THIS "SLUT" THING A LITTLE TOO SERIOUSLY, BABS. WE WERE JOKING.
YOU BETTER TAKE IT SERIOUSLY, LITTLE MISS ANAL DOESN'T COUNT.
BECAUSE WITHOUT ME AROUND?
YOU'RE THE SLUTTY ONE.

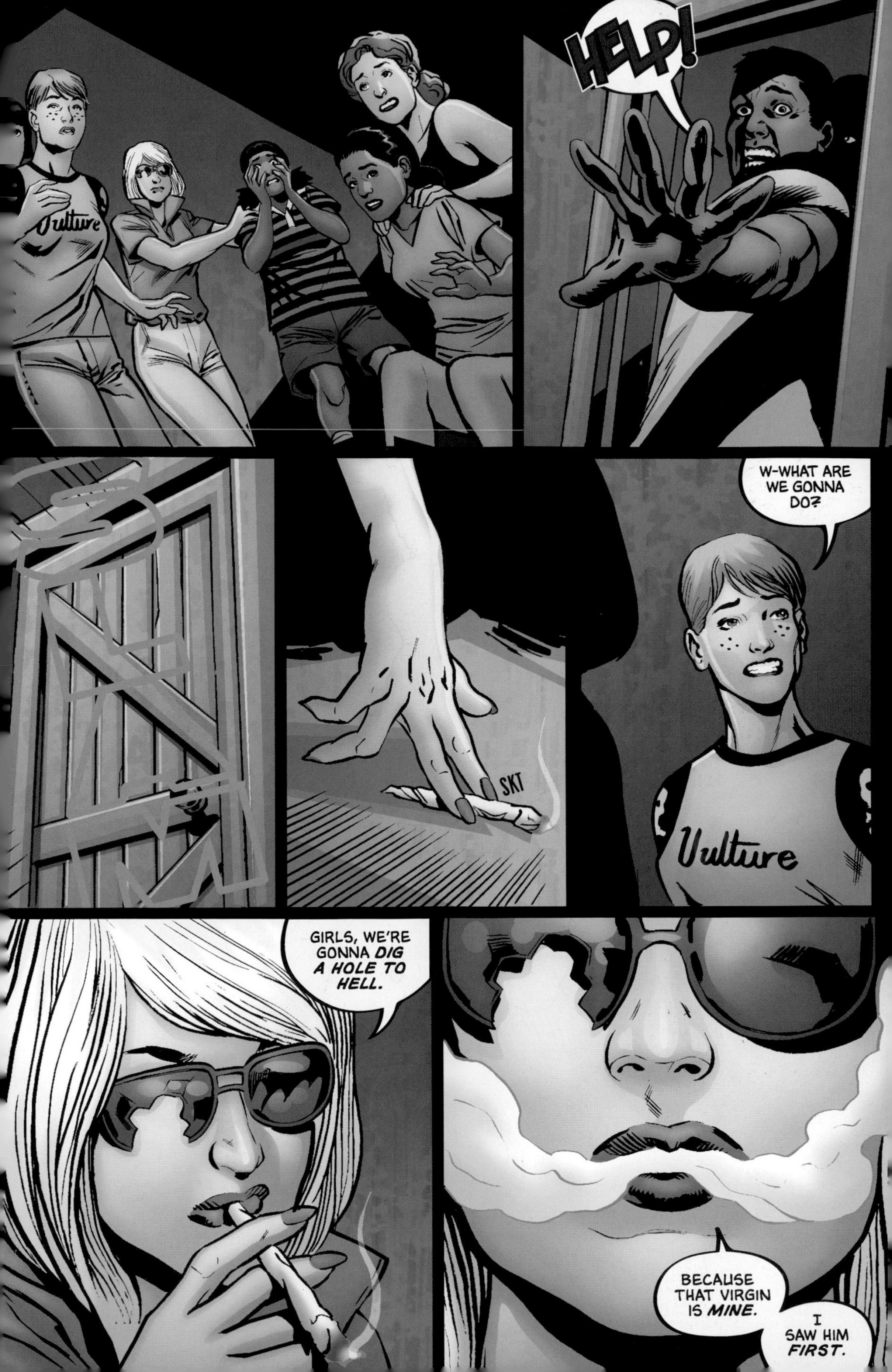
HELP!
W-WHAT ARE WE GONNA DO?
SKT
Vulture
GIRLS, WE'RE GONNA *DIG A HOLE TO HELL.*
BECAUSE THAT VIRGIN IS *MINE.*
I SAW HIM *FIRST.*

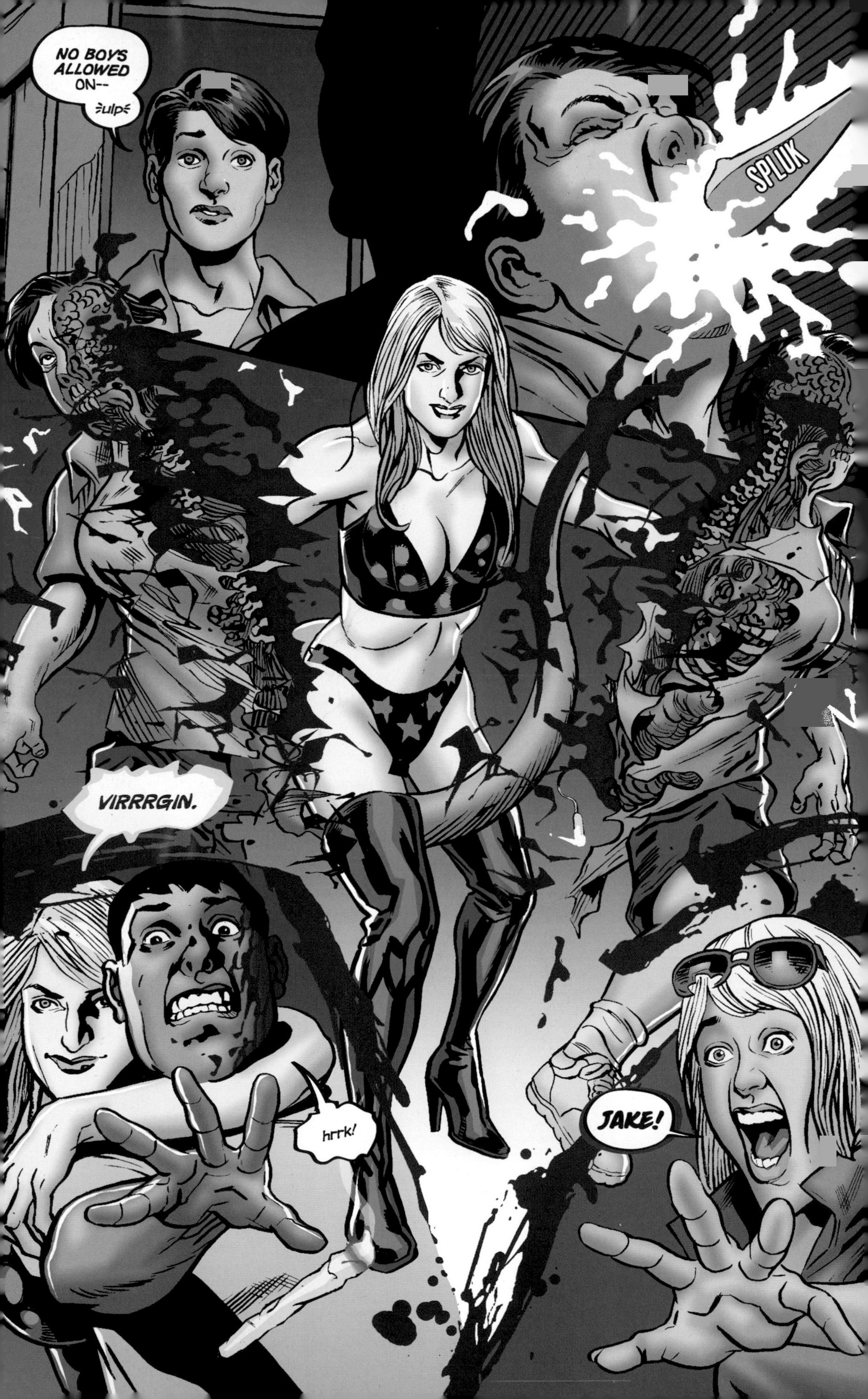
NO BOYS ALLOWED ON--
ulp
SPLUK
VIRRRGIN.
hrrk!
JAKE!

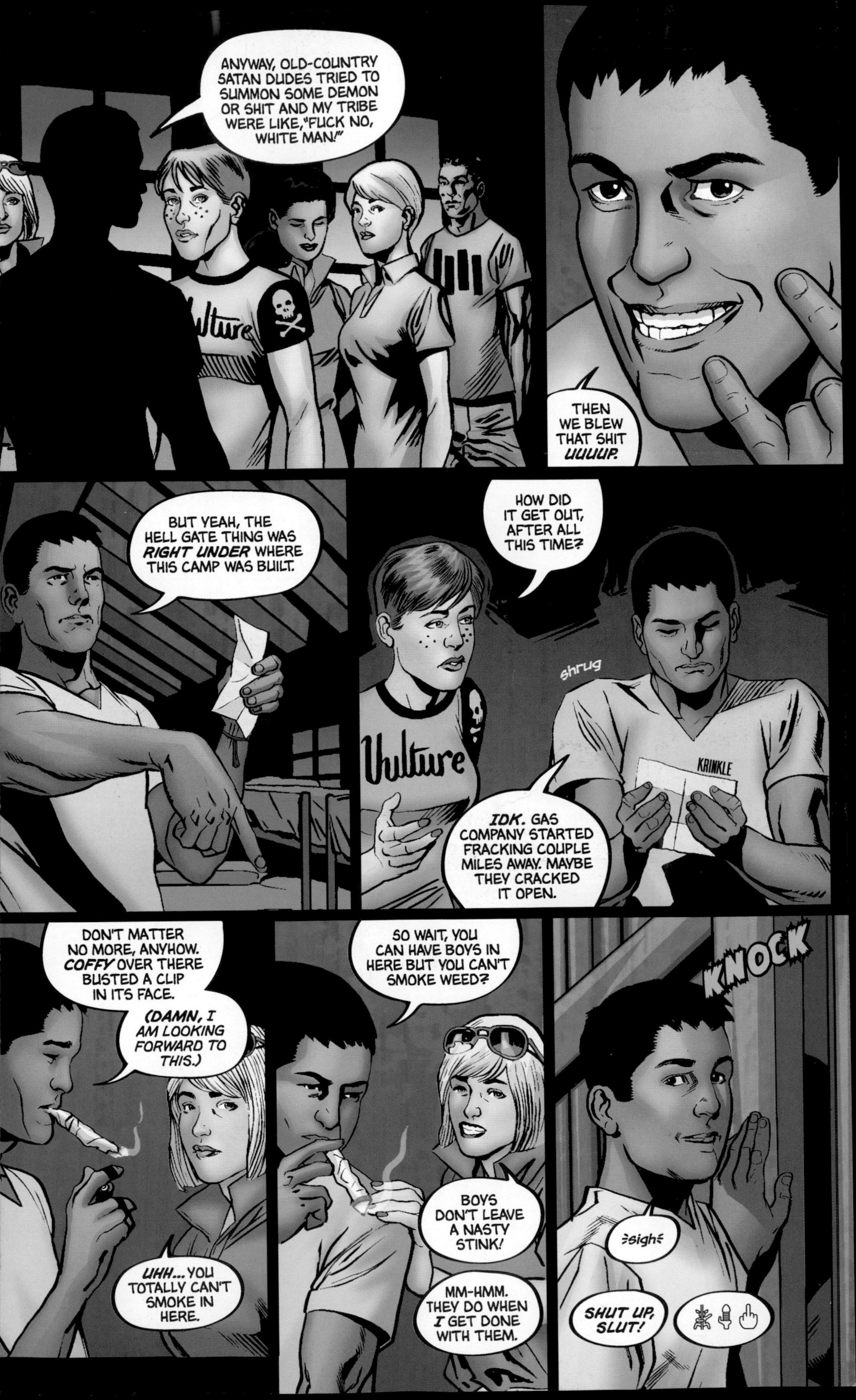
ANYWAY, OLD-COUNTRY SATAN DUDES TRIED TO SUMMON SOME DEMON OR SHIT AND MY TRIBE WERE LIKE, "FUCK NO, WHITE MAN!"
THEN WE BLEW THAT SHIT UUUUP.
BUT YEAH, THE HELL GATE THING WAS RIGHT UNDER WHERE THIS CAMP WAS BUILT.
HOW DID IT GET OUT, AFTER ALL THIS TIME?
shrug
IDK. GAS COMPANY STARTED FRACKING COUPLE MILES AWAY. MAYBE THEY CRACKED IT OPEN.
DON'T MATTER NO MORE, ANYHOW. COFFY OVER THERE BUSTED A CLIP IN ITS FACE.
(DAMN, I AM LOOKING FORWARD TO THIS.)
UHH... YOU TOTALLY CAN'T SMOKE IN HERE.
SO WAIT, YOU CAN HAVE BOYS IN HERE BUT YOU CAN'T SMOKE WEED?
BOYS DON'T LEAVE A NASTY STINK!
MM-HMM. THEY DO WHEN I GET DONE WITH THEM.
KNOCK
sigh
SHUT UP, SLUT!

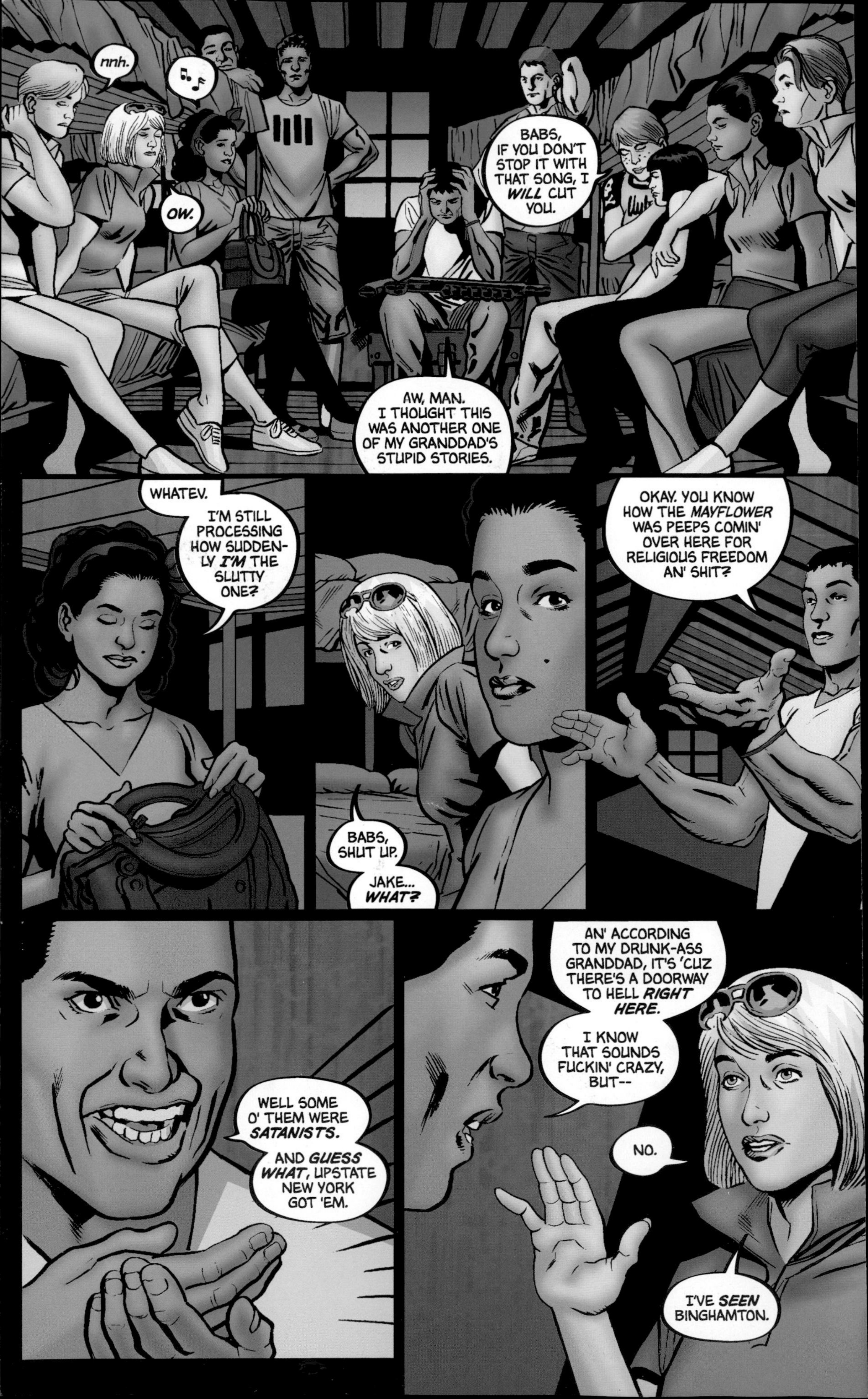
nnh.
♪♪
OW.
BABS, IF YOU DON'T STOP IT WITH THAT SONG, I *WILL* CUT YOU.
AW, MAN. I THOUGHT THIS WAS ANOTHER ONE OF MY GRANDDAD'S STUPID STORIES.
WHATEV.
I'M STILL PROCESSING HOW SUDDENLY *I'M* THE SLUTTY ONE?
BABS, SHUT UP.
JAKE... *WHAT?*
OKAY. YOU KNOW HOW THE *MAYFLOWER* WAS PEEPS COMIN' OVER HERE FOR RELIGIOUS FREEDOM AN' SHIT?
WELL SOME O' THEM WERE *SATANISTS.*
AND *GUESS WHAT*, UPSTATE NEW YORK GOT 'EM.
AN' ACCORDING TO MY DRUNK-ASS GRANDDAD, IT'S 'CUZ THERE'S A DOORWAY TO HELL *RIGHT HERE.*
I KNOW THAT SOUNDS FUCKIN' CRAZY, BUT--
NO.
I'VE *SEEN* BINGHAMTON.

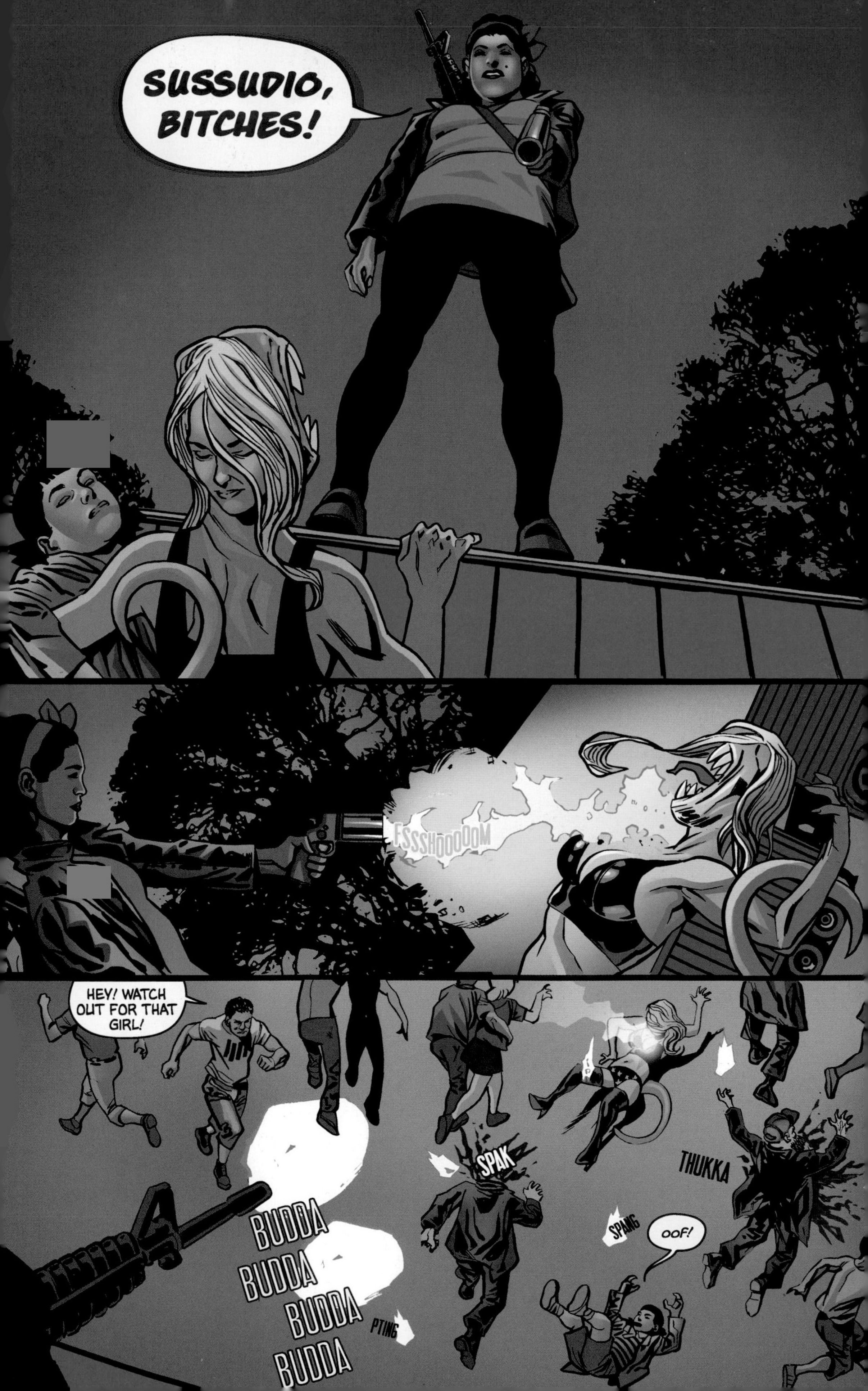
SUSSUDIO, BITCHES!
FSSSHOOOOOM
HEY! WATCH OUT FOR THAT GIRL!
SPAK
THUKKA
SPANG
OOF!
BUDDA
BUDDA
BUDDA
BUDDA
PTING

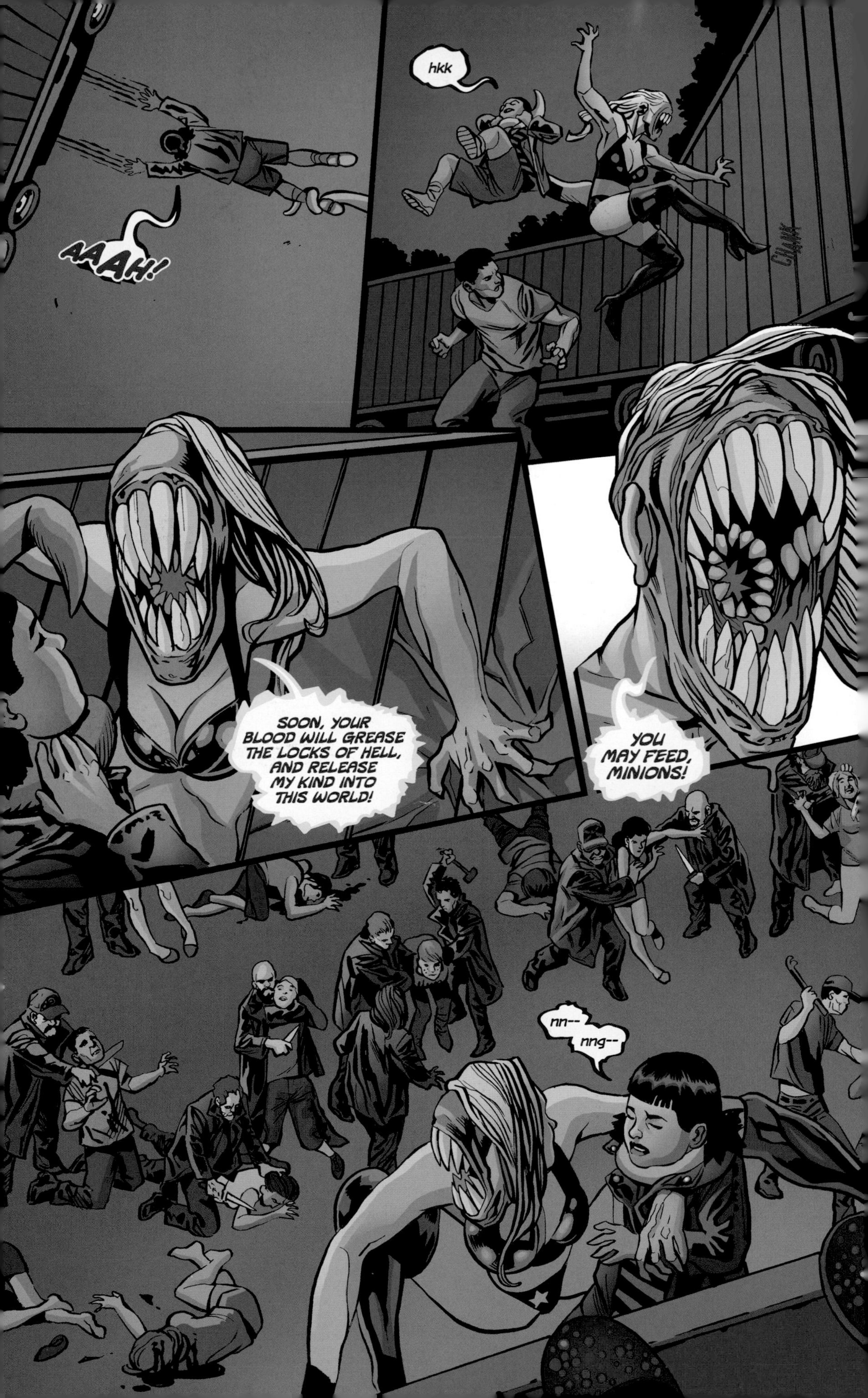
AAAH!
hkk
CHANK
SOON, YOUR BLOOD WILL GREASE THE LOCKS OF HELL, AND RELEASE MY KIND INTO THIS WORLD!
YOU MAY FEED, MINIONS!
nn--
nng--

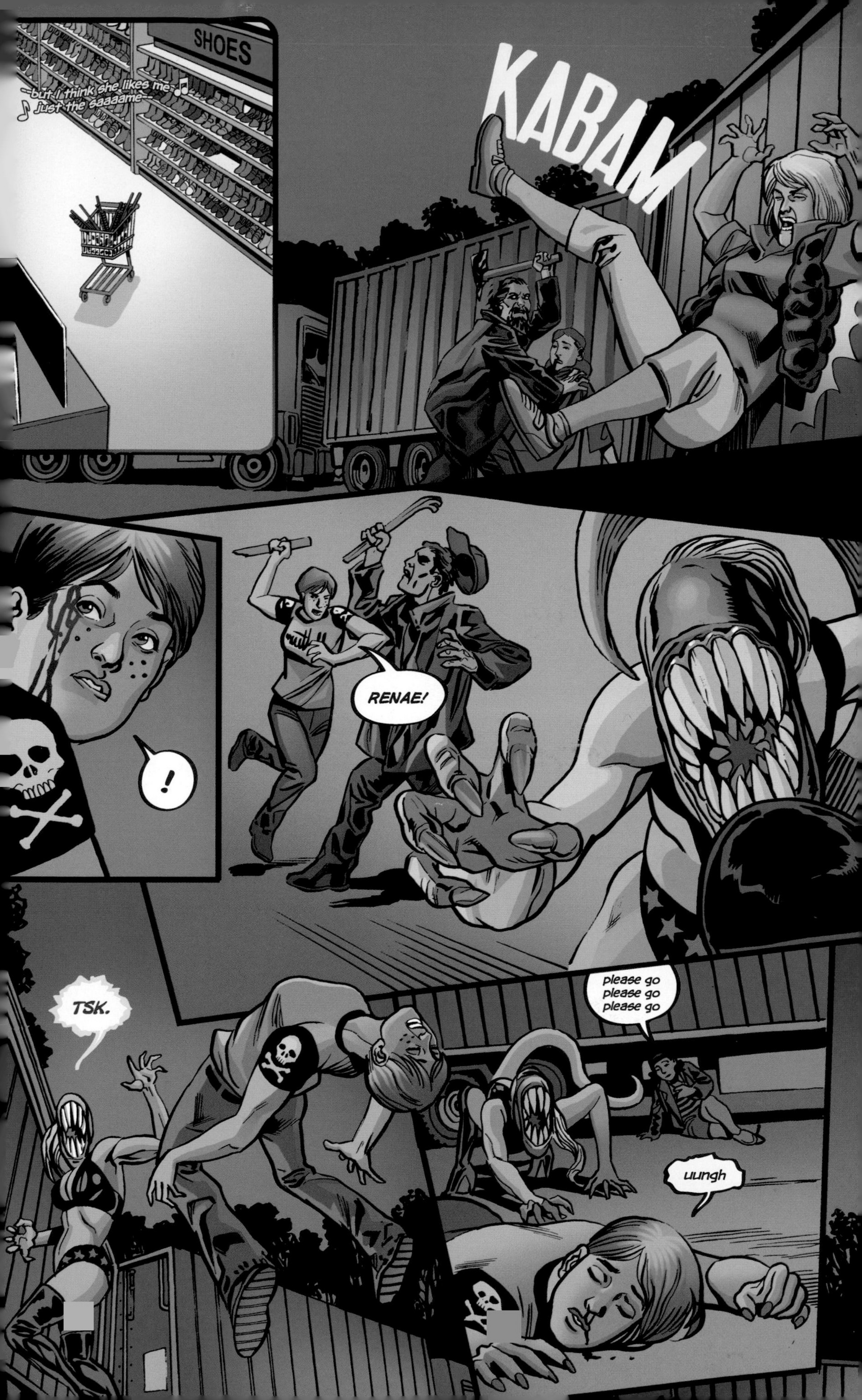

SHOES
—but I think she likes me—
just the saaaame—
KABAM
RENAE!
!
TSK.
please go
please go
please go
uungh

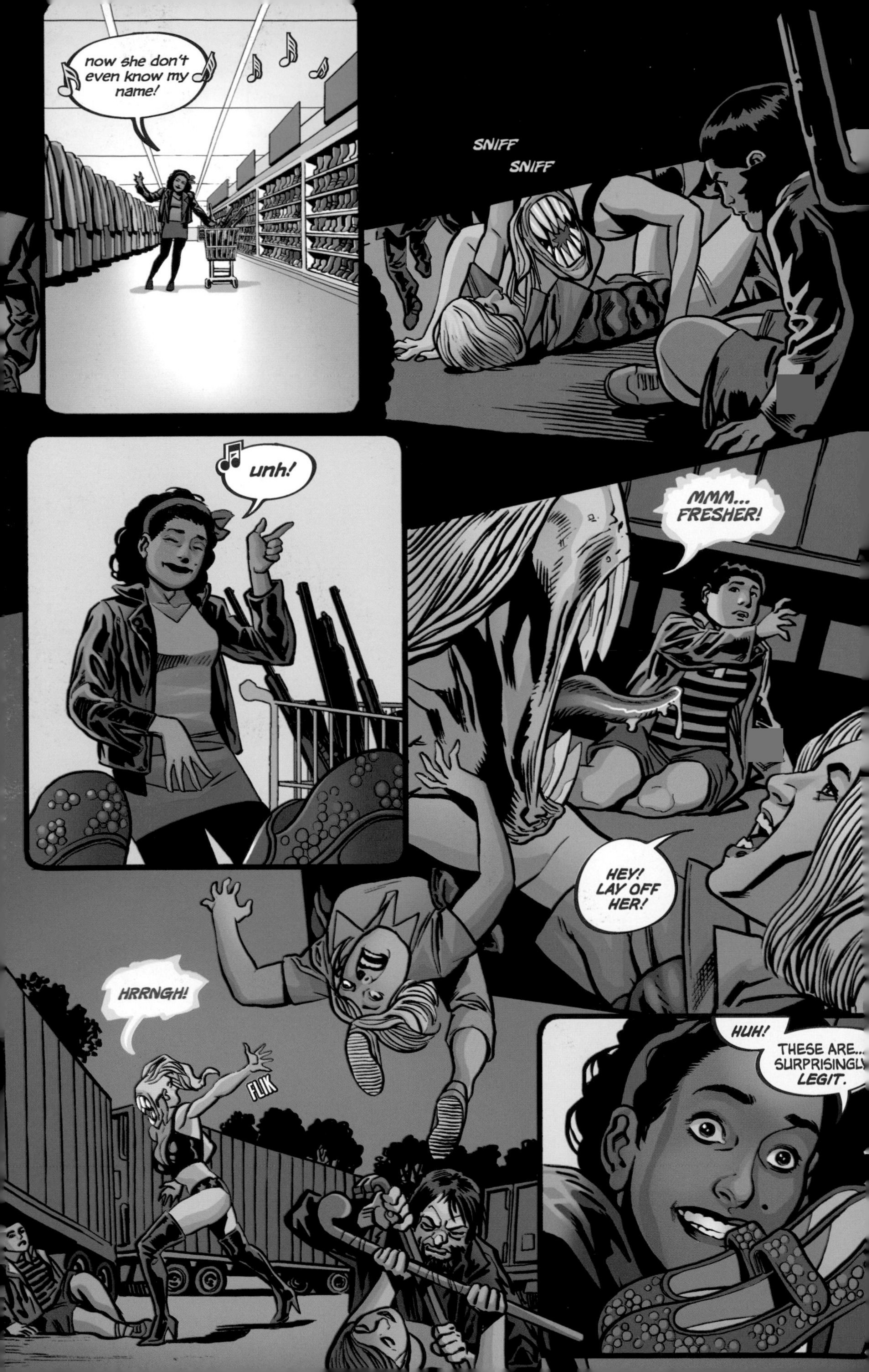
now she don't even know my name!
SNIFF
SNIFF
unh!
MMM... FRESHER!
HEY! LAY OFF HER!
HRRNGH!
FLIK
HUH!
THESE ARE... SURPRISINGLY LEGIT.

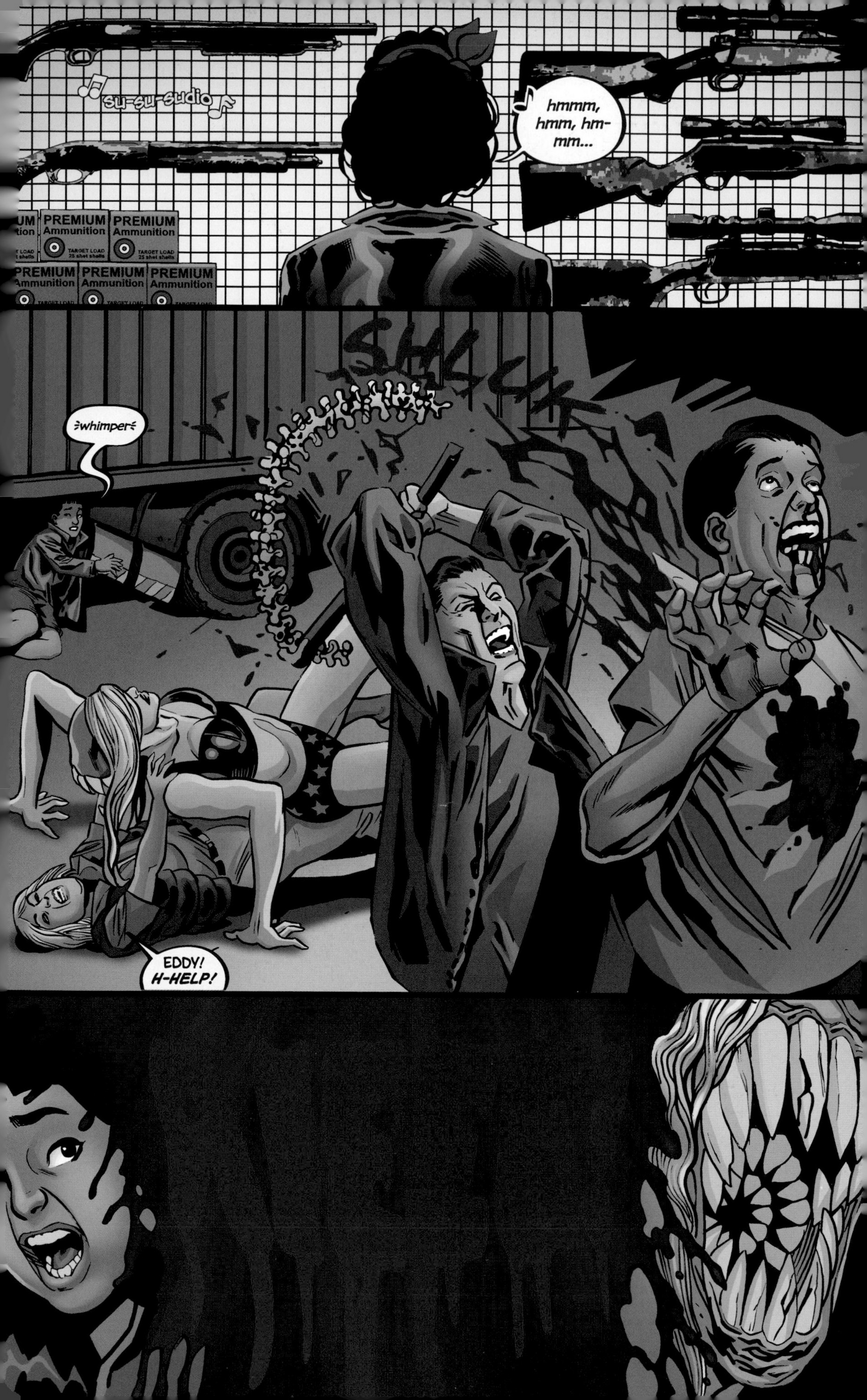
su-su-sudio
hmmm, hmm, hm-mm...
PREMIUM Ammunition
TARGET LOAD 25 shot shells
whimper
EDDY! H-HELP!

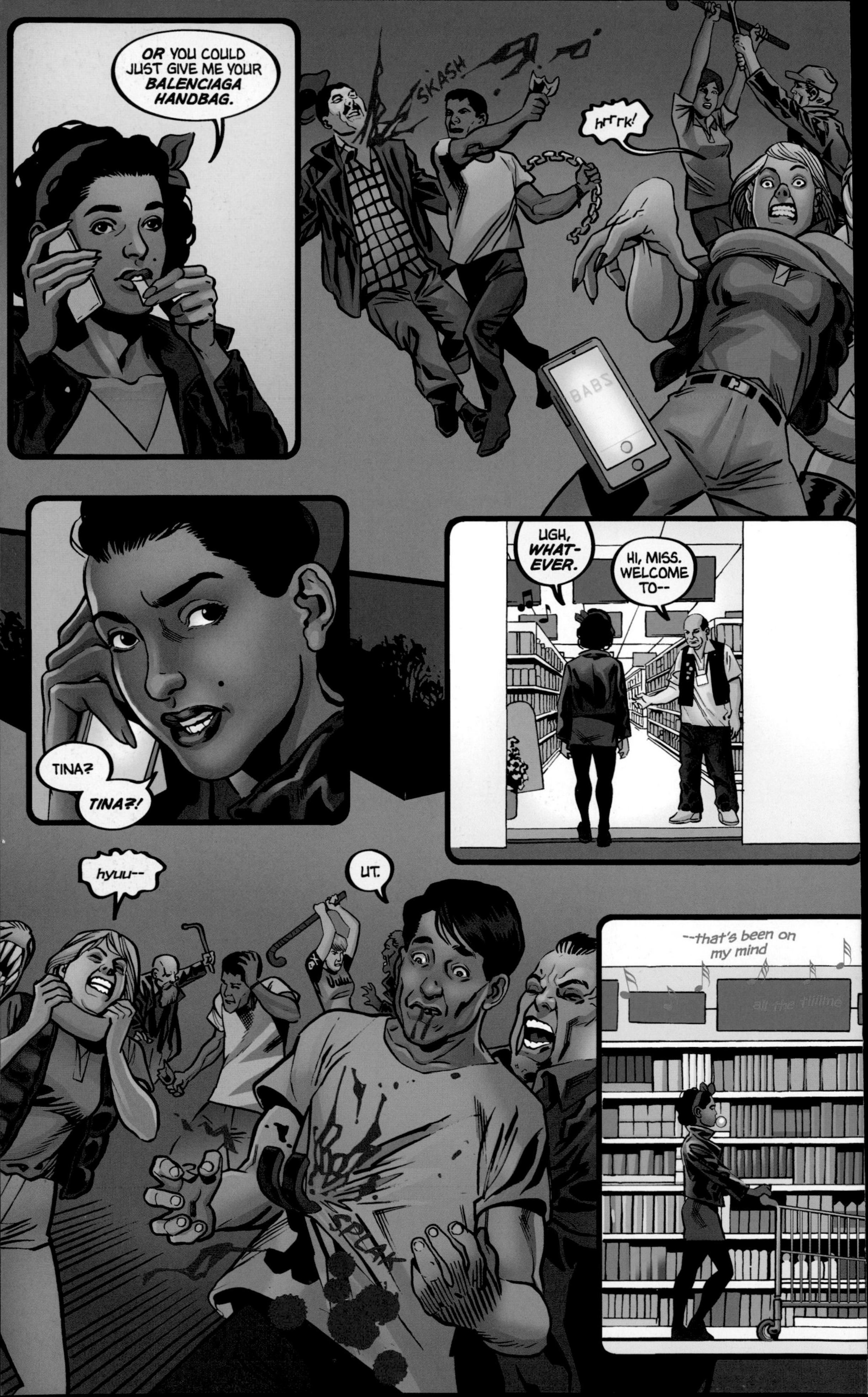
OR YOU COULD JUST GIVE ME YOUR BALENCIAGA HANDBAG.
SKASH
hrrrk!
BABZ
TINA?
TINA?!
UGH, WHAT-EVER.
HI, MISS. WELCOME TO--
hyuu--
UT.
SPLAK
--that's been on my mind
all the tiiiime

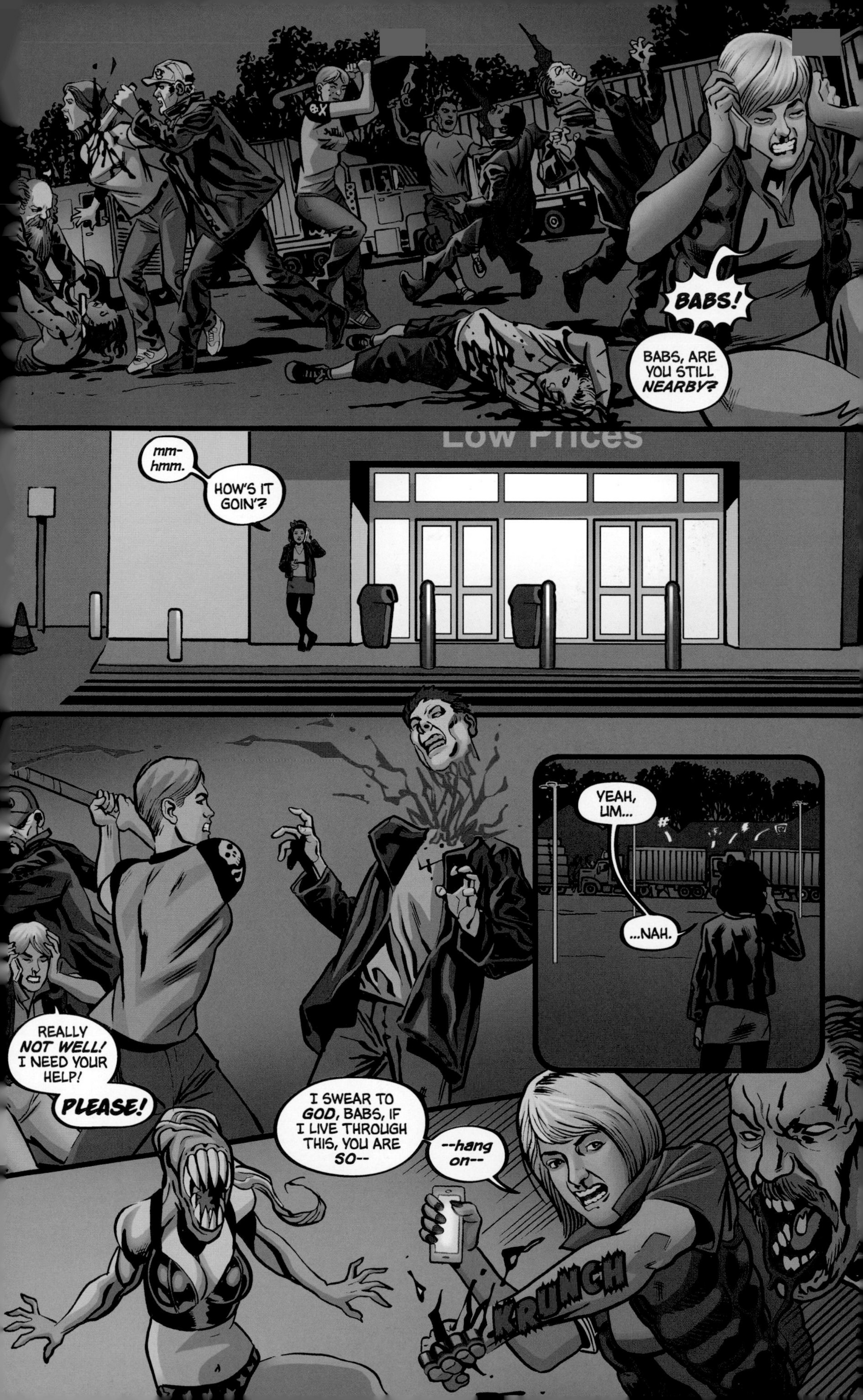
BABS!
BABS, ARE YOU STILL NEARBY?
Low Prices
mm-hmm.
HOW'S IT GOIN'?
YEAH, UM...
...NAH.
REALLY NOT WELL! I NEED YOUR HELP!
PLEASE!
I SWEAR TO GOD, BABS, IF I LIVE THROUGH THIS, YOU ARE SO--
--hang on--
KRUNCH

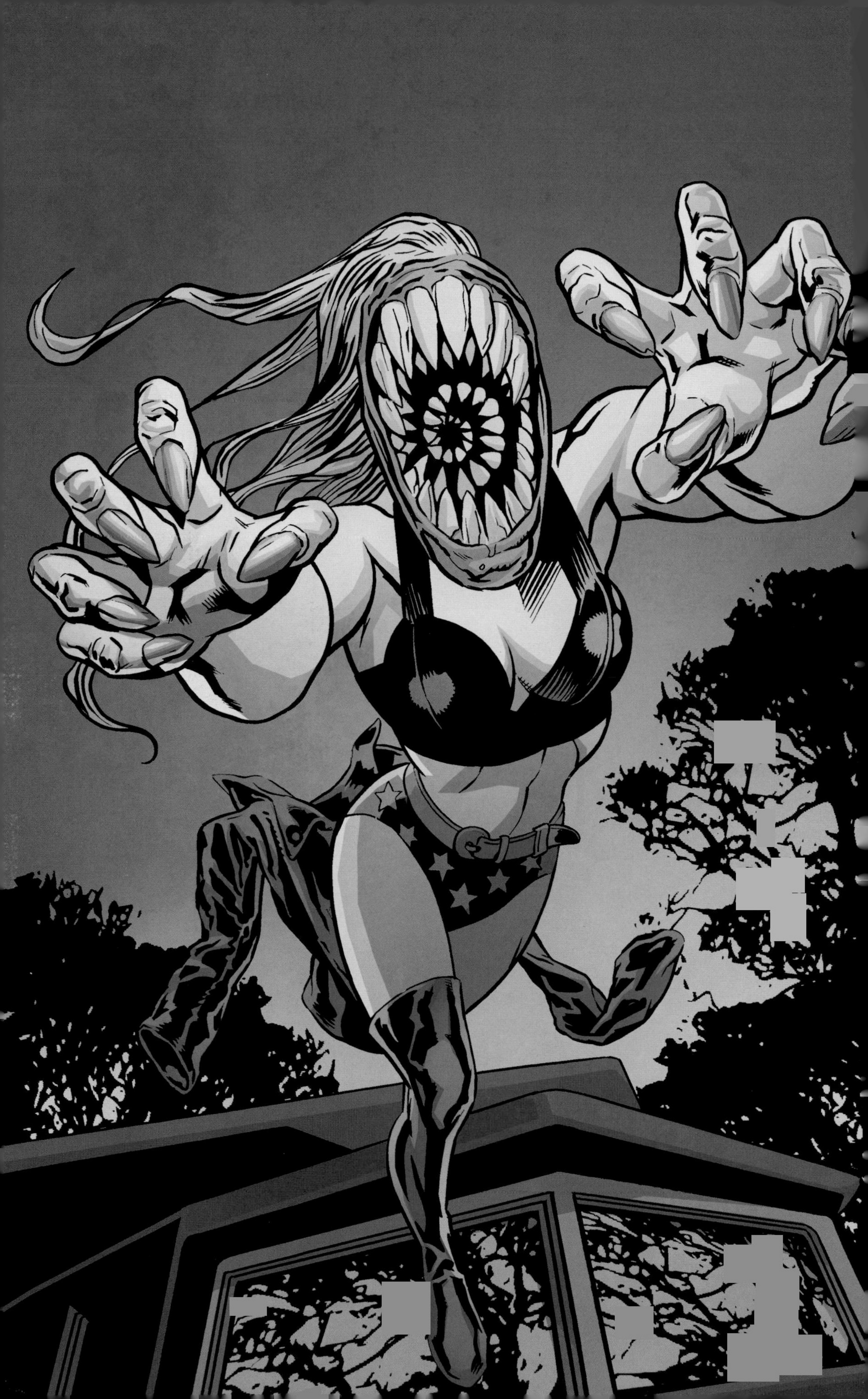

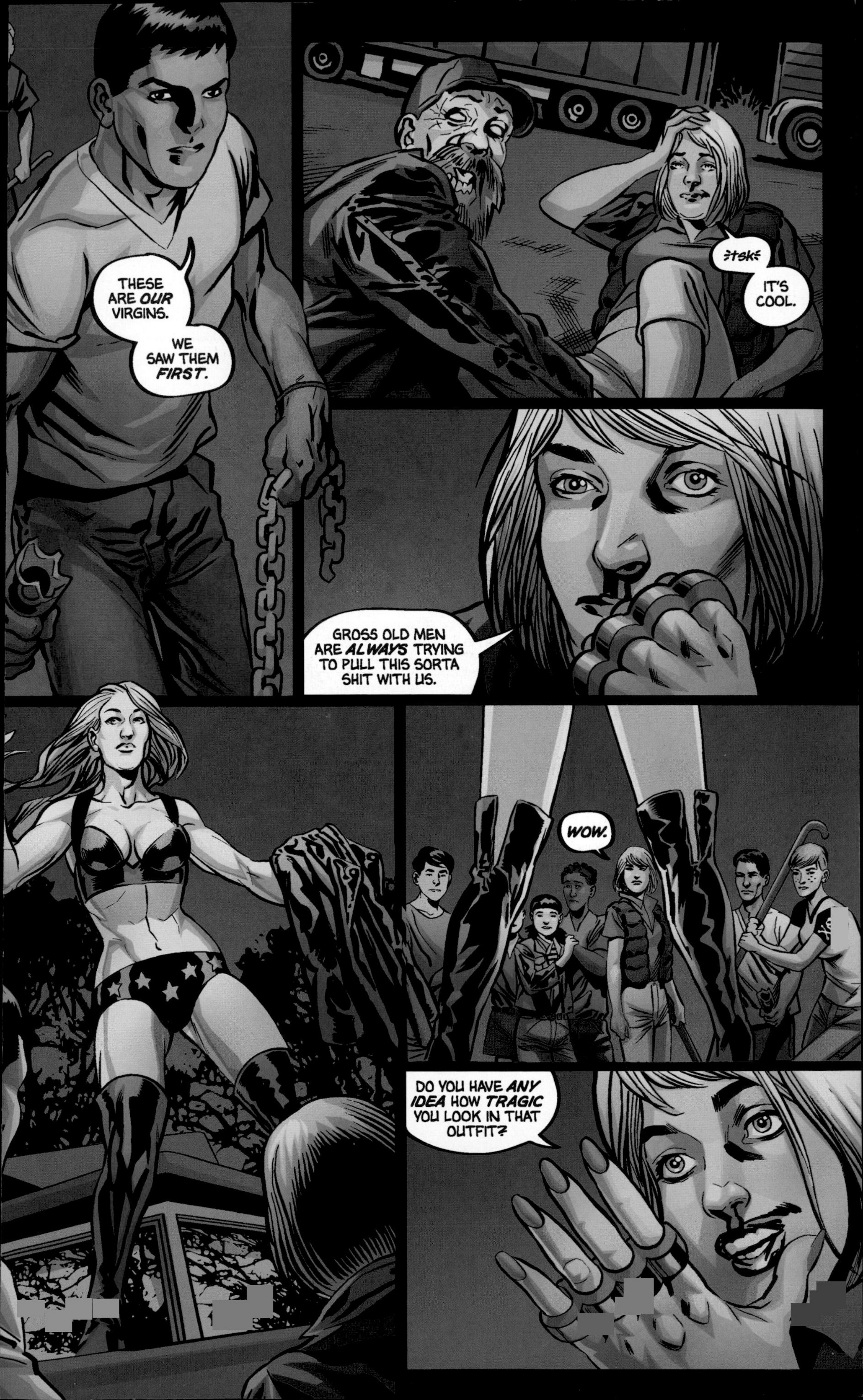
THESE ARE OUR VIRGINS.
WE SAW THEM FIRST.
=tsk=
IT'S COOL.
GROSS OLD MEN ARE ALWAYS TRYING TO PULL THIS SORTA SHIT WITH US.
WOW.
DO YOU HAVE ANY IDEA HOW TRAGIC YOU LOOK IN THAT OUTFIT?

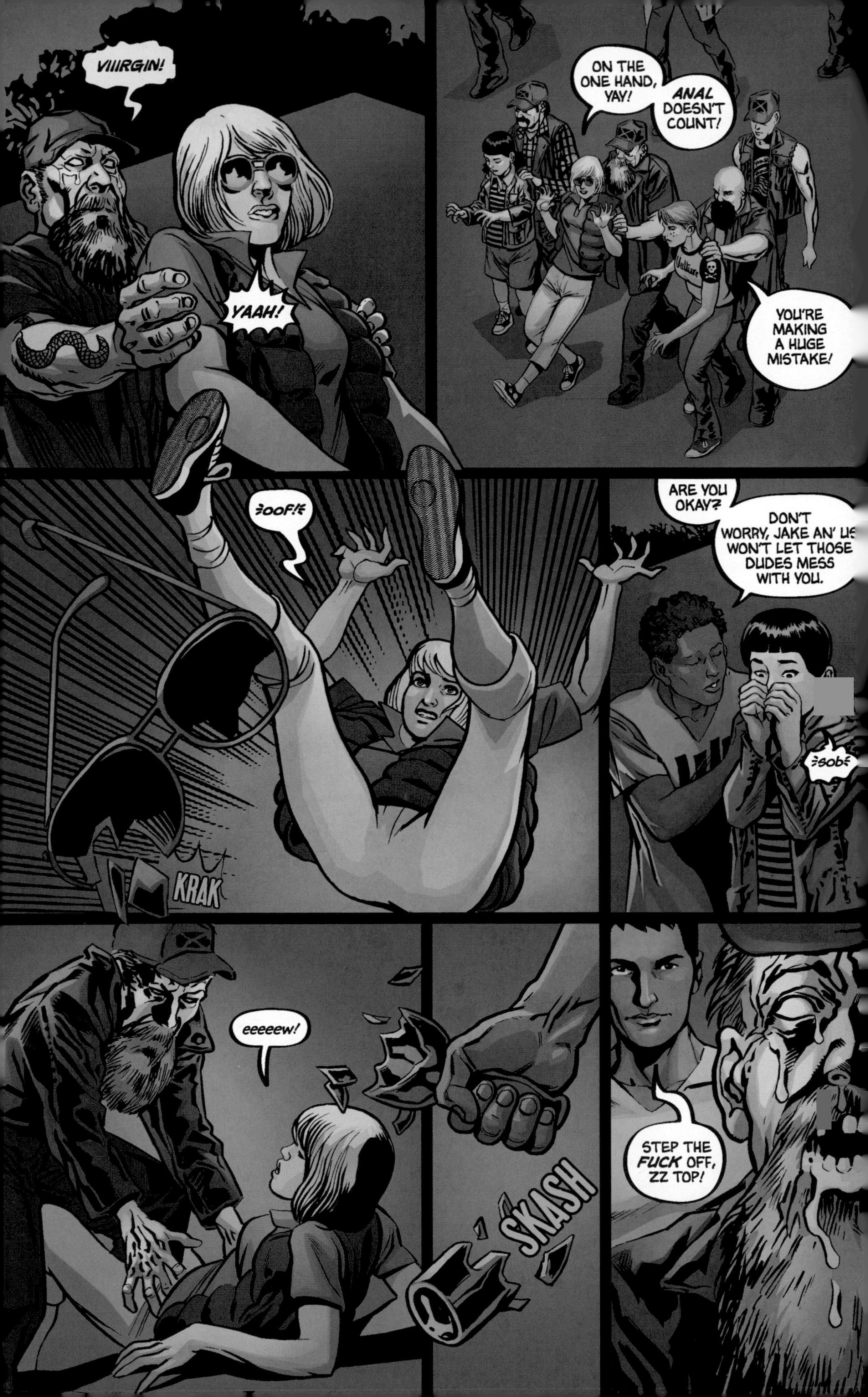
VIIIRGIN!
YAAH!
ON THE ONE HAND, YAY!
ANAL DOESN'T COUNT!
YOU'RE MAKING A HUGE MISTAKE!
OOF!
KRAK
ARE YOU OKAY?
DON'T WORRY, JAKE AN' US WON'T LET THOSE DUDES MESS WITH YOU.
SOB
eeeeew!
SKASH
STEP THE FUCK OFF, ZZ TOP!

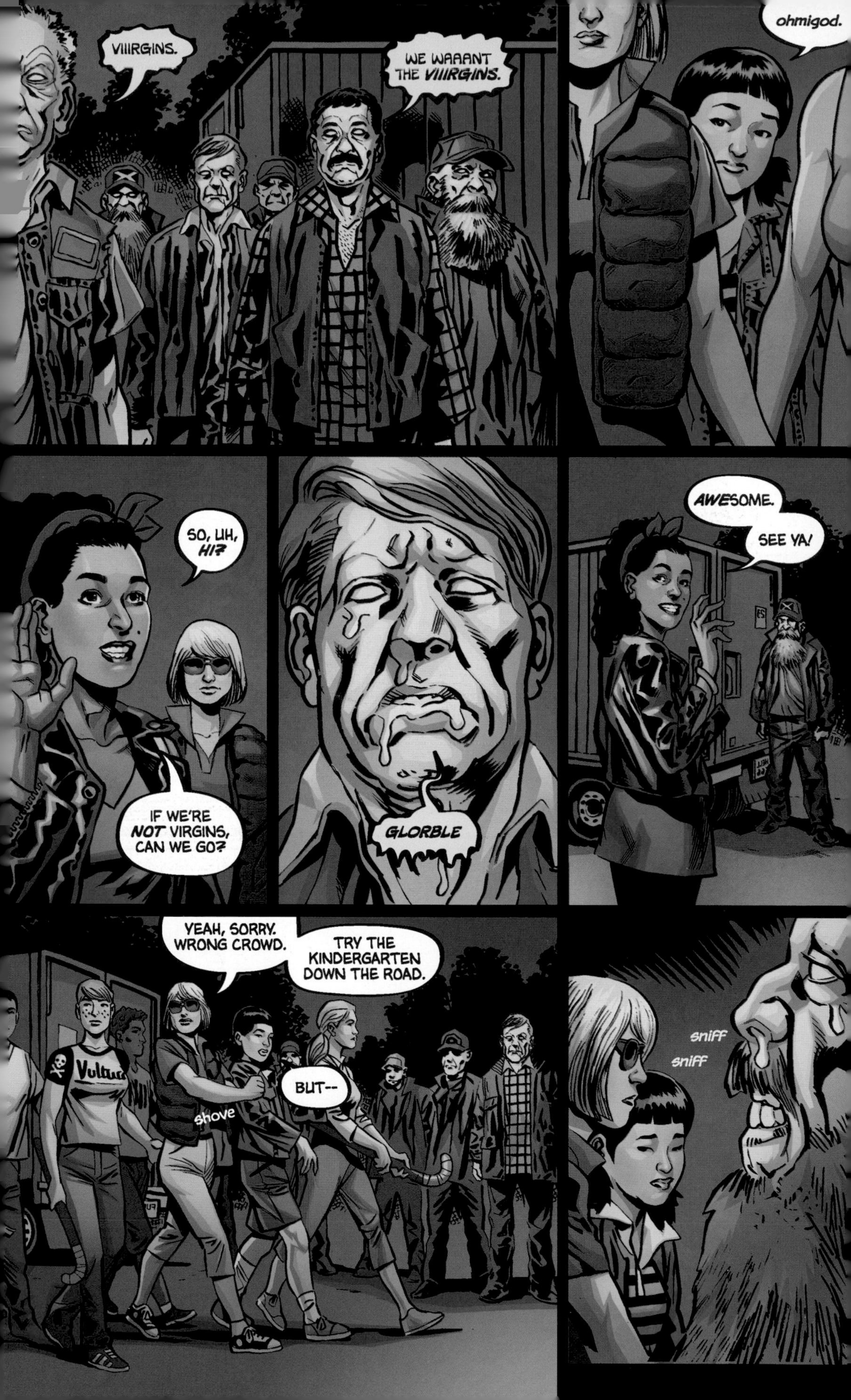
VIIIRGINS.
WE WAAANT THE VIIIRGINS.
ohmigod.
SO, UH, HI?
IF WE'RE NOT VIRGINS, CAN WE GO?
GLORBLE
AWESOME.
SEE YA!
YEAH, SORRY. WRONG CROWD.
TRY THE KINDERGARTEN DOWN THE ROAD.
BUT--
shove
sniff
sniff

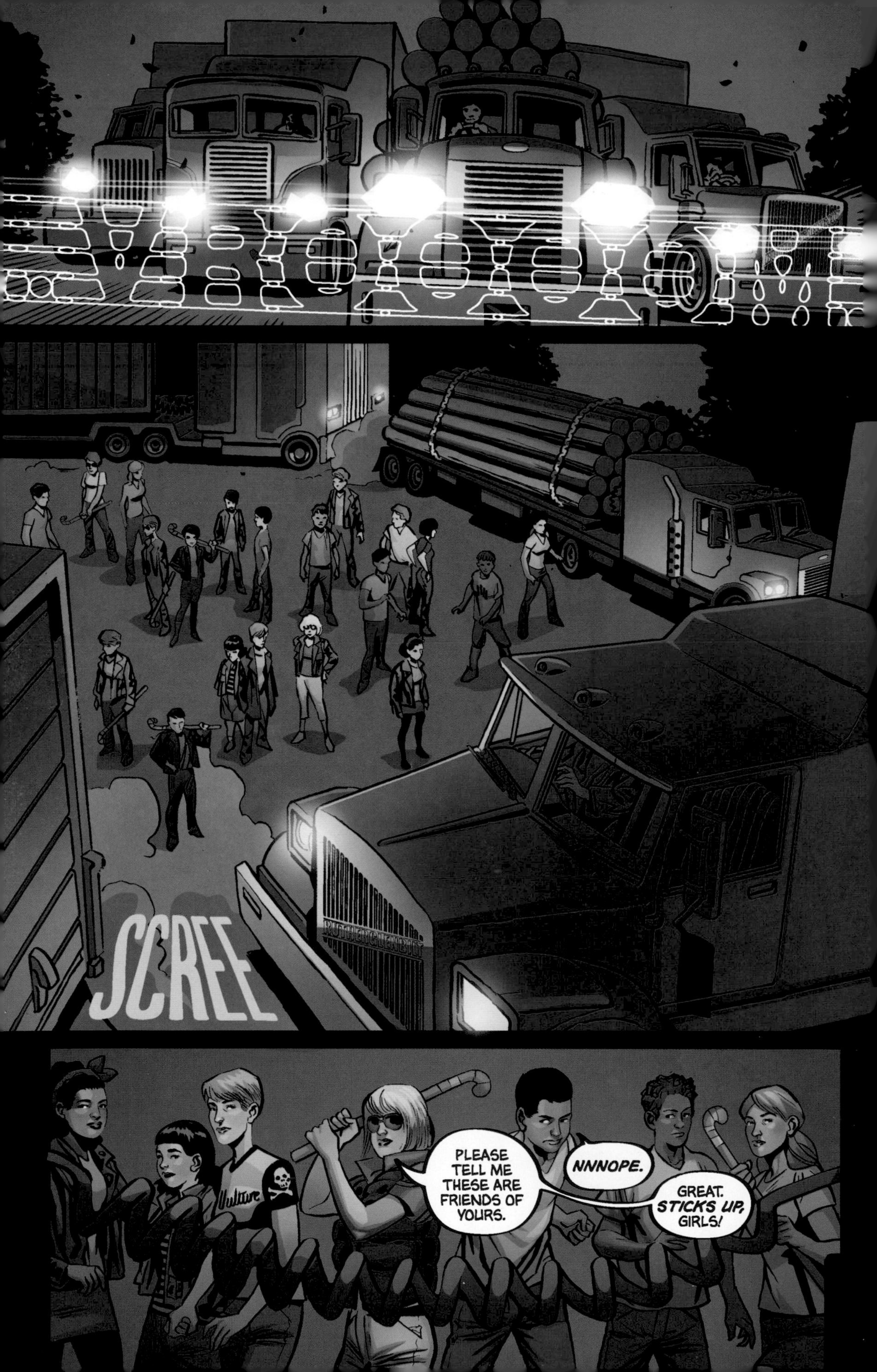
SCREE
PLEASE TELL ME THESE ARE FRIENDS OF YOURS.
NNNOPE.
GREAT. STICKS UP, GIRLS!

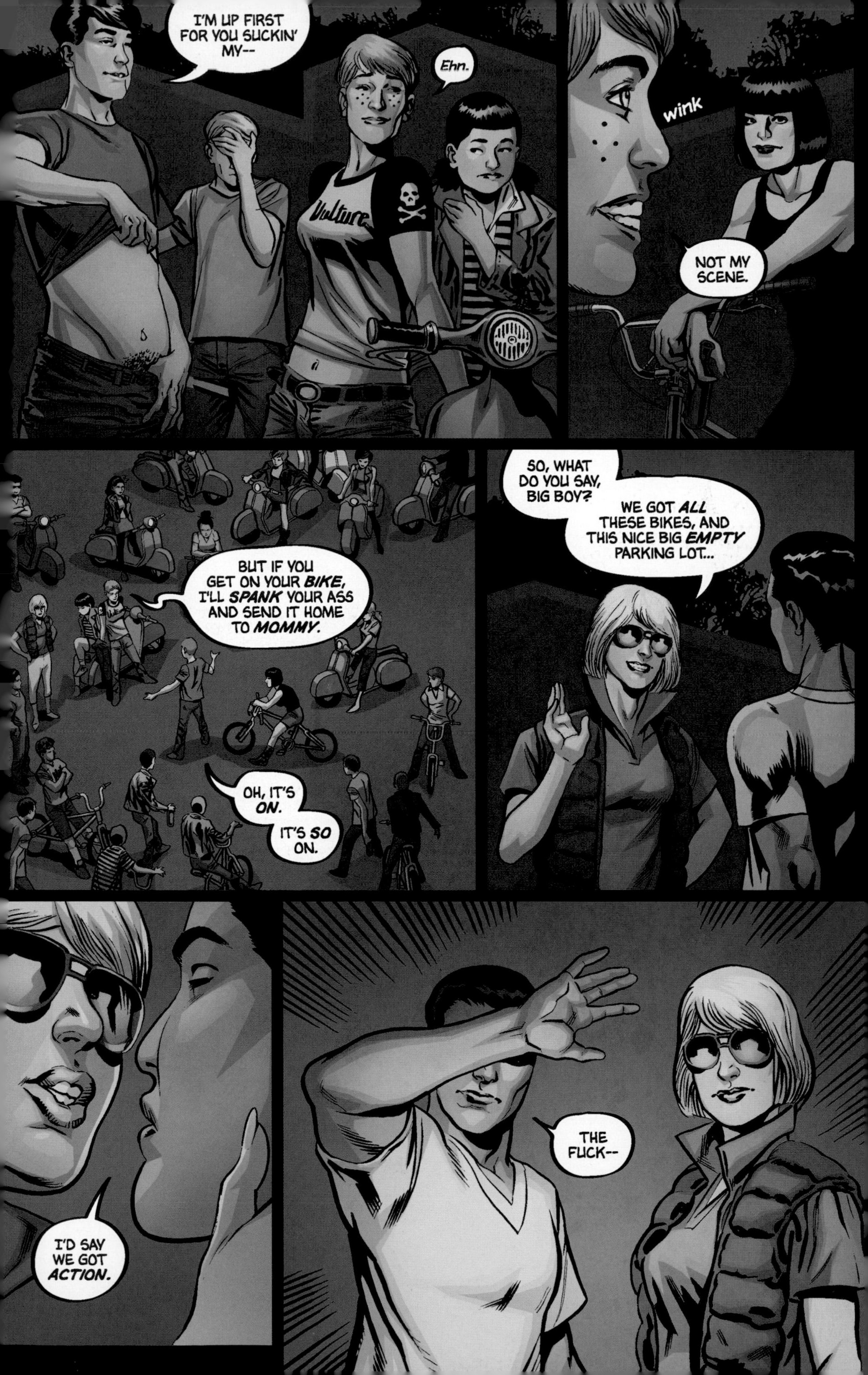
I'M UP FIRST FOR YOU SUCKIN' MY--
Ehn.
wink
NOT MY SCENE.
BUT IF YOU GET ON YOUR *BIKE*, I'LL *SPANK* YOUR ASS AND SEND IT HOME TO *MOMMY*.
OH, IT'S *ON*.
IT'S *SO* ON.
SO, WHAT DO YOU SAY, BIG BOY?
WE GOT *ALL* THESE BIKES, AND THIS NICE BIG *EMPTY* PARKING LOT...
I'D SAY WE GOT *ACTION*.
THE FUCK--

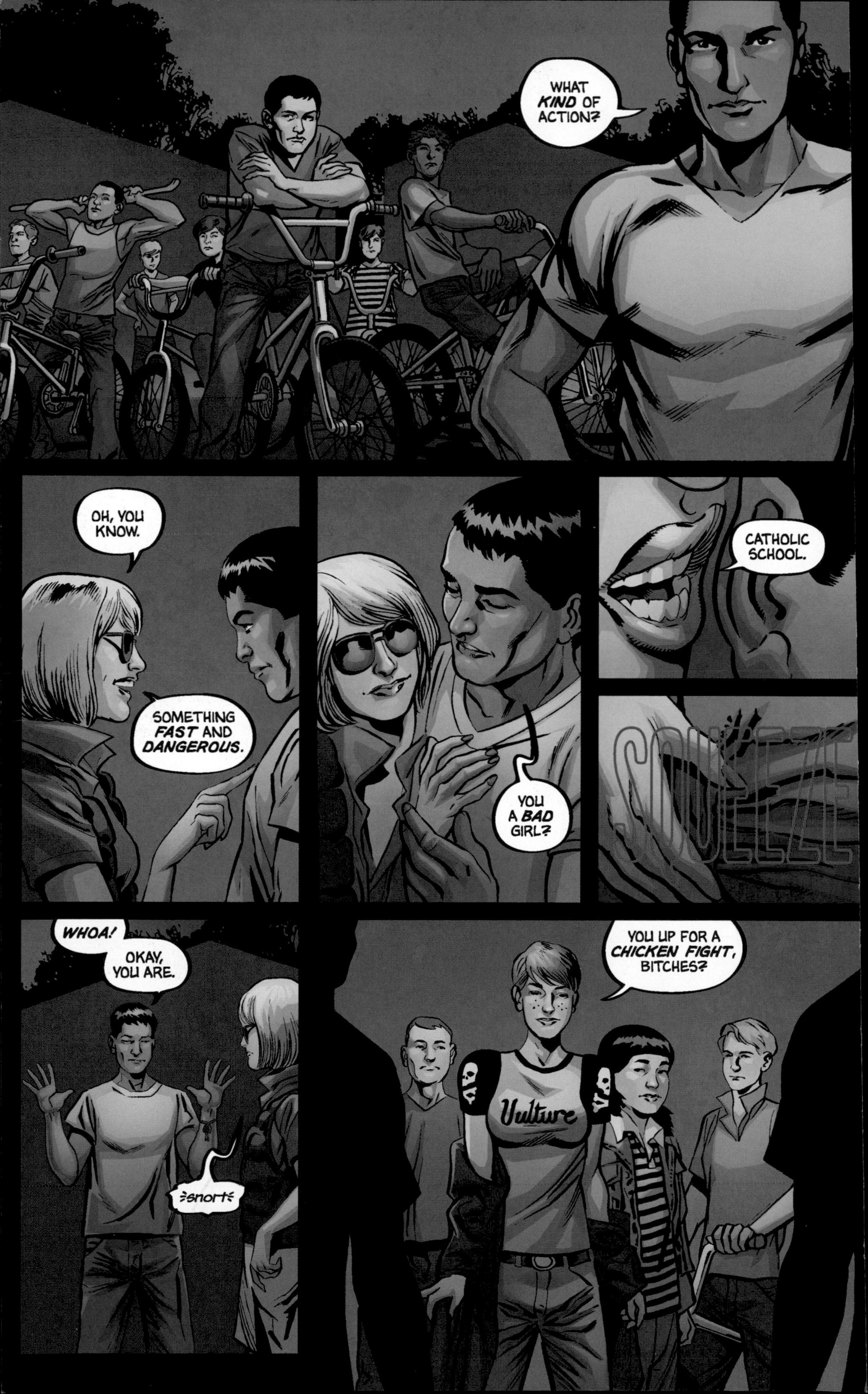
WHAT KIND OF ACTION?
OH, YOU KNOW.
SOMETHING FAST AND DANGEROUS.
YOU A BAD GIRL?
CATHOLIC SCHOOL.
SQUEEZE
WHOA!
OKAY, YOU ARE.
snort
YOU UP FOR A CHICKEN FIGHT, BITCHES?
Vulture

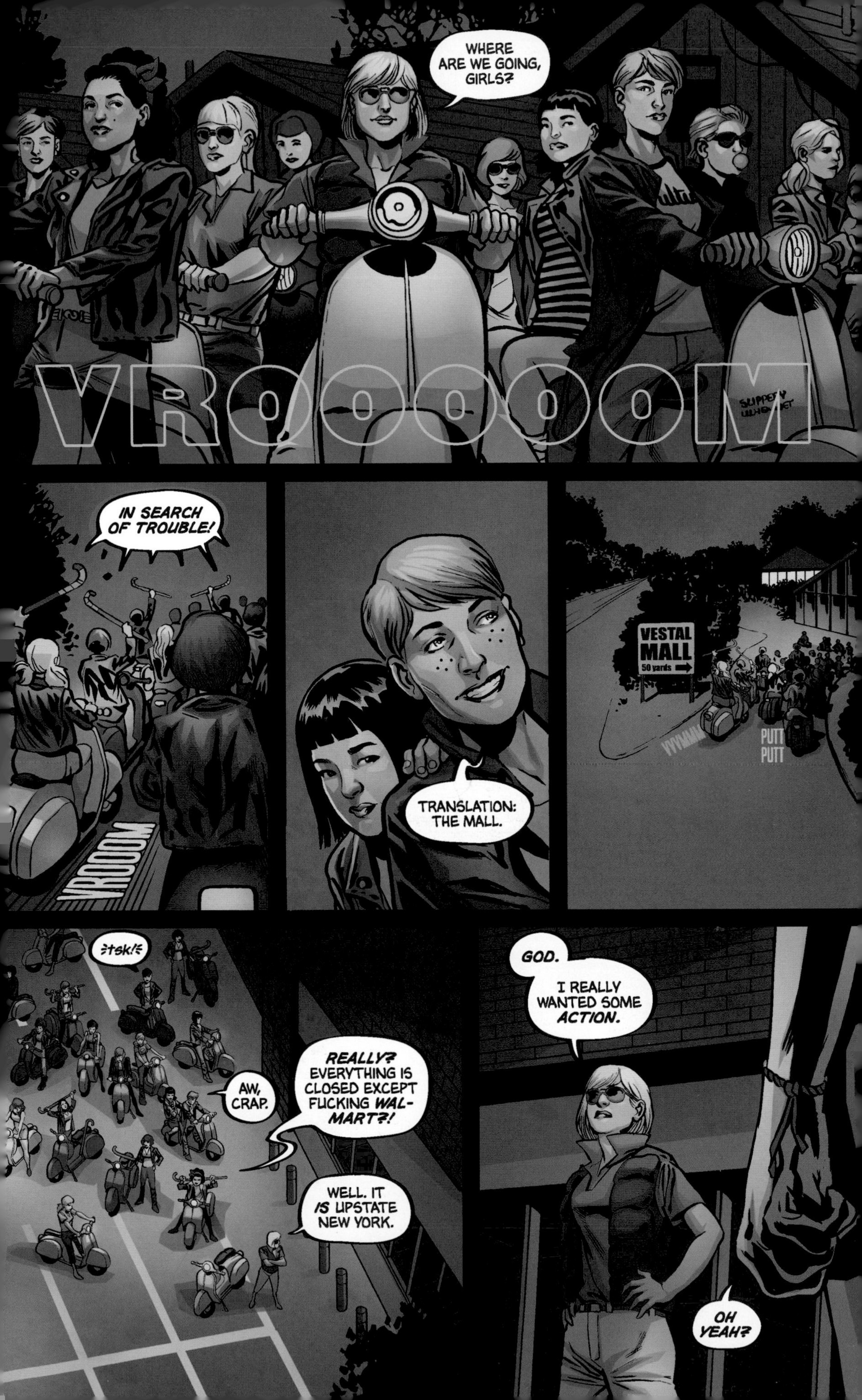
WHERE ARE WE GOING, GIRLS?
VROOOOOM
IN SEARCH OF TROUBLE!
VROOOM
TRANSLATION: THE MALL.
VESTAL MALL
50 yards
PUTT PUTT
tsk!
AW, CRAP.
REALLY? EVERYTHING IS CLOSED EXCEPT FUCKING WAL-MART?!
WELL. IT IS UPSTATE NEW YORK.
GOD.
I REALLY WANTED SOME ACTION.
OH YEAH?

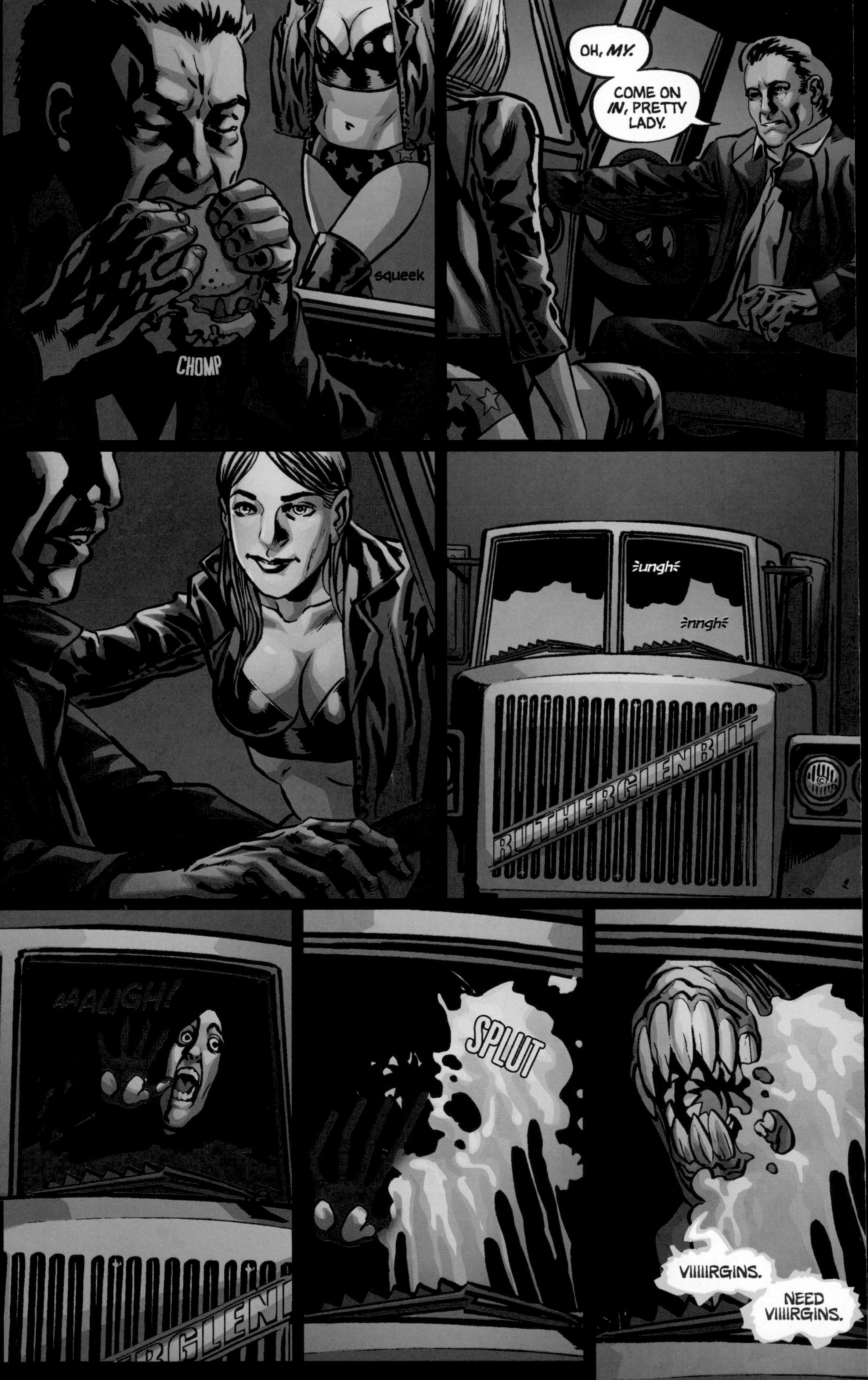
squeek
CHOMP
OH, MY.
COME ON IN, PRETTY LADY.
unghh
nngh
RUTHERGLENBILT
AAUGH!
SPLUT
VIIIIRGINS.
NEED VIIIIRGINS.

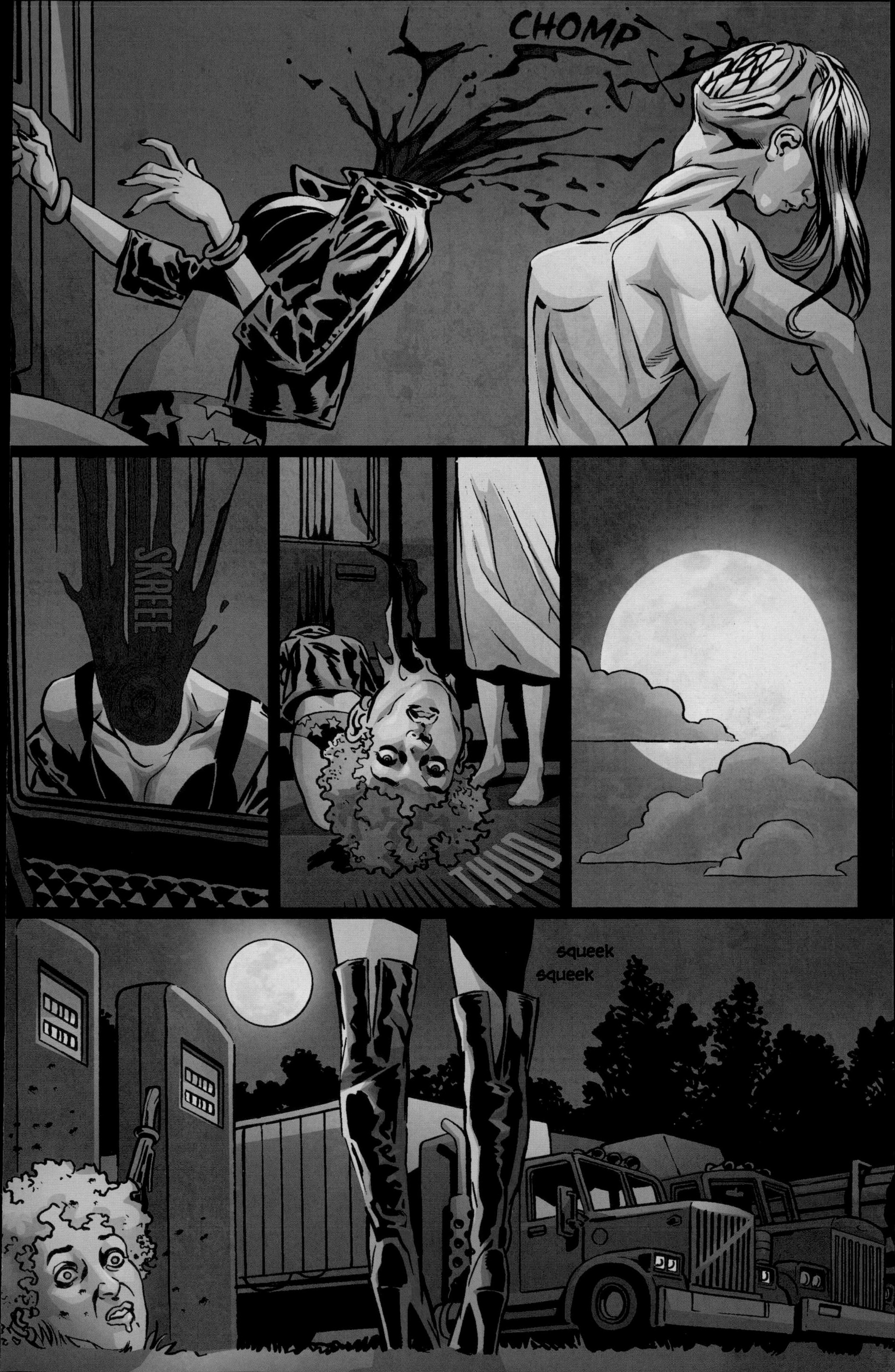
CHOMP
SKREEE
THUD
squeek
squeek

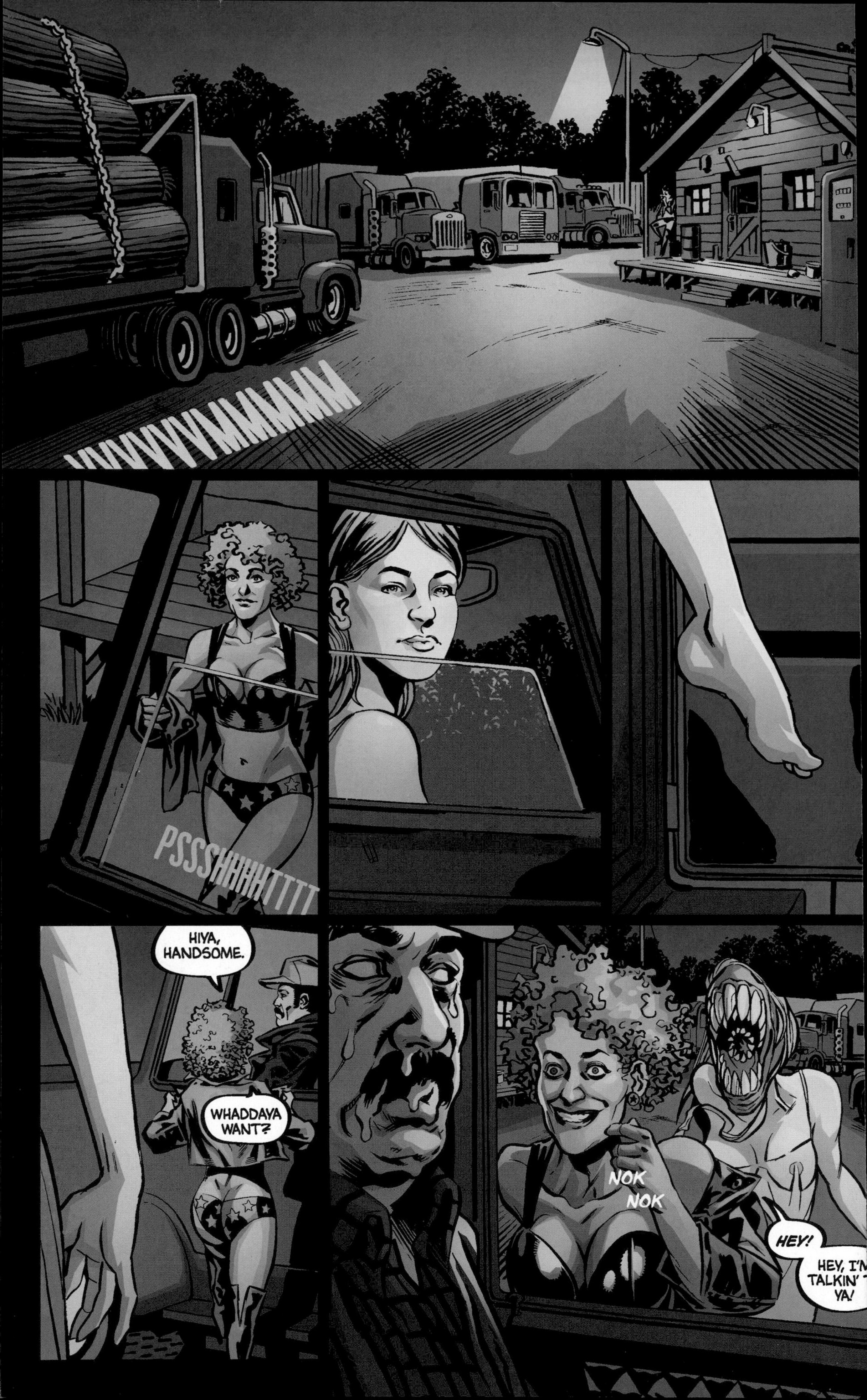
VVVVVVMMMMMM
PSSSHHHHTTTT
HIYA, HANDSOME.
WHADDAYA WANT?
NOK NOK
HEY!
HEY, I'M TALKIN' YA!

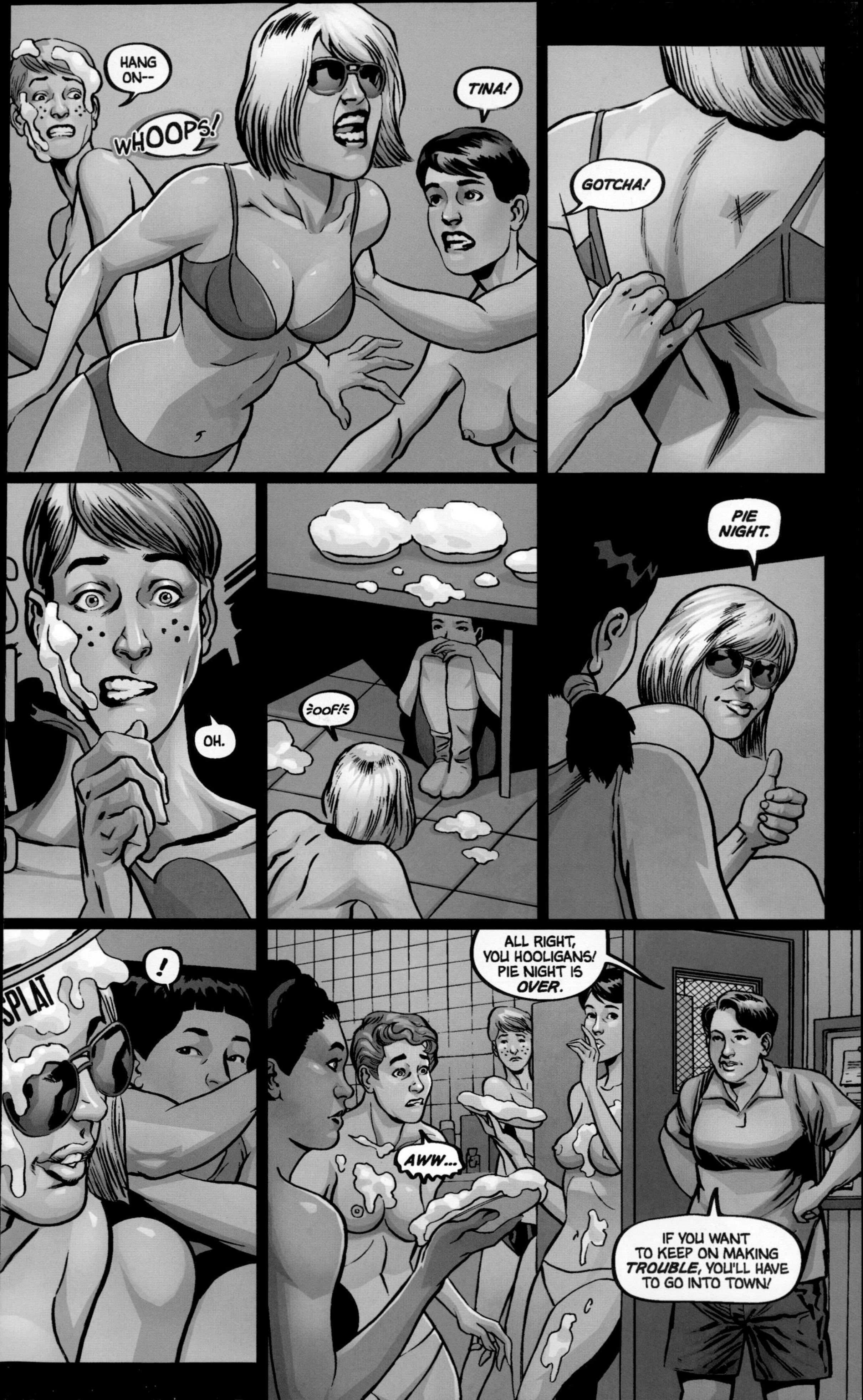
HANG ON--
WHOOPS!
TINA!
GOTCHA!
OH.
OOF!
PIE NIGHT.
SPLAT
!
ALL RIGHT, YOU HOOLIGANS! PIE NIGHT IS OVER.
AWW...
IF YOU WANT TO KEEP ON MAKING TROUBLE, YOU'LL HAVE TO GO INTO TOWN!

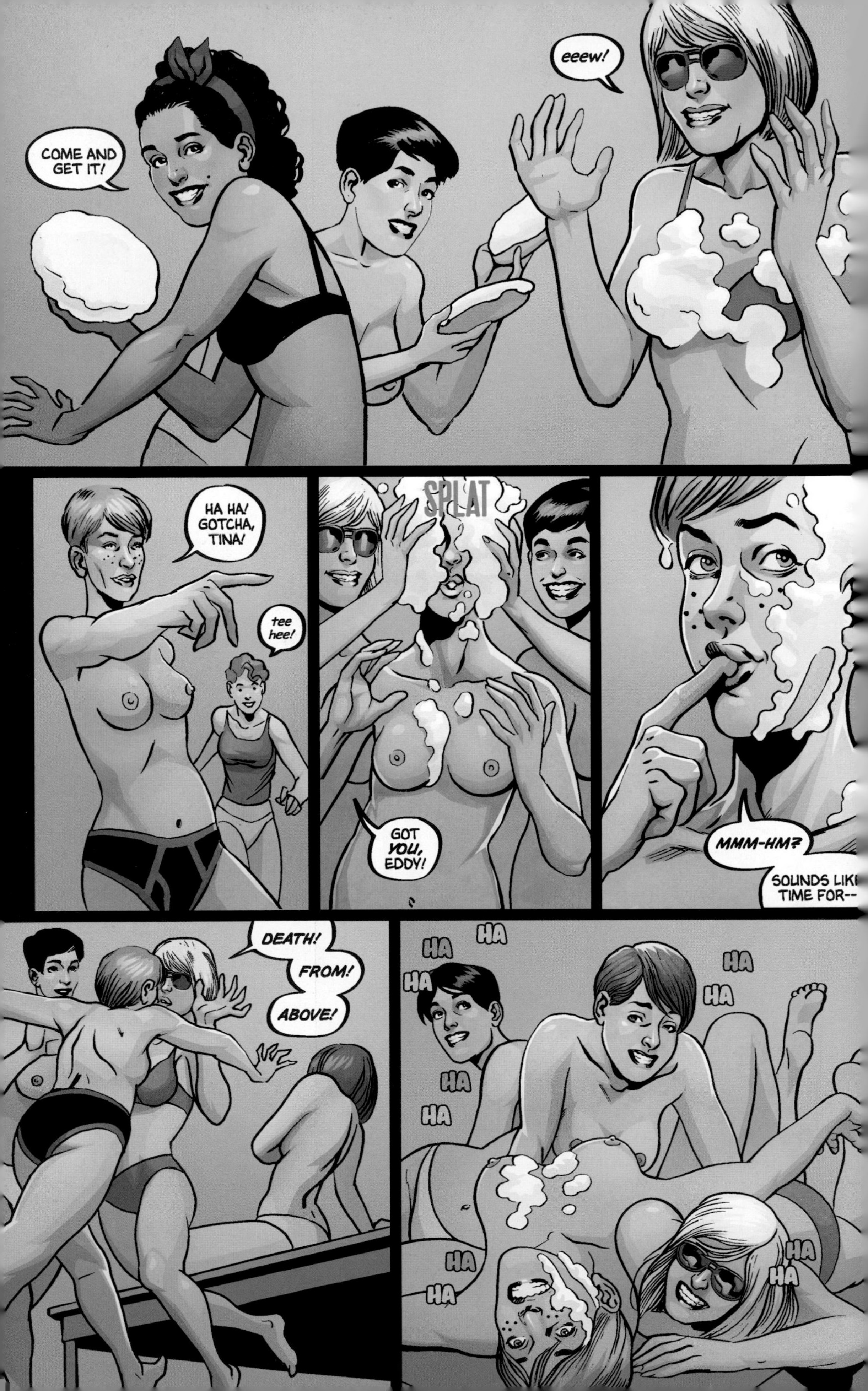
COME AND GET IT!
eeew!
HA HA! GOTCHA, TINA!
tee hee!
SPLAT
GOT YOU, EDDY!
MMM-HM?
SOUNDS LIK
TIME FOR--
DEATH!
FROM!
ABOVE!
HA
HA
HA
HA
HA
HA
HA
HA
HA
HA
HA

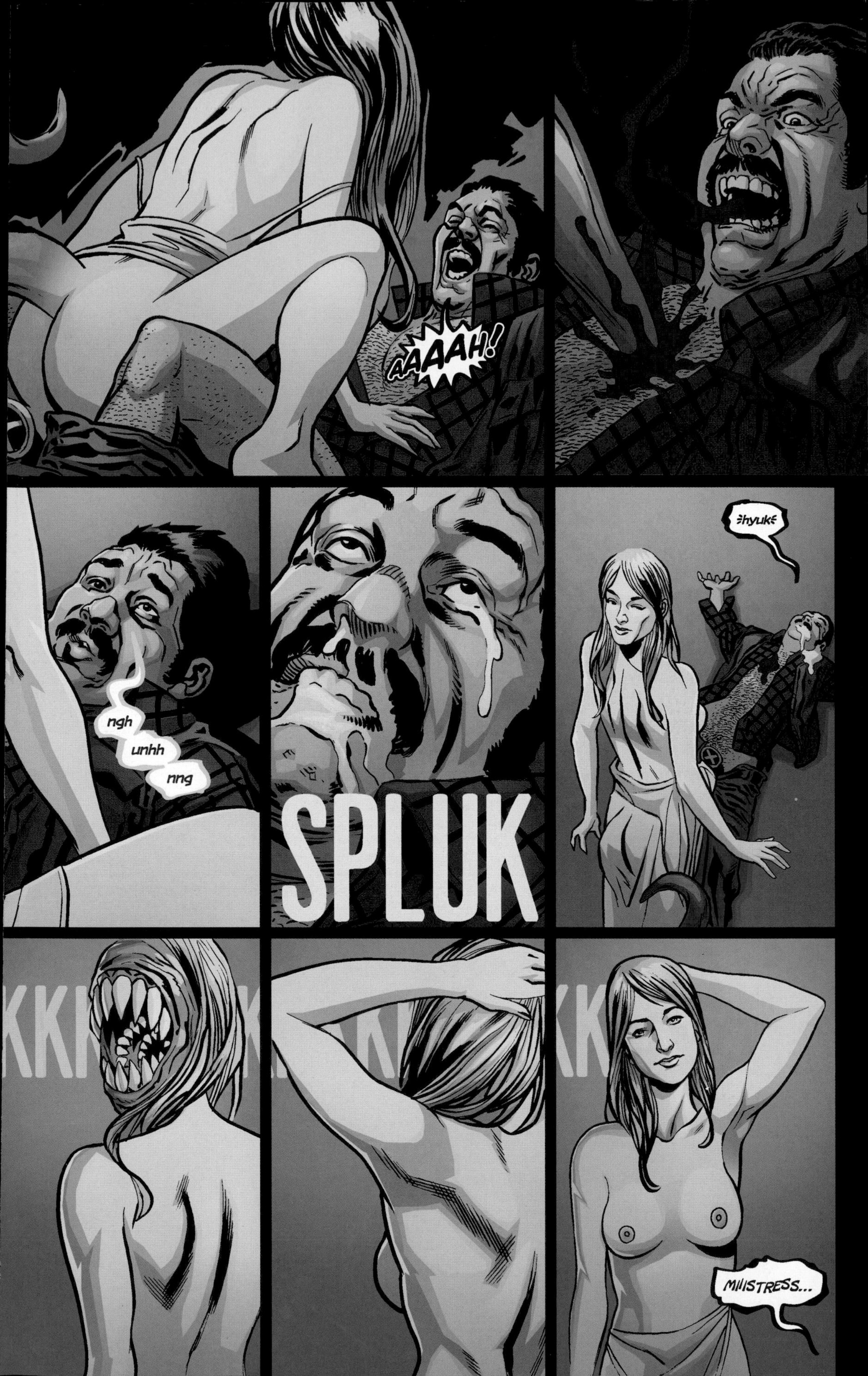
AAAAH!
ngh
unhh
nng
SPLUK
hyuk
MIIISTRESS...

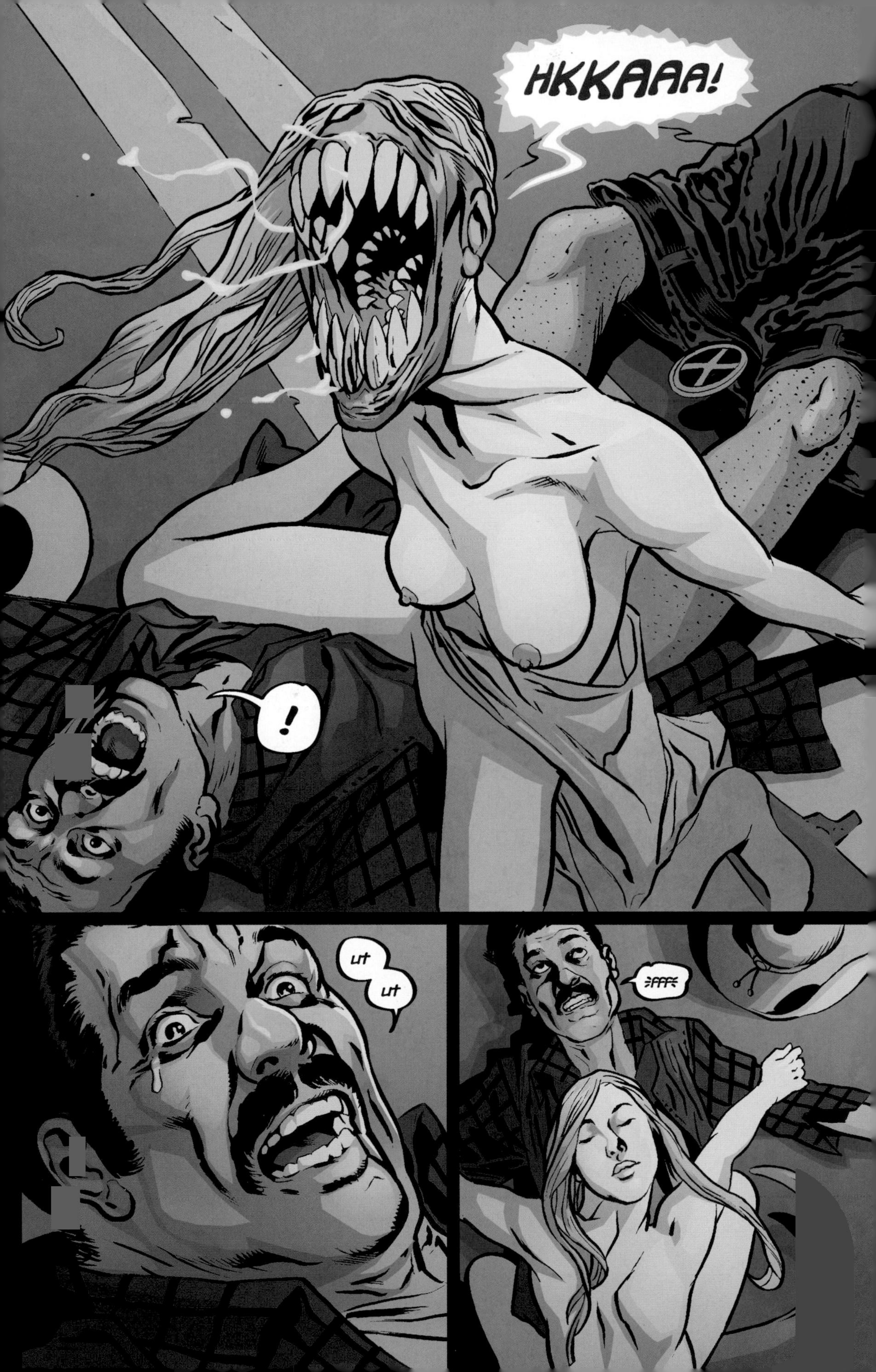
HKKAAA!
!
ut
ut
FFF

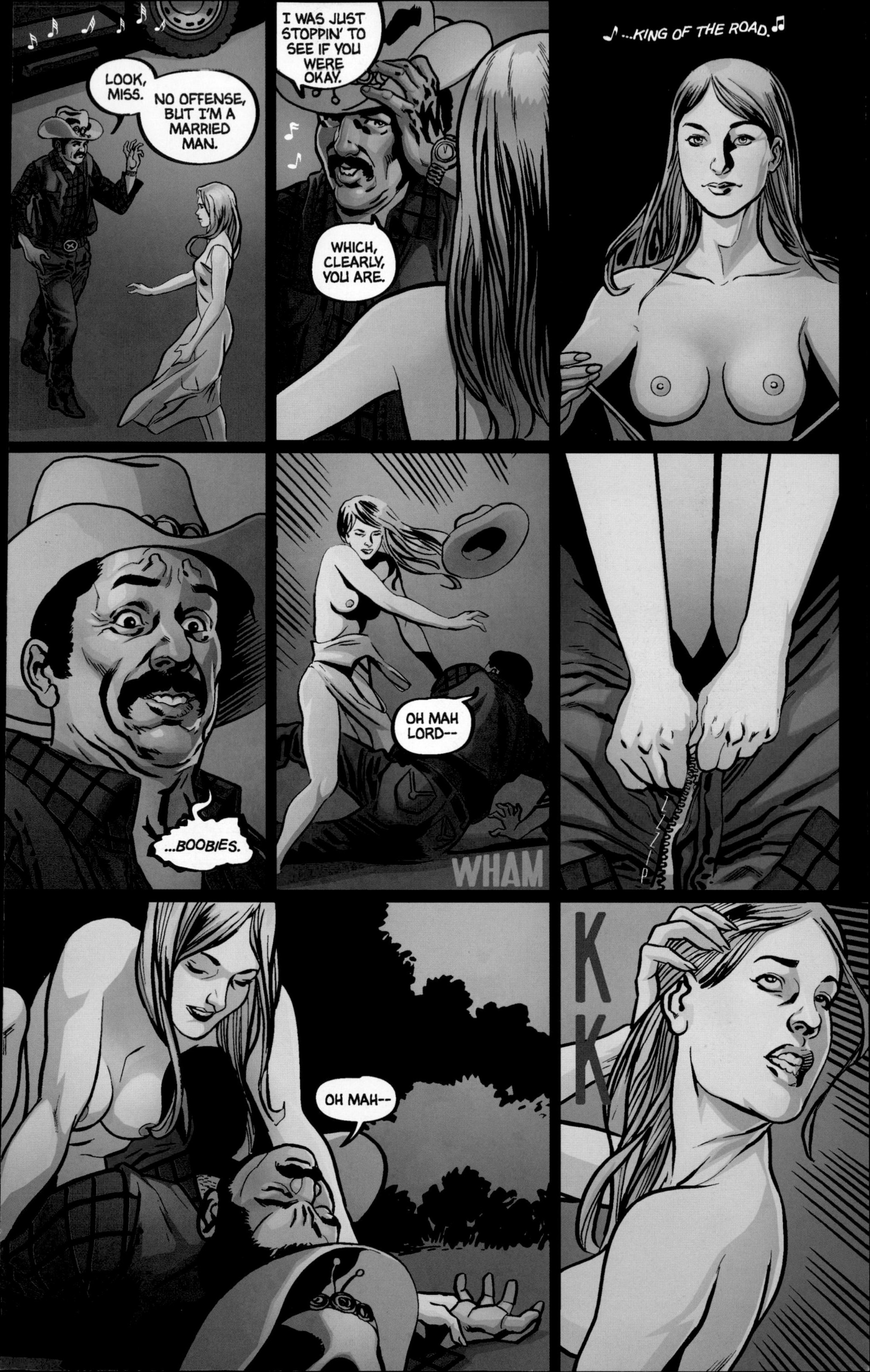
LOOK, MISS.
NO OFFENSE, BUT I'M A MARRIED MAN.
I WAS JUST STOPPIN' TO SEE IF YOU WERE OKAY.
WHICH, CLEARLY, YOU ARE.
...KING OF THE ROAD.
...BOOBIES.
OH MAH LORD--
WHAM
ZZZIP
OH MAH--
KK

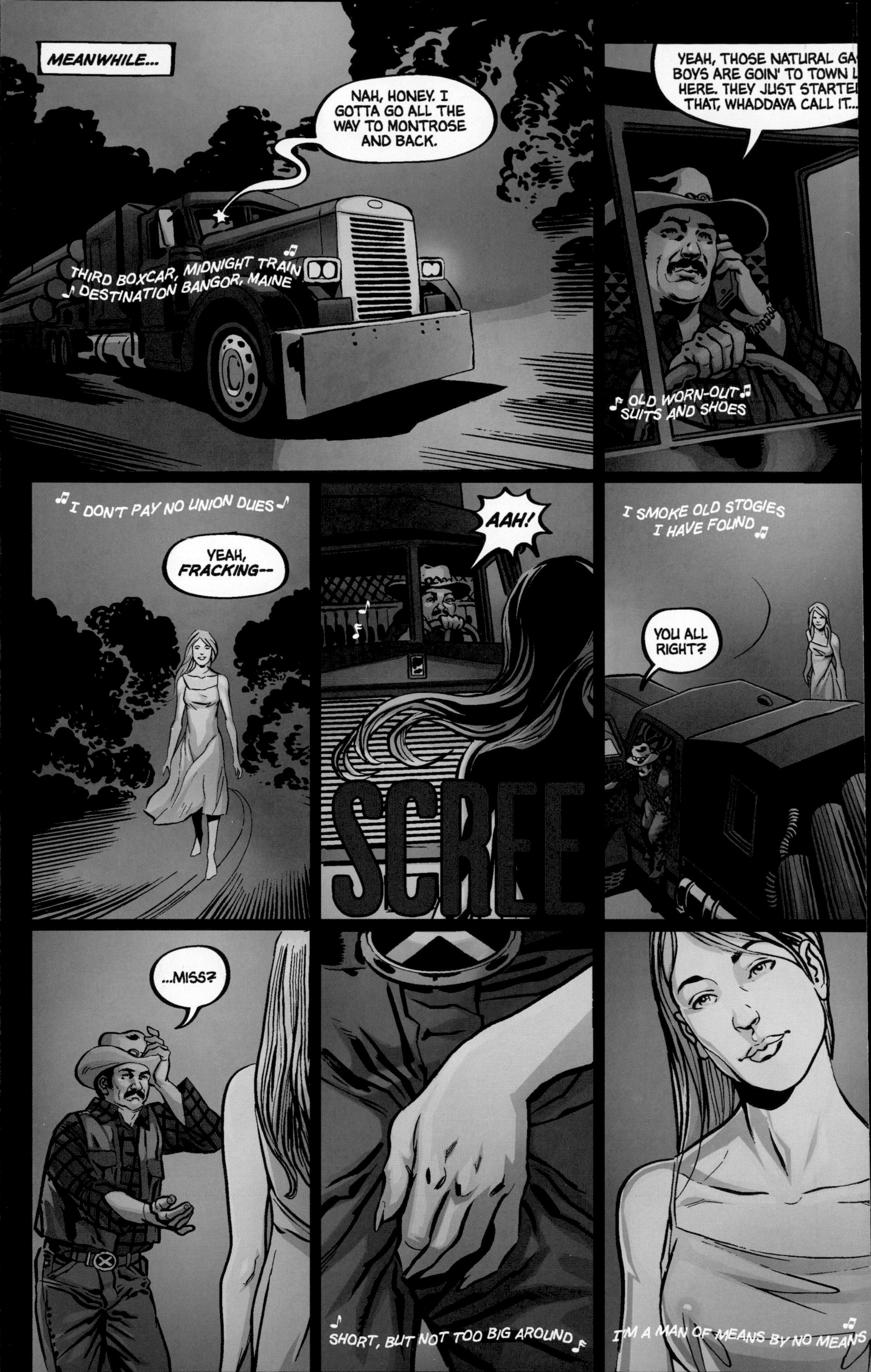
MEANWHILE...
NAH, HONEY. I GOTTA GO ALL THE WAY TO MONTROSE AND BACK.
THIRD BOXCAR, MIDNIGHT TRAIN DESTINATION BANGOR, MAINE
YEAH, THOSE NATURAL GA BOYS ARE GOIN' TO TOWN L HERE. THEY JUST STARTE THAT, WHADDAYA CALL IT...
OLD WORN-OUT SUITS AND SHOES
I DON'T PAY NO UNION DUES
YEAH, FRACKING--
AAH!
SCREE
I SMOKE OLD STOGIES I HAVE FOUND
YOU ALL RIGHT?
...MISS?
SHORT, BUT NOT TOO BIG AROUND
I'M A MAN OF MEANS BY NO MEANS

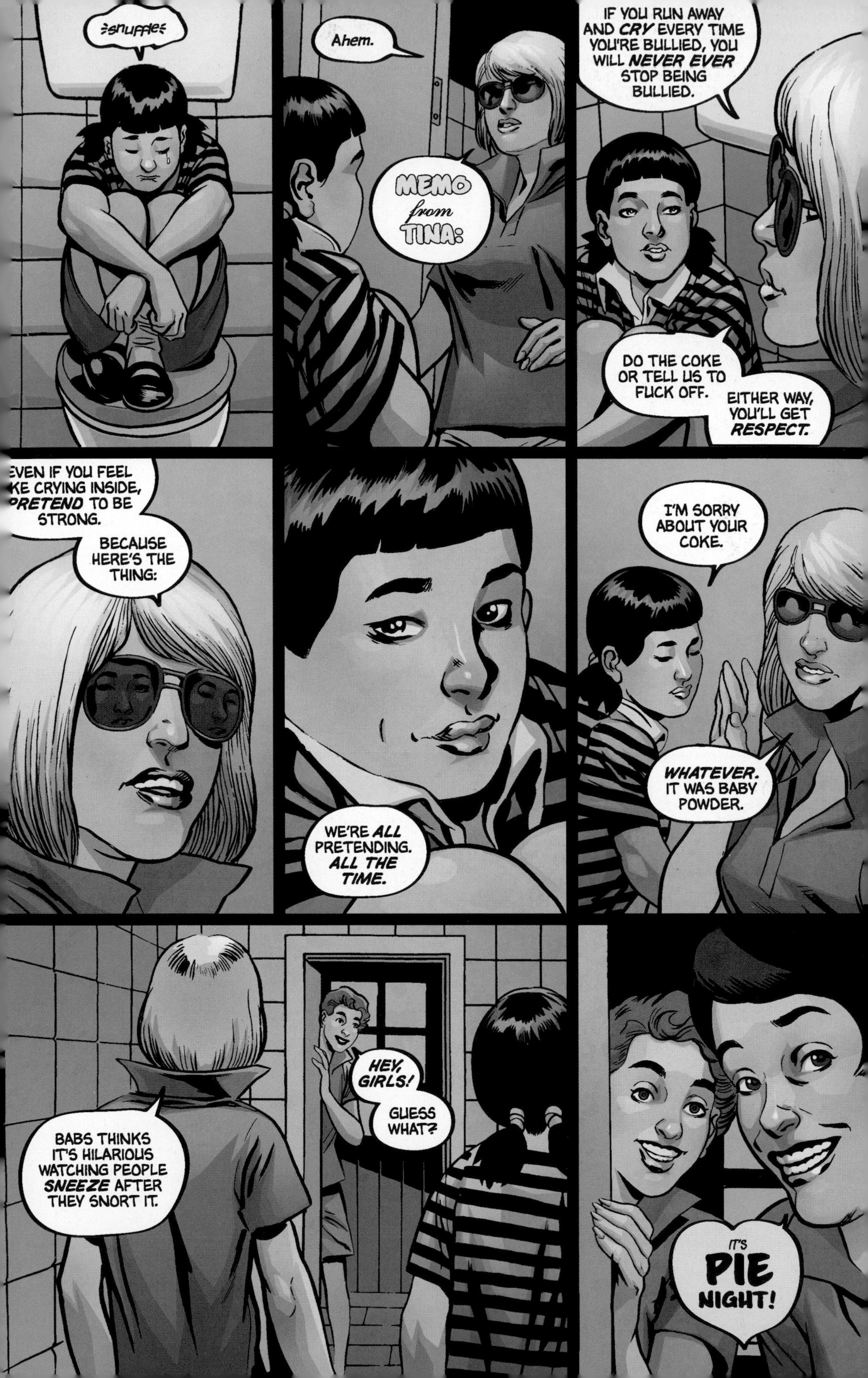

snuffle
Ahem.
MEMO from TINA:
IF YOU RUN AWAY AND CRY EVERY TIME YOU'RE BULLIED, YOU WILL NEVER EVER STOP BEING BULLIED.
DO THE COKE OR TELL US TO FUCK OFF.
EITHER WAY, YOU'LL GET RESPECT.
EVEN IF YOU FEEL LIKE CRYING INSIDE, PRETEND TO BE STRONG.
BECAUSE HERE'S THE THING:
WE'RE ALL PRETENDING. ALL THE TIME.
I'M SORRY ABOUT YOUR COKE.
WHATEVER. IT WAS BABY POWDER.
BABS THINKS IT'S HILARIOUS WATCHING PEOPLE SNEEZE AFTER THEY SNORT IT.
HEY, GIRLS!
GUESS WHAT?
IT'S PIE NIGHT!

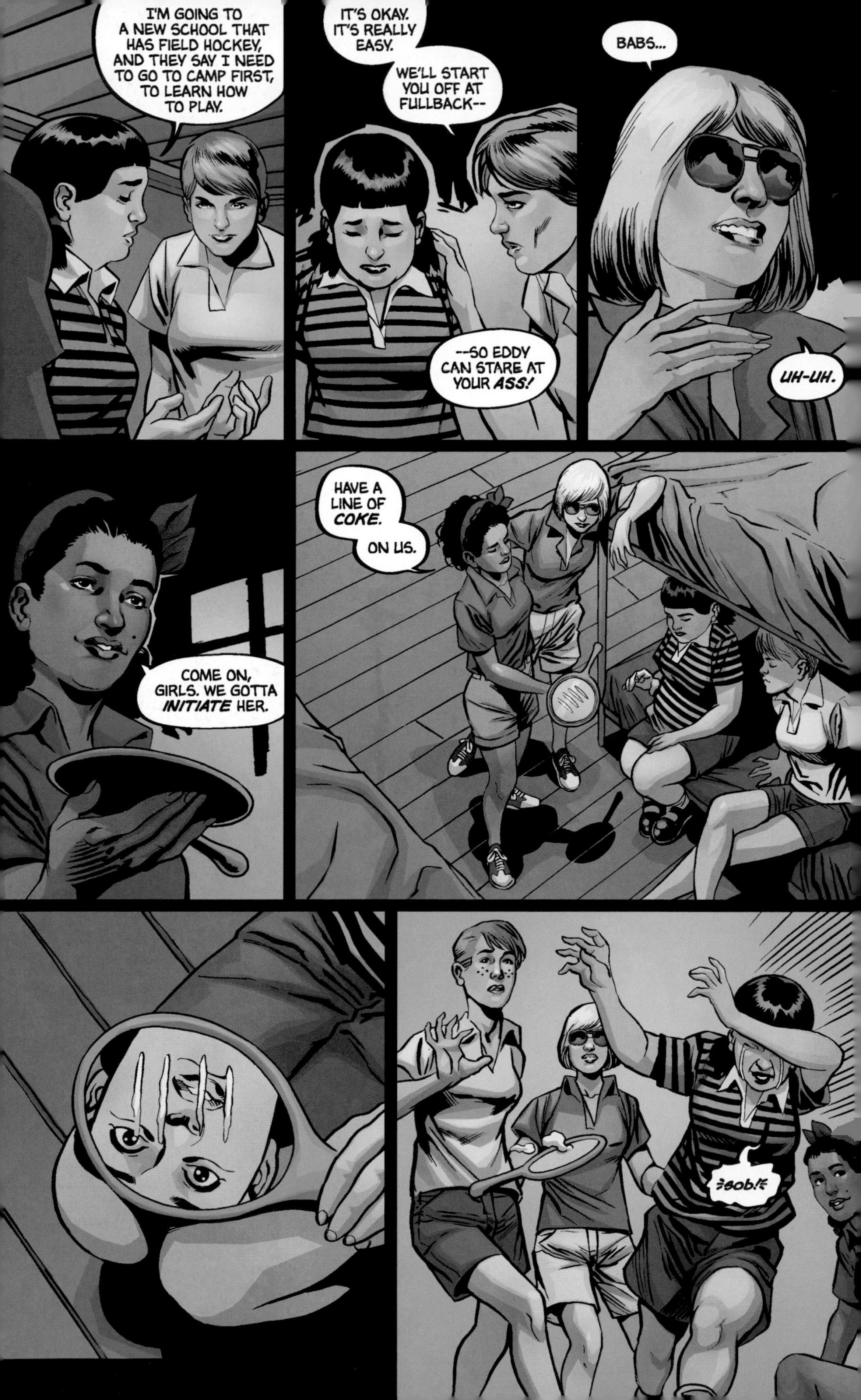
I'M GOING TO A NEW SCHOOL THAT HAS FIELD HOCKEY, AND THEY SAY I NEED TO GO TO CAMP FIRST, TO LEARN HOW TO PLAY.
IT'S OKAY. IT'S REALLY EASY.
WE'LL START YOU OFF AT FULLBACK--
--SO EDDY CAN STARE AT YOUR ASS!
BABS...
UH-UH.
COME ON, GIRLS. WE GOTTA INITIATE HER.
HAVE A LINE OF COKE.
ON US.
SOB!

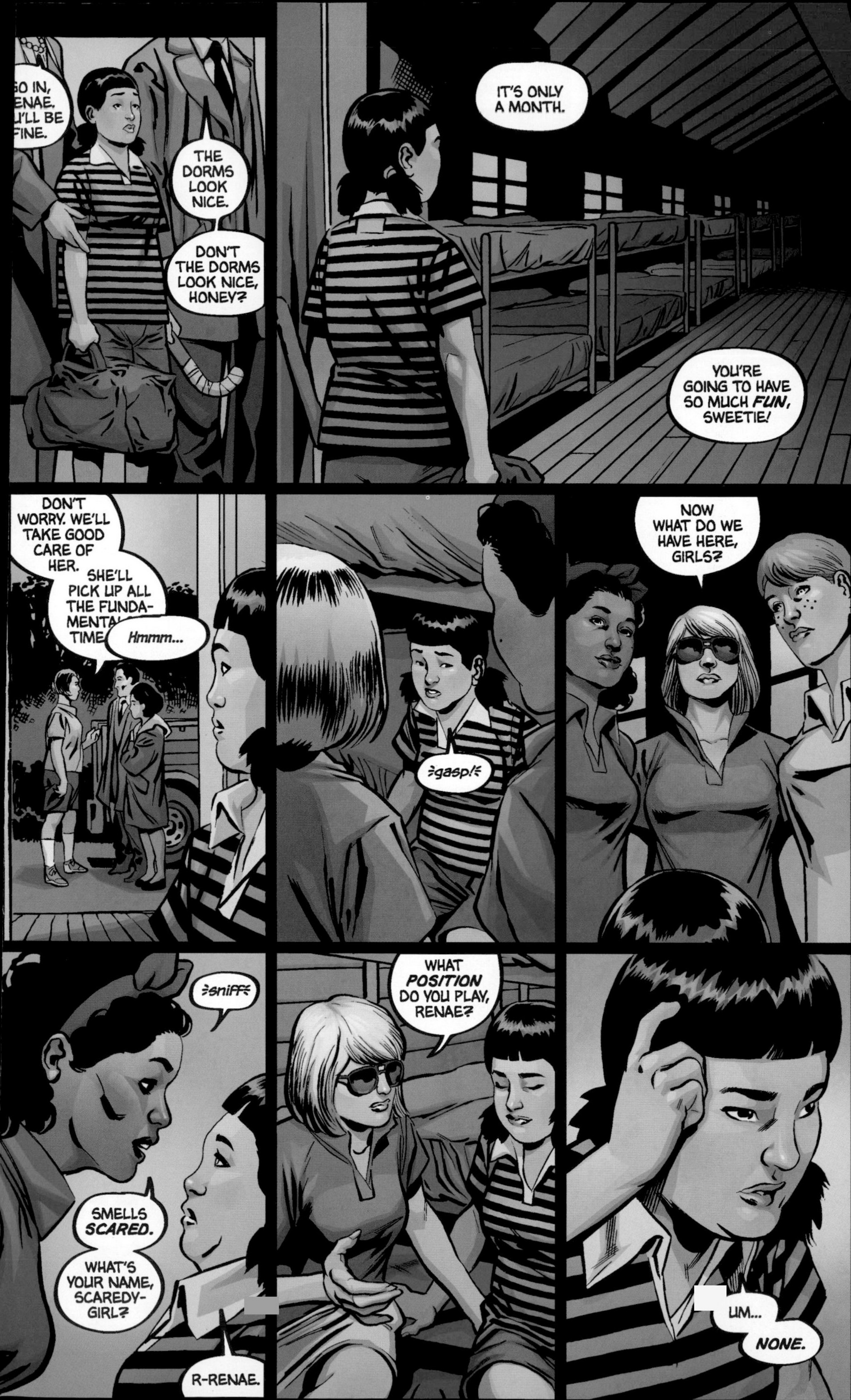
O IN, ENAE. U'LL BE FINE.
THE DORMS LOOK NICE.
DON'T THE DORMS LOOK NICE, HONEY?
IT'S ONLY A MONTH.
YOU'RE GOING TO HAVE SO MUCH *FUN*, SWEETIE!
DON'T WORRY. WE'LL TAKE GOOD CARE OF HER.
SHE'LL PICK UP ALL THE FUNDA-MENTA TIME
Hmmm...
gasp!
NOW WHAT DO WE HAVE HERE, GIRLS?
sniff
SMELLS *SCARED*.
WHAT'S YOUR NAME, SCAREDY-GIRL?
R-RENAE.
WHAT *POSITION* DO YOU PLAY, RENAE?
UM...
NONE.

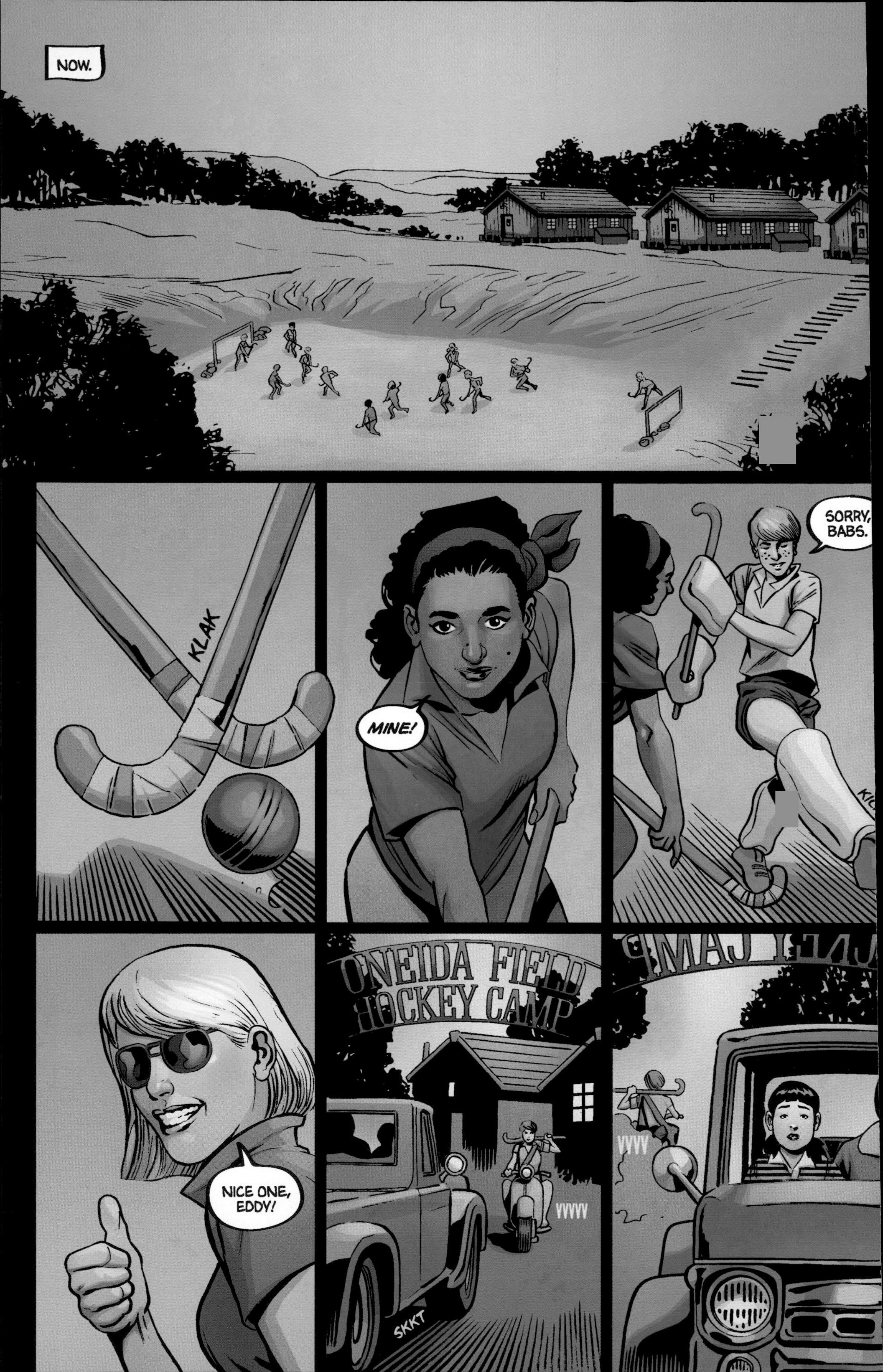
NOW.
KLAK
MINE!
SORRY, BABS.
NICE ONE, EDDY!
ONEIDA FIELD HOCKEY CAMP
VVVVV
SKKT
VVVV

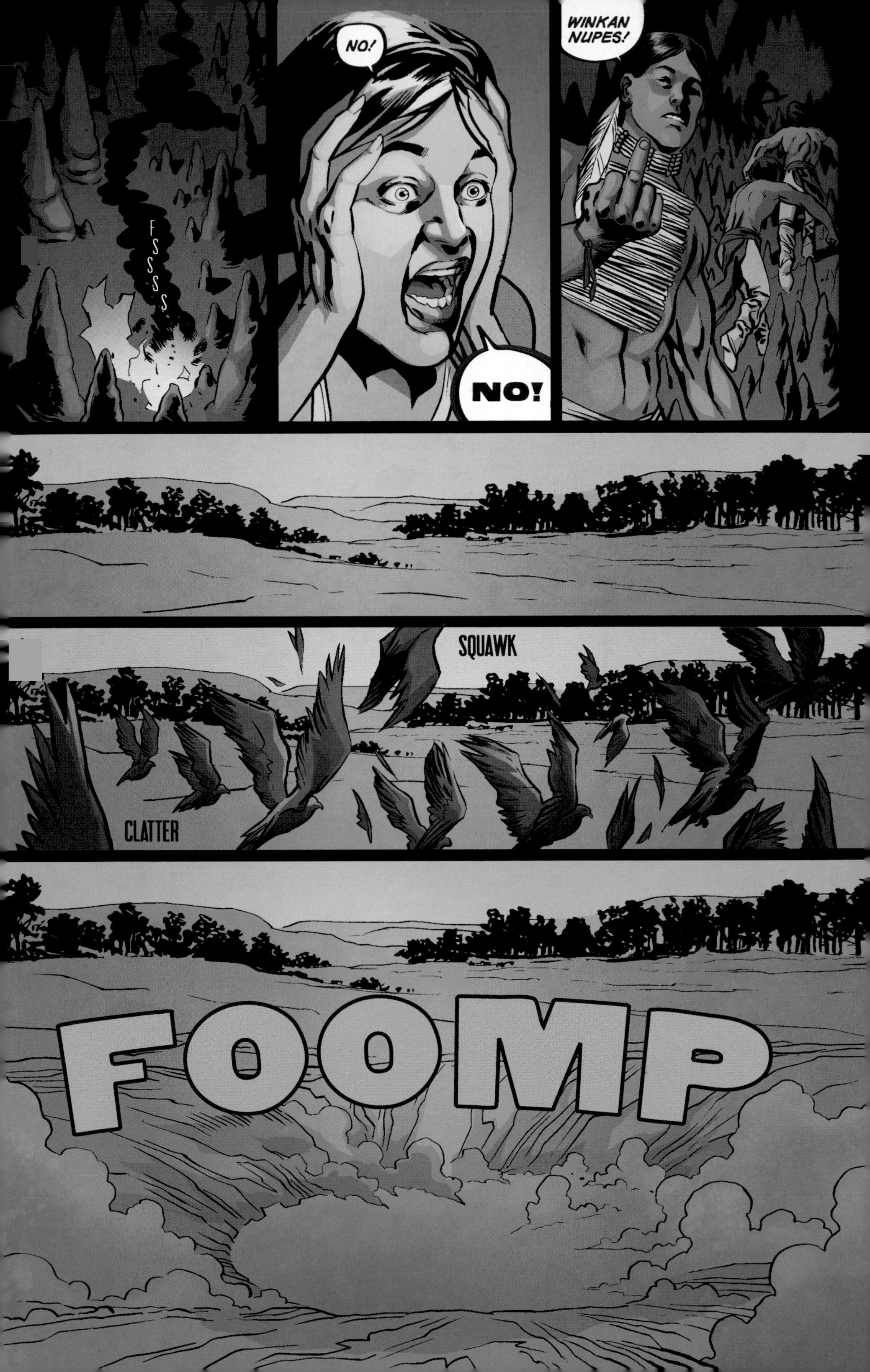
FSSSS
NO!
NO!
WINKAN NUPES!
SQUAWK
CLATTER
FOOMP

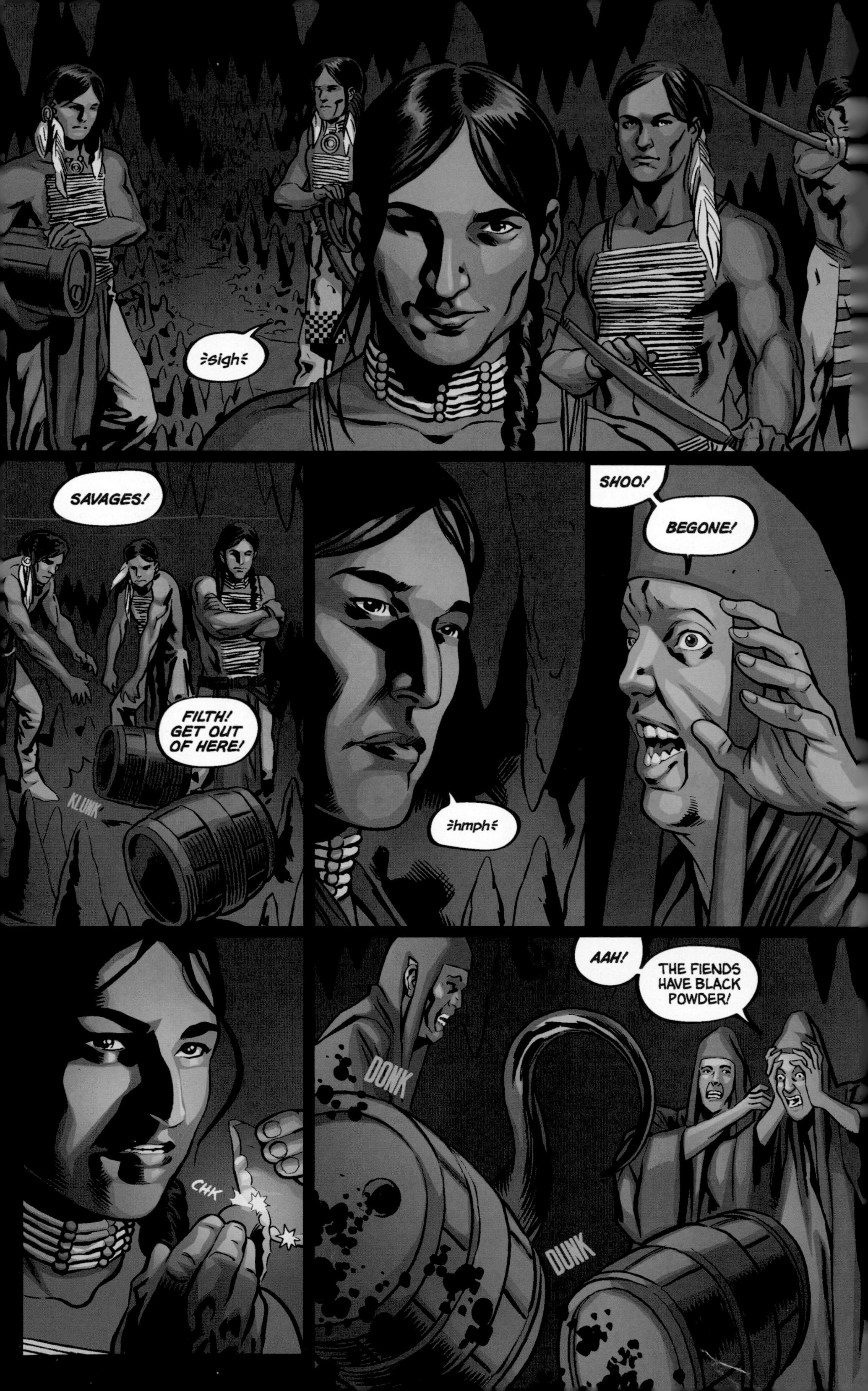
sigh
SAVAGES!
FILTH! GET OUT OF HERE!
KLUNK
hmph
SHOO!
BEGONE!
CHK
DONK
AAH!
THE FIENDS HAVE BLACK POWDER!
DUNK

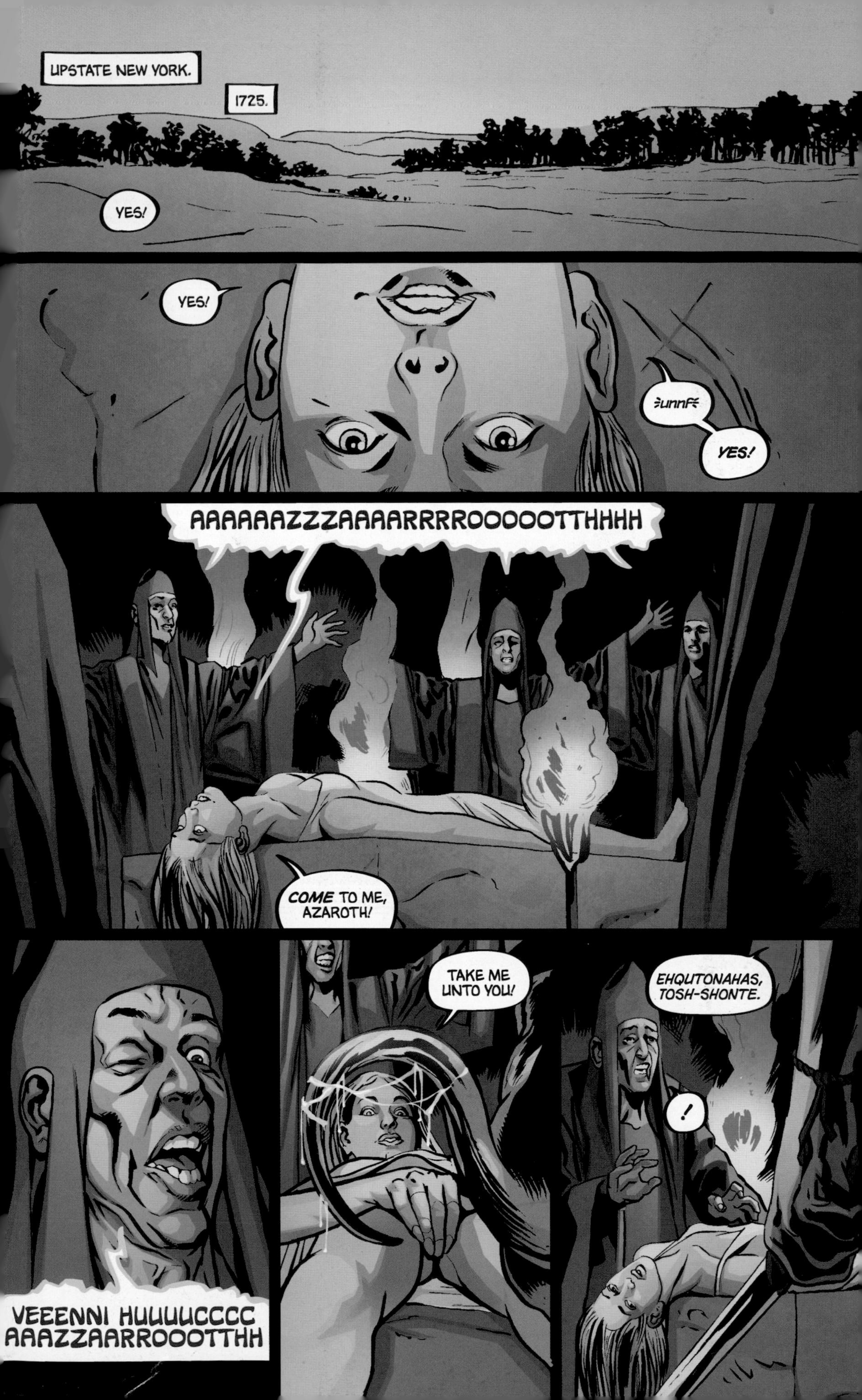
UPSTATE NEW YORK.
1725.
YES!
YES!
unnf
YES!
AAAAAAZZZAAAARRRROOOOOTTHHHH
COME TO ME, AZAROTH!
VEEENNI HUUUUCCCC AAAZZAARROOOTTHH
TAKE ME UNTO YOU!
EHQUTONAHAS, TOSH-SHONTE.
!

FLESH FEAST OF THE DEVIL DOLL

SCRIPT AND LETTERS
ALEX DE CAMPI

ART AND TITLE PAGE
GARY ERSKINE

COLORS
YEL ZAMOR
CHRIS BLYTHE
JAMES OFFREDI
HI-FI COLOR DESIGN

COVER
DAN PANOSIAN

DARK HORSE BOOKS

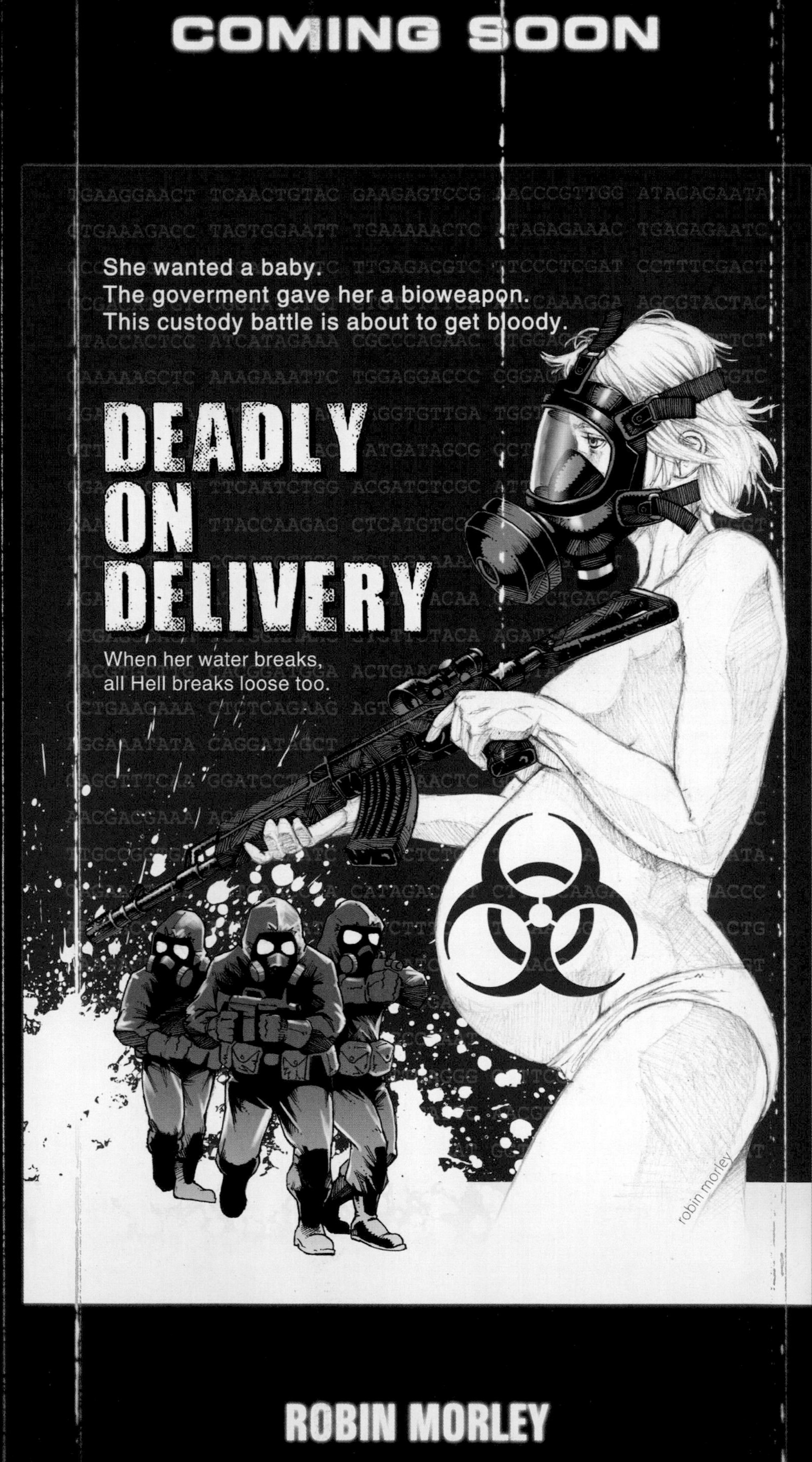
COMING SOON
She wanted a baby.
The goverment gave her a bioweapon.
This custody battle is about to get bloody.
DEADLY ON DELIVERY
When her water breaks,
all Hell breaks loose too.
robin morley
ROBIN MORLEY

COMING SOON

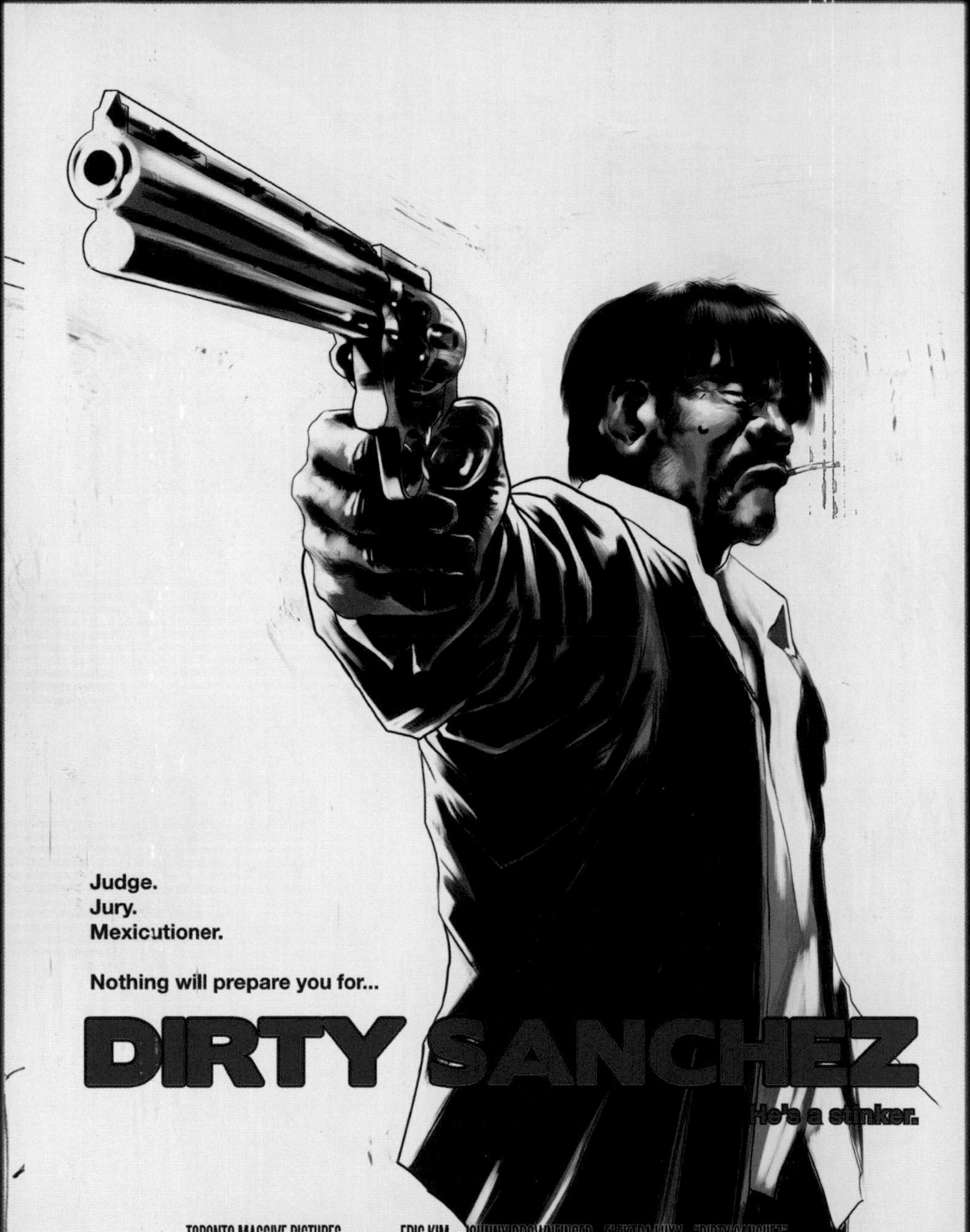

Judge.
Jury.
Mexicutioner.
Nothing will prepare you for...
DIRTY SANCHEZ
He's a stinker.
TORONTO MASSIVE PICTURES PRESENTS A FILM BY ERIC KIM JOHNNY BROWNFINGER ELEKTRA LUXX "DIRTY SANCHEZ"
MUSIC BY STEPHEN COATES COSTUME DESIGNER ERIKA MUNRO EDITED BY ALAN CAPRILES PRODUCTION DESIGNER HARRIET ZUCKER DIRECTOR OF PHOTOGRAPHY RAUL GONZO
EXECUTIVE PRODUCER BRENDAN WRIGHT AND SCOTT ALLIE PRODUCED BY IAN TUCKER STORY BY ERIC KIM
SCREENPLAY BY ALEX DE CAMPI DIRECTED BY ERIC KIM

ERIC KIM

GRINDHOUSE
DOORS OPEN AT MIDNIGHT
DOUBLE FEATURE